About the Author.

Rowland Crowland, sometimes known as, "that goblin poet," was born in Radcliffe, Lancashire and had always lived around North Manchester until recently, when after working in the NHS for thirty five years, he went peculiar and removed to live in a cave in Cumbria and write poetry. His poems concern nature, spirit, chip shops, factories, witches, the wind, the Buddha and goblins. All of the poems in this first collection have been read at venues around North Lancs and Cumbria.

Some Reviews...

If your idea of poetry is watching someone writhe about and wriggle and wretch up some mad shite from the depths of a tortuous and tormented soul, then Crowland's your man.

Anonymous Critic.

Mr. Crowland should keep his nosey beak out of other people's business.

Morris Schafter,
Stationery Consultant.

Rowland Crowland's a nob....

Anonymous street person.

BEGGARS.

by   Rowland Crowland.

To Sharena

Love Best Wishes

from

Rowland Crowland

For My Family.

Contents…

Sonnet Written in a Chippy.

Deep in your pocket there's coins jingling,
There's ready chips rustling and vinegar chinking
There's pies on a hot plate, puddings in a steamer,
This is the place to sit and dream
On the wooden bench that's under the window
And outside it's cold and forever the wind blows
And it's raining and dark and the window's steamed up
And people rush by they've clocked off and teamed up
And time stands still for some chips and a pie
And just for a moment you're warm inside
And safe and sound and the people in the queue
Are chatting and laughing, they're feeling it to.
Then it's "Hey you over there composing a sonnet,
Wake up cock, do you want gravy on it!"

Where Beggars can be Choosers.

Homeless in Lancaster.
Sit down but stand out.
Chilly but confident.
Expecting a handout.
I'm homeless in Lancaster.
At home with the losers.
But this is the place where beggars are choosers.

Homeless in Lancaster.
How did I get here?
I'm sat in a doorway.
It's terribly wet here.
But I've chosen my new friends
From smackheads and boozers,
Coz this is the place where beggars are choosers.

Homeless in Lancaster
Where nobody knew me.
I dropped to much acid
And dropped out of Uni.
I'm no longer a posh academic peruser.
I've dropped into the place where beggars are choosers.

Homeless in Lancaster.
It don't pay to be clever.
You just gotta get by
Whatever the weather.
It don't pay to consort
With thinkers and musers.
It pays to be here where the beggars are choosers.

Homeless in Lancaster.
No living wage there.
Living in Lancaster.
Living on welfare.
I could do some busking
And be a carouser
And sing of this place where beggars are choosers.

Homeless in Lancaster.
The people are kind here.
I smell like a shit box
And nobody minds here.
Nobody piss takes.
There are no abusers
In this lovely place where beggars are choosers.

It's Xmas in Lancaster.
Pissing with rain here.
The Rotary Club
And all of their reindeer
Have tipped me some pennies
In onesers and twosers.
Welcome to the town where beggars are choosers.

Homeless in Lancaster.
A sandwich from Asda,
A carton of couscous
With sweet corn and pasta.
The food is the business,
The people are groovers.

This sure is the place man, where beggars are choosers.

Homeless in Lancaster.
A caramel latte
A mouthful of thunderbird,
A glug of frascati,
A chance of some beer slops
Outside of the boozers.
There's a rave going on where the beggars are choosers.

Homeless in Lancaster.
I'm having a beefer.
A regular toff
With an occasional reefer.
It's not a big issue
In this town of old bluesers.
It's fab in this scene where the beggars are choosers.

But, homeless in Lancaster's
Not always so groovy.
You can't watch the telly
Or go to a movie
And life's a bit dodgy
Alone with the bruisers.
All on your own where the beggars are choosers.

Homeless in Lancaster.
Wherever I roam here
There's never a roof so
There's no place like home here.
I'm trickin for snaps
Like a right scooby doozer.

Things wear a bit thin when beggars are choosers.

Homeless in Lancaster.
My best friend's a thief!
Some of the beggars here
Beggar belief!
I can't call the coppers,
So what can I do sir?
The choices aren't easy when beggars are choosers.

Homeless in Lancaster.
The black Lune is flowing
Down to the quayside
Where the luners are going,
Dossing down in the dark
Where the dogs do their doozers.
I'm beginning to wonder if beggars are choosers.

Homeless in Lancaster.
Any chance of a bob sir?
Just give us a drink mate.
I can't do a job sir.
I'm seeing pink fairies
And crazy voodoozers.
It's scary in this place where beggars are choosers.

Homeless in Lancaster
I'm down on mi uppers
My defences are down
And I'm singing for supper.
A nice man and lady
Call me a nuisance

And it hurts in the place where beggars are choosers

Homeless in Lancaster.
I'm a right fuckin mess, me.
I'm losing my spirit.
Will somebody bless me!?
Prodders, Left-footers,
Muzzers or Jewsers.
Where gods are concerned
Need beggars be choosers?

Homeless in Lancaster.
My arse has gone numb!
I knew I'd end up
An insensitive bum!
Coz I can't leave my pitch
For a wee or a poo sir.
Is there any real choice
Where beggars are choosers?

Homeless in Lancaster.
Just when it gets nasty,
A kind passer-by
Stops and gives me a pasty.
Only one in the bag??!!!
There's usually two sir!!!
Coz this is the place where beggars are choosers.
Yeh this is the place where beggars can be choosers!

Little Tommy Tittlemouse.

Little Tommy Tittlemouse
Was the manager of a big warehouse.
He'd scurry about in a murine way,
While his workers grafted every day,
Then at night he'd drive quite far away,
To his cosy home where he lived with his family.
And he'd witter on about his busy day,
While his little wife hurried with his tea tray,
And he'd sit with it, on his knee,
While his children played in front of the TV
And after that he'd have a cup of tea,
And read for a while then clean his teeth,
And settle down in his comfy bed,
With dreams of his warehouse in his head.
And Little Tommy Tittlemouse at the drop of a hat
Would rat on folk, he'd pack your bags
If he'd a mind, he'd mark your card
And be so kind you'd drop your guard,
But he'd sharpen his knife behind your back,
And then surprise you with a smile and the sack.
Little Tommy Tittlemouse was feared by all,
No one knew how to take him at all,
He'd suddenly turn and scuttle off for a pen,
And then take your name...
And then....
And then....
And then you'd really have to watch your step,
And tiptoe around him, 'cause he wouldn't forget,
It could be months later on he'd produce that name,
Once he'd marked your card things were never the same.

One day Tommy Tittlemouse came for me,
"My office!" He said, and scampered off verminously.
I followed him there with that feeling of dread
That you get when your name's read out in assembly.
Once in his office he slammed the door,
Said I'd been three minutes late on the Monday before,
And instead of working I'd been chatting to Violet,
And he'd personally observed me taking too long in the toilet.
And he'd got mi card marked from some time ago
For some infringement that I didn't even know!
This, he said was a tale of woe,
So I'd have to redeem myself or go!
"So what have you got to say for yourself?"
He grinned up at me like a wicked elf.
Tommy Tittlemouse, I thought,
You really are a rat,
So I threw all caution to the wind...
And punched the little twat!

Thief.

A goblin stole mi DNA,
I didn't want it anyway,
But there's a goblin knocking about Manchester today
That looks like me in every way.
Someone saw him in Blakley Woods,
And casing houses on Heaton Park Road,
I think he might live in the woods,
I'm sure he's up to no good.
Someone saw him in the centre of town,
He was on Tib street walking up and down
Casually like he owned the gaff,
Pulling faces at the shopkeepers,
They were laughing at him.
In Harpurhey Asda he stole some beer,
The security man shouted "hey you, come here!"
He was caught red-handed then and there,
But vanished, they say, into thin air.
He just stalks about in broad daylight,
Ordinary people think he's frightening,
He pokes his big nose into babies' prams,
Then he pinches their mums' bums
And that really frightens 'em.
Jimmy saw him in Bolton Nevada,
He said this goblin was dancing harder
Than anyone else on the dance floor
Till the bouncers grabbed him and flung him out the door.
Not long after that the police came for me,
I was arrested and taken to Brutle Street,
But I explained to the Sergeant on duty that day
That a goblin had stolen mi DNA,
I think he believed me...
He let me go anyway!

Pity the Lune.

Rain falls pure from the heavens
On the fell where ravens hail
And gathers as the River Lune
In Ravenstonedale,
Then laughs and trills in falls and rills
And innocently glides
Towards the foot of Borrowdale
Where Romans killed or compromised.
Then youthful and exuberant
Gorging mountains downward flows
Where trains dash and cars crash
And every day bloody the roads,
But pretty lies the prospect
Of green Lonsdale past the kirk
And underneath the bridge that lies
Where Christians did the Devil's work.
Then hesitant and faltering unsure of what's to come
Twists and turns to plot a course back home.
But drawn away inexorably
Westwards to the sea,
And crooked destiny now leads
And creeps inevitably
Into the town where black clouds hung
And righteous hymns to Him were sung,
Whilst all the time His traps were sprung
On Gallows Hill where witches swung.
A town where beggars still doss down
In the dark...
In the municipal park...
Deserted and doomed...
Past the quayside, where slaves festooned
With chains, in pain, stood
Marooned in their new home,

Never to return to Sierra Leone,

Lost and alone...

Leave them all alone!

And rush down to the strand

To the wet sand,

Where plovers land,

And flee..

Far out into the Irish Sea,

And bathe in equanimity

And drown...

Far, far away from people and towns!

Pie Tin.

She had an enamel pie tin,
And everybody craved it.
Everybody else just played at gravy,
But she really made it.
Everything was on the table
Just as she laid it,
And she never gave anything at all away
If she could possibly save it.

Values,
Working class values,
The values that made our world,
Values,
Real values,
The birthright of every girl.

She was a homely woman,
With a household full of ornaments,
She wasn't a comely woman,
She had very few personal adornments.
She always had two pinnies though,
A sign of status,
And the smell that came through her kitchen door
Was braised onions and potatoes.

She had a pot horse on the mantle piece
And she donkey-stoned the step,
And on the geraniumed window-sill
A secret door key was kept.
A spit and polished sideboard
Just to spit and polish on,
On Mondays it was washing day,

"Where's all this washing come from?!!"

Values,
Working class values,
The values that made our world,
Values
Real values,
The birthright of every girl.

And everyday's a cleaning day,
And everyday's a godly day,
And every stick of furniture's
Been all but spit and polished away.
A pledge to Him in heaven
To keep the parlour clean,
In return for blessings on a Sunday
From Jesus,
And maybe an ice cream.

She's weaving yarn all through the week,
Working her fingers to the bone,
Running ragged in the cotton mill
And threadbare in the home.
It was always the Protestant ethic
To work for the Father and Son,
And on Sunday you're seen by the Holy Ghost,
So she'd have to put her best frock on.

The clock...forever ticking,
The cross...forever begging pardon,
But there's no rest for the wicked
While there's rhubarb in the garden.
Thin custard on a Friday
On a little piece of sponge cake,
A few tiny random salad items,

A sliver of hake.

Values,
Working class values,
The values that made our world,
Values,
Real values,
The birthright of every girl.

And everybody understood
That nothing should be said,
Nothing bad would be talked about
Till after she was dead.
So all the loves, the lies, the leers,
The lechery was hidden,
Frustrations, flirtations, failures, fears
Just festered in the midden.

It was all about appearances,
And keeping things from others,
She couldn't share her feelings
With her sisters or her mother.
So not far beneath the surface
The nightmare's bleeding real,
It's a bloody lifetime's bloody stains
Two pinnies have to conceal.

But it's never use your crying
Over anything that's spilled,
When all your life's spent dying
And your living's long been killed.
It's all just something and nothing,
It's nothing to shout about,
So calm yourself, and dry your tears,

And get your pie tin out.

Values,
Working class values,
The values that made our world,
Values,
Real values,

The birthright of every girl.

Solstice.

Hunkered down in a winter storm
In a bunker to keep us safe from harm,
We've oak and ash logs in our arms,
We need a fire to keep us warm.
I strike a spark from flint and steel,
With kindling in mi hands I'm kneeling,
I'm going to tell you how I really feel
And then I'll cook us one last meal.
I'm scared and hungry, I'm tired and cold,
I don't know when I got so old,
Unless there's fire I'll never hold
You again, our story wont unfold,
But this tiny spark wont ignite the tinder
And look right there outside the window,
It's bleak and black and the great north wind blows
And it's surely death that it's bringing us.
Our lives are spent in cheating and lying,
There's nobody left who isn't crying
Inside themselves while endlessly trying
To live a life thats not spent dying,
And all along you've seen me here,
I'm cold and dark and I'm disappearing,
There's nowhere any warmth in this dreary
Life that's so very nearly leaving.
But wait, little flames are burning bright,
Something's happening here tonight,
And in our hearths something just might
Melt the ice that holds us tight.
It's in the very firelight,

The tiny flame that's been ignited,
Within the black and endless night,
It's sparks have set the stars alight.
Life is here and is for living,
Things are ending but just beginning,
And at the very point of leaving
Is the light you must believe in.
Something deep inside is stirring,
Something sprung from endless yearning,
It's just the firelight that's burning,
But something magikal's returning!
Solstice!
    Solstice!
        Solstice!

Alice Taylor's Wood.

School's taking us for a picnic,
In Alice Taylor's Wood.
Everybody's going....
Because everyone's been good.
Even the naughty ones are coming,
Because everyone felt they should.
It's going to be great!
Are you coming today?
To Alice Taylor's Wood.

The Cubs and Scouts are camping
Out in Alice Taylor's Wood.
They've got a fire going,
Frying bacon that smells good.
They're tying knots and using knives,
Like pioneers should.
Shall we join the scouts?
So we can camp out,
In Alice Taylor's Wood.

I used to go and sit alone
In Alice Taylor's Wood,
And climb a tree and sit quietly,
Amongst the leaves and buds,
And Alice Taylor would blow the leaves,
And whisper when she could,
"I see you there,
Without a care,
Sitting in my wood."

We're going to build a rope swing,
In Alice Taylor's Wood.
We'll hook it on a high branch
And swing over the brook.
All the lads are going,
We've got the rope and wood.
Come on let's go,
They won't wait you know,
In Alice Taylor's Wood.

The grown-ups are having a party,
In Alice Taylor's Wood.
They've got some stalls and games with balls,
Like only grown-ups would,
And they're cooking sausages.
Doesn't that sound good.
I've got sixpence you know,
Shall we go?
To Alice Taylor's Wood.

The Council are cutting some trees down
In Alice Taylor's Wood.
They've cut back loads of branches
And made everywhere look good.
They've made a place for kids to play.
It's like they've understood.
Shall we go?
It's free you know,
In Alice Taylor's Wood.

Someone's built a fishpond
In Alice Taylor's Wood.
They've dug it from the reed bed
And lined it all with mud.
There's coots on it and newts in it
And little frogs and toads.
Shall we take
A jam jar?

To Alice Taylor's Wood.

Something once had happened
In Alice Taylor's Wood.
Some man had been where he shouldn't have been,
And he'd been up to no good.
A little girl was missing,
And they'd found some blood.
Was she Alice?
Alice Taylor?
And why they named the wood?

There's a stream runs through the bluebells
In Alice Taylor's Wood,
And sitting there one day I heard,
"You can play with me if you would,
Just look around, I'm in the ground,
And in the trees above.
I'm on the swing,
I'm in everything
In Alice Taylor's Wood."

Light My Fire.

Summer solstice wort,
Yellow sun,
Bleeding red,
Nothing to do with St. John,
Healing,
With true feeling instead
Of medicine that's prescribed,
Your drops imbibed
By my tribe
Since time begun,
Set my heart ablaze,
Like in ancient days,
Leaves me golden,
Like I've swallowed
The sun,
My blood fires red
And what was dead
Lives again
And plays
Through the long summer days
And only then wanes
Like autumn lanes
Till the winter solstice
Lights my fire again.

March of the Hobgoblins.

Hobgoblins,
A party of them,
Slick and sly,
And stealthy
Follow me down the road.
What strange company I keep
Whenever I'm alone.
Come Flouncer,
Come Trouncer,
And Three-quarter-ouncer,
Come Dipper and Kipper,
And Cheeky-bottom-nipper,
Malingerer,
Fingerer,
Little freckled Flea-ringer,
Stuck-in-tethers,
Scraggy Crow-feathers,
All together,
Gay,
On our way,
To the horse fair,
Along green lanes,
And summer paths,
Stealing silently,
We laugh,
We skirt the edges
Of cornfields,
Over hedges,
Of haw and blackthorn.
Will there be a horse there
That we can ride to anywhere?
Will there be a woman there
Who's fair?
Will we see the gallows there,

And pretend that we don't care?
We'll make camp over night,
And dance by firelight,
And at daybreak wash our hair
In the bright beck,
I expect,
And we'll give the horse an apple,
And give our dogs a bone,
And we'll sink a keg of cider
Before we go rolling home.

Dog Shit Valley.

All's not well in Dog Shit Valley,
All's not what it seems,
The mills are shut,
The market's caput,
And nobody's selling ice cream anymore,
Yeh, no one's selling ice cream.

If you were born in Dog Shit Valley,
Your life not what it seems,
You're hung out to dry
On a washing line
And the wind blows away all your dreams,
Because there's no point having dreams.

Dog Shit Valley's the only place,
The only place not to be.
You grow up hard,
You have a small back yard
And kids by the time you're seventeen,
Yeh, three at least at seventeen.

Dog Shit Valley's not a happy valley,
Even when you're pissed,
Because smack and crack
And paki black
Are on your shopping list.
They're on everyone's shopping list.

I remember when Dog Shit Valley
Was a green and pleasant land.
Everyone had a job,
Everyone earned a bob
And a lot of blokes even owned a van,
And you can do all sorts with a van.

On Friday nights in Dog Shit Valley
You drink until you're numb,
You get well pissed,
Then buy some chips,
And have a fight on the way home,
Yeh, you fight your way back home.

It's lawless down in Dog Shit Valley,
There ain't no laws at all,
They live on crime,
Shit happens all the time,
And it makes Dodge City look like Bramhall,
Or any other big posh hall.

The River Irwell runs through Dog Shit Valley,
It'd rather not...
Because it's full of old prams,
Used johnnies and beer cans,
It's not happy with its lot,
But it's the only choice it's got.

There was a man in Dog Shit Valley,
Bill Berry was his name,
He bit off the head
Of a rat that wasn't dead,
And nothing was ever the same,
He raised everybody's game.

Mi grandad lived in Dog Shit Valley,
The hardest man you'd meet,
He had no fear,
And he earned his beer,
By clog fighting in the street,
He'd clog a few shins of a neet.

So if you go down to Dog Shit Valley,
You'd better go in disguise,
Because it's no picnic there,
There's no teddy bears anywhere,
Just the dog shit and the flies'
Not a teddy bear's paradise.

You've got to get out of dog Shit Valley,
You've got to get away,
Leave the shite,
Get a normal life,
Then maybe come back one day,
But just for a look around, don't stay!

Just get away from Dog Shit Valley,
Just go and don't look back,
And try to get
Your life on track,
Not back on smack and crack,
And wacky paki black.

So enough's been said of Dog Shit Valley,
There's only so much can be said,
It's a place of misgiving,
Not a place for the living,
Unless you're the living dead,
Or you're living right out of you're head!

So that's the fate of Dog Shit Valley,
The whole town's up on bricks.
A community dies
For the rise and demise
Of Manchester 26
Because all politicians are dicks,
Yeh, all politicians are pricks!

Freddy and the Ghost.

Freddy was possessed by a ghost,
There were no two ways about it.
There are never two ways about these things,
It's a one way ticket for two and don't doubt it.
It all happened quite innocently,
When he went in for a minor operation,
And came out hosting a major entity,
That slipped in during his anaesthetisation.
He just felt unusual at first,
Muzzy head, bad back and sore joints,
And a feeling that something had happened,
And a tingle in some of his acupuncture points.
But what can you do about that?
Any doctor would give you short shrift,
So Freddy got on with his day to day life,
Till the ghost started talking to him.
It was just a few phrases at first,
And whisperings that sounded like "I'm here."
But as the days became weeks and the weeks became months,
There's a full on ghost monologue in his ear.
"I'm here, I'm with you and I always will be,
I'm your friend to the end, I'm not lying.
I'll confide in you, chide you, I'm riding you,
I'm an angel you're a bum and you're dying."
It wouldn't let Freddy think for himself.
It said everything he did was wrong,
And sometimes it'd even try taking the reins
By commandeering Freddy's own tongue.
It called Mrs. Sattersthwaite a bugger
And it spat at the post man as well.
It called reverend Fidler a perverted old fucker
Who should be locked up in a cell.
The only time that the ghost would be quiet

Was when Freddy was driving his car,
So he'd drive round the block,
And then drive to the shop,
To get peace he didn't need to go far.
But then he would have to go home,
And the ghost would be angry and moan.
It'd call Freddy a dick and say the car made it travel sick,
And it'd punish Freddy when they were alone.
It'd roar in his ears that it'd kill him
By pushing him under a train,
Or by choking him while he was sleeping
Or by growing a big tumour in his brain.
It wouldn't let Freddy answer the phone
Or talk to any of his friends,
It wouldn't even let him open the curtains,
He'd be a prisoner for days on end.
The first time Freddy went to his Doctor's,
He said he'd write the Psychiatrist a letter,
But in the meantime prescribed him some Prozac
And said in three weeks he'd be better.
So Freddy went home and got worse
Because the ghost wouldn't now be placated,
So the Doctor prescribed him some extra Prozac
Because if you can't beat it, medicate it!
The first Psychiatrist that Freddy saw
Said "I'm sure you've psychotic depression,
You'll have to take this Olanzapine,
And attend for another ten sessions.
A Community Nurse came to see him,
He was a nice guy and seemed realistic,
So Freddy told him all about the ghost,
And that made the ghost go ballistic!
It accused Freddy of telling bad tales,
And betraying their mutual trust,
And said it'd make things a whole lot worse
If Freddy told anyone else.
So Freddy then drunk loads of whisky,
Desperate to drive the ghost away,

But the ghost actually seemed to thrive on the stuff
And proclaimed his intention to stay.
So he tried smoking weed and tried ecstasy,
But that made the ghost ecstatic and loud,
And made Freddy believe that the ghost wouldn't leave
Until he was dead in the ground.

But then Freddy stumbled on a Shaman,
Or a Shaman stumbled upon him,
And this man seemed kind and seemed to understand
And so Freddy liked talking to him.
He talked to Freddy like he was normal
And he treated the ghost normal as well.
In fact he talked to the ghost more than Freddy,
And he seemed to be working a spell.
He touched Freddy at certain points on his body,
And he burned some sweet smelling herbs,
And he made some nice noises that sounded like bird calls,
And then said some magikal words.
He said....
"Come with me to where you should be,
 There's a place in me where you can be free,
 Just let go and come to me,
 And you will rest in tranquility."

Freddy felt fine straight away,
When the ghost was gone from his mind.
He cried with relief. It felt strangely like grief.
But he felt like human kind.
And he basked in the paradise of normality,
And bathed in the thrill of release,
And he phoned all his friends and just chatted with them,
And he pulled back his curtains and breathed.
He came down off the tablets real slowly,
And Freddy was Freddy again,
Just happy and lovely and normal,

Like before the ghost had slipped in.
And the ghost was happy as well,
When the Shaman showed it how to be free,
And it lived happily ever after,
In what was its right place to be.
And the Psychiatrist was puzzled by the remission,
But he lived on happily too,
And he attributed Freddy's cure to Olanzepine
And prescribed it to everyone he knew.

Sitting.

The buddha's wife came home,
"Have you been sitting there all day?"
She said...
"I don't know what's the matter with you,
You might as well be dead!
You said...
You'd do the washing,
The cleaning wont do itself!
Look at these bits on the carpet!
Look at this dust on the shelf!
You what?
You've no self?!
You're unhealthy!
In fact you're self-ish!
You've no ego?!
What does that mean?!!
What about us normal people,
Where do you think we go?!
I've been to work and done the shopping,
I think you've forgotten what that meant!
You could at least have done the hoovering,
What do you mean, you've no attachment?!!!
There's no excuse for laziness,
Bone -idleness is next to craziness.
It's cleanliness that's next to godliness
Not sit on your arse with your eyes closed looking odliness!!!
I don't know what I ever saw in you!
Look at your face now, am I boring you?!
I'm sick to death of just ignoring you,
Just do something! I'm imploring you!"
And Lord Buddha smiled, and lifted his eyes
And said "all around us is dukha
But, today, by way of a surprise,
I have put a casserole in the slow-cooker!"

Sad Ending.

Hung up on a hook,
A sad ending somehow,
Waiting to be cooked,
Or rendered,
Blended
In a stew,
Hung up askew,
Skewered through,
Nothing left to do.
I'm glad mi friends can't see me now,
I'm thinking,
Or mi children,
Hanging like this,
Stinking,
Upside down,
I think,
I'm dead,
No head,
No dignity,
Not me,
Reduced
To soup,
Or sandwiches for someone's tea.
Dying hurt me,
Hands on me,
Mean,
Men who didn't know me,
And a machine,
Clean through mi head,
Not dead right away,

But noise, knives, confusion,
Terrible pain,
Something's an illusion…
Something's an illusion…
Again and again,
Drowning in mi own gore,
Then,
No more,
Don't have to breathe anymore,
It's a relief,
Is this like grief?
I remember being young,
Strong,
I remember bird song,
And green meadows,
And woods,
And buttercups,
And gulping cool fresh air,
Free to wander anywhere…
But where am I?
Oh yeh, I'm just over there,
Cold,
Not even old,
Just out of luck,
Waiting to be cooked,
Hung up on a hook.

Sambo's Grave.

A blackbird lands,
His eyes black suns,
Two swans at home
Where the pylons hum,
The tracks all mud
Where the water comes
When the tide gets high,
Where the river runs.
There's no crows here
But a scarecrow stands
And points both ways
With the palms of his hands
To Sunderland Point
Between Sea and sand,
Between heaven and earth
Where plovers land.

I don't think
You can stand here today,
You'd better go back,
Go back the way you came,
Go back before you drown
In the sea's impartial waves
In a Lune-grey grave
With a forgotten black slave.

This is the place
Where fortunes were made
By the whiteman's trade

That his god forgave,
He forgot that his son
Was sent here to save
The very souls
He sold into slavery,
In those dark days,
All our yesterdays
And tomorrows are the same,
Nothing's changed,
We're all deranged
And stand here estranged,
Exposed as we gaze
Into destiny's black face.

I don't think
You can stand here today,
You'd better go back,
Go back the way came,
Go back before you drown
In the sea's impartial waves
In a Lune-grey grave,
With a forgotten black slave.

In unconsecrated ground!?
An unmarked mound!?
Stop and look around!
Yeh look all around
Where hypocracy abounds
And where deluded clowns
Who consecrate our earth
Are blind and bound
In chains, their minds
Can't see our sanctity
Regardless of our creeds,
Our colours, our abilities,
And this god of theirs
Demands only servility
And his piety's profanity

And idolatry, It's insanity!

And I don't think
You can stand here today,
Go back, go back,
Go back the way you came,
Go back before you drown
In the sea's impartial waves
In a Lune-grey grave
With a forgotten black slave.

It's a cover-up
In desolation!
Yeh here lies hidden
The shame of our whole nation,
One poor little soul
Who's not worth saving
Shoved down a rabbit hole,
Forever degrading,
While the holy depraved
Pretending they're praying
Are enslaving us all
By everything they're saying,
And it says everything
In their guilty engraving,
It's not forgiveness they're giving
But power they're craving.

And I think you should
Stand here today,
Because the tide has to turn
And was all this away
And we can stay here forever
Washed clean as a slate,
Because it's never too late
To change our ways
Or the way we behave,
But we'll have to remain

In this forgotten place
And accept the sea's embrace
For the rest of our days,
Tended only by waves
In this lonely enclave...
Sambo's grave...

Holy Ghost.

This goblin told me he was the Holy Ghost,
I know most people wouldn't have believed him,
But I was compromised at the time,
I was only young,
I was lonely,
And I was grieving,
I was living on the street
And I was thieving,
And yeh, so I believed him.
Looking back now it all seems so strange
To think that I was...
I was so deranged,
And now so many things have changed,
And I'm me!
And I'm here!
And mi mind's clear!
And I'm saved!
But at the time mi path was paved
With crazy paving,
And one strange day
There's someone waving
At me saying
He's come to save me,
And saying he's the Holy Ghost,
And he's the most
Beautiful person I'd ever seen,
And I stagger towards him,
And I lean on him,
And he lifts me,
And he leads me,
And I'm no longer struggling,
And I'm no longer hobbling,
I'm with God the Father,
God the Son,
God the Goblin!

Oystercatchers.

Oystercatchers
Hard by the bay,
Steadfast,
Braced against the rain,
Legs rigid,
Wings folded,
Fixed into the wind,
Bold, sea-cold
Birds of the coastal plain.
I first saw them from Fegla Fawr,
Big red beaks like I'd never seen before,
I sat and spied on them from afar,
Oystercatchers! Wow!
And now they're here on Morecambe Bay,
Unmistakeable, standing that way,
A panoply of piebald
All facing Ireland
Through the sea-spray.
Look!
For flying in a straight line
There's got to be no match.
There's no time to deviate
When there's oysters to catch!
I can see them from Marine Road.
It's the place where oystercatchers go
For cockles and mussels by the tractor load,
I've never seen one catch an oyster though!
But there they go,
Stepping staccato
Red stiletto
Legs with backward knees,
Rooting, tooting,
Whistling like referees,

Pied pipers
Shooting the breeze,
Red-eyed, intent
On serious deeds.
You can keep your peregrines
You can keep your golden eagles,
Here's majesty enough for me
Standing proud amongst the seagulls.
And then as one,
They're gone!
I'm going to get a cup....
With an Oystercatcher on!

In the Shadow of the Church.

St. John's Church,
On the hill,
Very big,
Very still,
Very dark,
A holy place,
A black steeple full of grace,
Where people congregate.
The spire-shadow finger
Creeping through the school gates,
Choosing children's fates
Points at me
In my classroom in St. John's C of E,
Singles me out
As nothing to shout about,
As a low-achiever,
As one who likes Jesus
And fairy tales,
And at play times
Just stares through the rails
At the spire-shadow finger
As if impaled.
At dinner time you walk in pairs
Down the road in heavy rain
Past the black church with the stone stairs
And the shadows where heaven reigns,
To the canteen,
The same every day
Slops,

Then walk back with raindrops
Down the necks of your plastic macs,
Back to your classroom for maths and facts..
While inside the church it's still and dark,
There are candles and a gold cross
And it's next to the park,
But things seem always dark in there,
In the church up the stone cold stairs.
There's a pulpit...
Where the vicar doesn't say much,
There's an altar
That children mustn't touch.
There's a verger with an everlasting frown.
The church had been there forever
And then they knocked it down.
What would St John do?
Now he only had a school to belong to?
Does anybody know?
And where would God go?
"To St. Thomas's" they said,
"It's the one that has a bell
And it's only a few streets away
And God lives there as well!"
A pile of cold stones is where God used to be
No black spire rising up through the trees.
You can see St. Thomas's now,
Now that the spire has gone!
But I don't think God's happy,
And neither is St. John!

M and M Schafter Ltd.

"So, Hello, M and M Schaffer Ltd.,
Bringing our Clients Considerations to themselves."
How can I help? For sure, For sure,
Not a problem, I'm on it, no worries,
Hey anyway, you enjoying your day?
That's the one, stay safe, no fears.
How long have you been trying to get through?
Did you you know there's nobody here?
Press one for if you know what you want,
Press two for if you don't,
Press three if you think you want some more,
And if you don't, press four,
Press five for sure, for sure, for sure,
Press six when you just can't take any more,
If you press seven you'll be back out the door,
Press eight for a mocha and nine for a cappuccino.
If you want to go somewhere but you're not sure where,
We've a complex algorithm that'll take you right there,
You'll have to be on hold forever
But I don't really care,
Because I'm suddenly going to disappear,
And you'll realise there's no one really there.
So hey, hey, if that's ok,
So let's say you're having a great day...
Can I get a signal here ?
Can I get a good to go?
Can I get a piece of this?
Can I get a soya frappaccino?
So we've created?

A cool space?

That'll bi-pass?

The rat-race?

And lead you back?

At your own pace?

To where you started from?

In the first place?

It's an investment?

That'll divest you?

And leave you destitute?

In a Rest Home?

So shall we say yeh?...

Yeh yeh yeh yeh yeh yeh

Yeh yeh yeh yeh yeh yeh yeh?...

So what we gotta do here...

So we share some ideas...

So we're brain-storming, blank-paging,

Blue-skying, level-playing-fielding,

Sorta thing yeh,

So we gotta input this yeh

And throughput that yeh,

And pump-prime this yeh,

And ring-fence that,

So let me run it by you,

So you can run with it,

Right so we're running.

We're running?

No not raining! Running!

But if it's raining, no worries, we're nowhere near you...

We're based in Shaharazarabad....

That's why I can't hear you...

Anyway, so give me your account number,

And your sort code and your password,

And the keys to your car,

And hey, if I may, just one last word...

I'm so sorry for your wait,

Yeh so sorry, had you been waiting long,

Thank you so much for waiting...

Have I mentioned you waiting at all?

Anyway, anyway, so you're having a great day,

I'm having a grrreat day!

I'm somewhere near...I think it's Bombay,

With a blueberry muffin,

And a caramel latte,

So what else is there to say?

So, does anybody care anyway?

So no, yeh yeh, you're right ...Nobody really cares,

That's why whenever you ring this number..

There's no one really there,

Now, Is there anything else I can patronise you with

And keep you on the phone for years?

We're M and M Schafter Ltd,

"Bringing our Clients Considerations to themselves...."

The Ballad of Billy Openshaw.

Billy Openshaw was my best friend,
He lived in the next street, down at the end,
His mother was a seamstress,
She was always making dresses,
His house was full of sewing machines
And things like trouser-presses.
I'd call for him nearly every day
And wait for what his mother would say,
"Is your Billy coming out'
Mrs. Openshaw?" I'd stand and shout.
"Now I know you want to play" she'd say,
And this might seem a little rotten,
But I'll be very busy sewing today,
So I've sent Billy out. To get some cotton."
It didn't matter when you came,
The answer would just be the same,
His mother smiling, needle in hand,
Would apologise but make a stand,
I'd ask if Billy was coming to play,
She'd look down at me and kindly say,
"I know that this will be a pain,
And that your plans will be misbegotten,
But I've just sent Billy out again,
He's gone to get some cotton.
Then when Billy did come out,
We'd play and play all day,
Through the fields we'd run and shout,
Over hills we'd stray,
Down the river building rafts,
Up the street lamps acting daft,
Anywhere the fun would be,
Was just the place for Billy and me.
But every morning when I'd come

To Billy's door there'd be his mum,
"Now I hate to be a kill-joy,
But today I've got such a lot on,
I've had to send Billy out again,
He's gone to get more cotton.
But then one day when she answered the door,
She looked at me and cried,
"Billy's not playing out today,
Because last night Billy died!"

His funeral was a sad affair,
His brothers, sisters and aunties there,
All their tears flowed with the rain
Into the ground where Billy lay.
It surely was the saddest day
Standing mourning in the mud,
But something there did lift my gaze,
To where his little gravestone stood,
And there the strangest thing I saw,
It was inscribed at the bottom,
"Here lies Billy Openshaw,
Gone, but not for cotton..."

Tea for One

Tea for one
Is not what I'd planned.
We should be down Market street holding hands
Or laughing together at the burger stand.
No, tea for one wasn't planned.

Tea for one's
A fragile deal,
Brittle bone china on teaspoon steel,
In an empty room,
With a ready meal,
Tea for one has little appeal.

Tea for one,
Not two for tea.
Tea's for two or even three.
I'd give anything
To have tea with you,
Because tea for one is not for me.

"Tea for one sir?"
Is a haunting call,
When you're sat by yourself in the market hall
On a table for two
Pushed up against the wall.
"Tea for one please,
Yeh, that's all!"

Charlie Peace.

I was walking up a back street when I was a kid,
When a big lad jumped out and held a gun to my head,
"Do you want plugging?" "No!" I said,
"Then you'll have to be my friend instead."
So I agreed that I would be his friend,
And thought that that would be the end,
But we shook hands and that was that,
I'd just made a pact with the ultimate twat.

Charlie Peace,
Charlie Peace,
If you ever see him just call the police.
He's pure evil,
In fact he's the devil,
In fact don't call the police, go straight for the priest.

Charlie Peace was a scary guy,
We'd walk out at night when the moon was high,
Out in the town while everyone slept,
"Grubbing" he called it, I don't know why.
He made me go in houses and put things in a sack,
He said if I didn't then I couldn't go back
To my own house to my mum and dad,
Charlie was round the bend, Charlie was real bad.

Charlie Peace had an evil grip on me,
He'd tie me up and then set me free,
He'd threaten me with a "hanging tree"
Then sit me down and make some tea,

And talk of the fun we'd have together,
"Stirring up storms and making bad weather"
For the ordinary folk who lived close by,
Who Charlie said deserved to die.

He had an evil face,
He had evil ways,
He had evil eyes,
He wore evil disguises,
He was evil outside,
He was more evil inside,
He was evil by day,
He was evil at night,
He was evil from his head
Down to both his evil feet,
He had an evil monster mind
He had evil teeth,
From the evil smile on his evil lips,
He was evil to the grease on his evil fingertips.
He had an evil little song
That he sang every night..,
"Charlie Peace is always near!
Sleep tight!"

One night Charlie said to me,
"Tonight we're going "feathering"...You'll see,"
He meant stealing chickens from someone's farm,
He said it'd be alright, it'd be no harm,
And it only needed one twist of my arm,
And I'm crawling round a chicken coop all on my own,
And all of the clucking must've sounded the alarm,
Because suddenly there's a farmer with a firearm.

We'd got two chickens and made it away,
Like urban foxes back to the estate.
Charlie took the chickens just as he'd planned,
And I had to go home with blood on my hands.
And then I wouldn't see him for days on end,

And it was nice to knock about with my usual friends,
But sooner or later the time would always come,
When Charlie would pop up with his gun.

Charlie Peace,
Charlie Peace,
If you see him just call the police,
Don't let him anywhere near you please,
Or he'll be all over you like a disease.

Charlie had a den in a derelict mill,
Everything in there was dark and still,
He'd make a little fire to brew some tea,
And plan his evil deeds with glee.
He had an old tea pot he'd found on a tip,
And two enamel cups that burned your lips,
He'd grin and sink a nip of whisky,
And he'd laugh and choke on his stolen biscuits.

He'd wear a woolly hat like a baby's bonnet,
He had a wooden cupboard with a padlock on it,
He'd sit in a chair that was old and dusty,
He had a cushion for me that was mouldy and musty,
And we'd sit and talk about things to do,
And sometimes he'd hurt me and sometimes he wouldn't do,
And I'd stare at his scary face looking at me,
And I'd see it again in my scary dreams.

Then one day he had a girl in there,
With freckles and giggles and ginger hair,
He made her take off her underwear,
And then made me touch her everywhere.
She carried on giggling but it wasn't funny,
And when she got dressed Charlie gave her some money,
After she'd gone he said "That was swell!"
And he made me some tea and a biscuit as well!

Charlie Peace,

Charlie peace,
Don't mess about just get the police,
He's not like anyone living or deceased,
He's Evolution's monsterpiece!

Other kids would run away from him,
Mrs Rowbottom said she'd pray for him.
Grown up people were appalled by him,
Oh how did I end up in thrall to him!
You couldn't even plead to him,
It didn't mean a thing to him,
Charlie Peace had no feelings in him,
And tears would only make him grin.

We strolled into a church in the middle of the day,
There were a couple of people there quietly praying,
Charlie took a drink from the water in the font,
Which brought the vicar over shouting "What do you want?!!"
"We want a crucifixion" Charlie said to his face,
"And if you can't provide one, we'll wreck the fucking place!!"
We covered all the altar with obscene stickers,
Then Charlie poured Domestos all over the Vicar.

Charlie Peace,
Charlie Peace,
He should've been done for "Bleach of the Priest"
His hands are dirty,
His mind's diseased,
Wherever he went he made people uneasy!

Charlie found all bad things funny,
Like we'd threaten kids and take their pocket money,
Like we'd wreck people's privets and wouldn't run away,
We'd take biscuits from the corner shop and wouldn't pay.
Then one night at home I was having my tea,
When the police came to our house and said they wanted me.
They told my mum and dad there'd been some burglaries,
And they reckoned it was all down to me and Charlie peace.

So I was in the cop shop in a cold dark cell,
And Charlie was in another one, locked up as well.
I could hear him whispering through the walls,
That if I spilled he'd slam my balls
In his padlocked cupboard in his dirty den.
He'd keep them there forever and then
He'd tell everyone I'd stole the chickens,
There was blood on my hands and no mistaking!

I was scared that I'd be in prison for years,
Like Strangeways or Alcatraz behind iron bars.
But the policemen were kind and gave me some tea,
They said that I was alright to go free,
They said that Charlie had "manipulated" me,
And that the truth was there for all to see,
And they told my mum and dad all the lies he'd spun,
And they said that his gun wasn't even a real one.

Charlie Peace,
Charlie Peace,
He ended up in the hands of the police,
Pray to god that he'll never be released,
And kids will be safe from this evil beast.

Charlie"s sudden absence hit me like a bomb.
My dad said, "He'll get no peace where he's gone!
He's been sentenced by the judge to a House of Correction,
Where even bigger kids than he is wont leave him alone!"
I stopped being haunted by the evil things we did,
It was great just to go and play with other kids.
People often get bored with leading normal lives,
But when you've lived in Charlie's world, normality's paradise.

Charlie was a bully and crazy to boot,
I saw him years later, he'd been in an Institute,
"Do you want plugging?!" came the voice one afternoon,
And my heart sank fast like I was doomed!
But "Fuck off Charlie," I said, "You don't scare me at all!
And far from plugging me, I'll be slamming your balls
Because I've been told you're a fake and a farce,
Now fuck off or I stick that toy gun up your arse!!!"

Crest-fallen Charlie Peace slinked away,
And I've never seen him again to this day.
I've often wondered what became of him,
Wether he's a criminal now or a politician.
But I learned a lot from his evil ways....
About how to live my life day to day
I walk my own path...
I lead my own life...
I be my own person always! Always!

Charlie Peace,
Charlie Peace,
If you ever see him just dial the police,
He should be in Broadmoor
And never be released,
He's the bogeyman, he's the devil, he's the beast

No one.

The sound of people having fun,
And I am nowhere,
I am no one.

Jimmy Nipples.

He's Jimmy,
He's the man with the guts,
He'll turn everybody's nipples to nuts,
He chain smokes his fags right down to the butts,
He's got his gang by the spanners
And he likes his crew cut.

He's Jimmy an' he's on his way in he...
Knows how to earn much more than a crust,
Every morning he has a full breakfast,
An' every dinner time four pints or bust.
In the clockin' out queue he's always the first.

He's Jimmy an' he's on his way in he...
Said to clock in for him coz he'll be on the minutes,
He's got a lovely ford Capri but he isn't comin' in it,
Coz it's "too long a story" to even begin it
So just clock him in its easy innit.

He's Jimmy an' he's on his way in he...
Looks after his tools with a boyish glee,
He tightens all his nuts with an Allen key,
He has five sugars in a man-sized mug of tea
An' he goes for a shit everyday at half past three.

He's Jimmy

He's the man with the guts.
He'll turn everybody's nipples to nuts.
He chain-smokes his fags right down to the butts.
He's got his gang by the spanners
An' he loves his crew cut.

He's Jimmy an' he's on his way in he...
Always buys a Sun and a packet of cigs,
"Coz that's what life is son, tits and politics,
And if you don't fit in with it then you're a misfit,
And all managers are dicks and all politicians are tits!"

He's Jimmy an' he's on his way in he'll...
Fettle any metal an' make a meal of it,
He'll tackle any job with the appropriate drill bit,
He says he's good at everything and says he's tough an' fit.
He had a trial for Bolton but they said he was shit.

He's Jimmy an' he's on his way in he...
Talks real dirty all over the shop floor,
When the women are leaving he lingers by the door
And he whispers them things that'd embarrass a whore
And he says he's had Ivy Rowbottom who manages the store.

He's Jimmy,
He's the man with the guts.
He'll turn any woman's nipples to nuts.
He chain-smokes his fags right down to their butts.
He' got his gang by the spanners
He's lookin good with his crew cut.

He's Jimmy an' he's on his way in he...
Can't wait for Friday's when he's on his way home.
His tea will be ready an' then he'll be gone
Straight into Bolton where he's never alone,
He'll get to the Nevada if he gets his skates on.

He's Jimmy an' he's on his way in if...

There's a dodgy job, he's the man with the balls,
He'll climb over any roof, he'll scale any walls,
Any dangerous machine's just "Fuck all!"
There's nothing but grit underneath his overalls.

He's Jimmy an' he's on his way in he...
Over did the ale on the Sunday night,
An' on Monday mornin' I could see he wasn't right.
The last time I saw him, he asked me for a light,
It wasn't till the Tuesday we discovered his plight.

He's Jimmy but he's NOT comin' in he...
Must've fallen into a pulping machine
And gone right through the system albeit unseen,
Thereby ironically fulfilling his dream
Of ending up in the papers, if you know what I mean.

He's Jimmy.
He's the man with the guts.
He'll turn everybody's nipples to nuts.
He chain-smokes his fags right down to the butts.
He's got his gang by the spanners and they've all got a crew cut.

Raggy Trousers.

Don't be fooled by my pleasant smile
Or by my laid-back demeanour,
Don't think I'll go the extra mile,
Or invite you back for dinner,
And if you're expecting a handout,
It's likely I'll snap your wrist,
I might be wearing raggy trousers
But I'm no philanthropist!

A homeless man approached me once
And asked me for a dime.
I said "Buddy go ask someone else,
Because what I've got is all mine!"
He said "I'm sorry to have troubled you,
It was something that I missed...
I saw your raggy trousers
And thought you were a philanthropist.

From time to time people knock on my door
And ask me for charity,
And I say what are you knocking on my door for?
Why are you picking on me?
I'm sat on my own, in my own home,
Eating scones and feeling blissed,
And although these pyjamas may be raggy indeed,
They're not those of a philanthropist.

A blind man tapping along the pavement,
Unsure of where to go,
Tapped straight into me and said,

Would I lead him across the road.
But I had to insist that he stayed right there
And suggested he was being myopic.
I am actually wearing raggy trousers sir,
But by no means am I philanthropic.

I worked on Tib Street in Manchester,
The crank central of the town.
But I'd always put on a smile for the tramps
And never pass them with a frown.
And they came to know that an approach to me,
Was something to resist,
I'd hear them whisper, "He might have raggy trousers mate,
But he's no fuckin filanfropist!

Out at the shops on a Saturday,
Down to Aldi in the Ford Capri,
And Saturday can't come soon enough
Because shopping's therapeutic to me.
But an elderly lady laden with bags,
Started begging me for a lift.
"These might be raggy trousers madam,
But this is not a philanthropist!

I went to the chip shop one Friday night,
It's a Dog Shit Valley thing.
The moon and stars they shone so bright,
What a joy to the Valley that brings.
When a sultry lady stopped me
And asked me to give her a chip.
I said, it seems you've mistaken these trousers miss,
For those of a philanthropist.

And now I'm living in Lancaster,
Where there are beggars on the street.
Some are on uppers, some can be quite down,
But nicer beggars you couldn't meet.

But invariably they'll approach me
And they have to be dismissed,
Although my trousers are a lot raggier than theirs,
It doesn't mean I'm a philanthropist.

Someone asked me if I'd sponsor them
To climb Mount Everest.
They were collecting for a worthy cause,
To open a Community Centre in Hest.
"But the people of Hest are communal enough,"
I said, if you get my gist,
So begone! I've got my raggy trousers on,
But I'm no philanthropist!

And so in life you have to be careful,
Because people can want a quick buck,
And it's never the posh and the powerful,
It's those that are down on their luck.
They'll pop up sudden and ugly
Like gorillas in the mist
And they see you're wearing raggy trousers,
And presume you're a philanthropist.

So I never fall for their bravado,
They're often three parts pissed,
I wear my raggy trousers with pride,
I don't want to be a philanthropist.
And I always consider others
To be totally round the twist,
And I aspire to be, I strive to be
A Raggy Trousered Misanthropist!

Tip Man.

As I pulled up he was stalking about.
Now I know that tip men can curse and shout,
But he was effin' and jeffin' and spitting it out,
Someone had rubbished his day, no doubt.

I couldn't tell if it was me that upset him,
Or whether this was just his normal Touretting,
In any case, I tell you, that I'll never forget him
And he'd deeply disturb my unconscious if I let him.

He was effin about this and effin about the other
And effin, eff knows whose effin mother.
It doesn't usually bother me one way or the effin other
But I tip-toed past him hoping he wouldn't bother.

He shouted "Aye! Where you going with that piece of hardboard,
It goes in with the wood not in with the cardboard!"
And you've not even shut your effin car door,
Now eff off from the port and get over to effin starboard!"

"Hang on, hardboard, cardboard...it's similar tipman
It's not like I've just gone ip dip dip man,
Like some people must do when they visit this shit pan,
So you can hardly accuse me of having no wit man!"

He shouts..."Excuse me for not being too cooperative
But I'm not a tipman I'm a Refuse Operative,
So I'll thank you not to be so effin provocative
Or the next time you speak will be effin post-operative!"

"Look, all I want to do is dump this stuff,
So I'd appreciate civility, if you'd be good enough.
I don't want to split hairs with the Corporation tough,
So I'll just dump this board and then I'll be off!"

So he's over to me with assertive strides,
And standing up straight with his hands by his sides,
All badged up with Local Authority pride,
He says, "Tipping's what we do in here, Dumping's what you do outside!"

It was too much to bear...and try as I might,
He'd flicked on the switch that flips on my attack light.
"What's this? What's that? I don't give a shite!
Now move or I'll dump you from a very great height!"

"You really had better button your effin lip man,
Or I'll be dumping you in that dirty effin skip man
And your mates will be brushing up your every effin bit man
And tipping it all in the Corporation shit van!"

"And when it comes to Xmas and you're expecting a tip man,
You'll have a long effin wait coz I'll give you zip man,
Coz you effin really have got on my effin pip man,
You horrible, cheeky, ugly, dirty, smelly effin tipman!!!

The Buddha in Manchester.

The Buddha was walking along Deansgate,
When he came across this guy,
And he told him of a technique you can use
At the point at which you die.
You intone some sacred syllables
And instead of then being dead
Your consciousness will simply leave
Through a point at the top of your head.
The buddha gave the guy the syllables
And showed him how to meditate,
And taught him how to lead his consciousness
Through the bardo state,
Until he should reach enlightenment
In everlasting bliss,
And wouldn't return to the suffering
That we all experience,
He'd instantly be freed from all our
Hate and greed and crime,
And the guy listened to the Buddha
And thanked him for his time,
He said, "I really am so grateful
And so thankful that you care,
But why don't you try the Northern Quarter mate,
Coz you get more cranks up there!"

We'll Be Alright Tonight.

There's a scrape of Branston in the bottom of this jar,
There's some cheese rind here that hasn't gone too far,
And I've found these cigarette dimps in Crumpsall Park,
We'll be alright tonight.

We've got some old books we can read again,
There's some comics here that I've just been given,
We can do the crossword in the Daily Mirror,
We'll be alright tonight.

You get paid tomorrow and we'll buy some spuds and stuff,
And we'll think ourselves lucky that we're not living rough,
Coz out there it's ice cold and that's really tough,
We'll be alright tonight.

And when I get some money we'll go for early doors,
And we'll soon forget what it's like to be poor.
And to have no telly and sleep on the floor,
We'll be alright tonight.

Yeh, we'll go to the pub and we'll buy twenty fags,
Then we'll stagger back home with two massive bags
Of shopping and make steak puddings in rags,
Oh we'll be alright tonight.

We'll get a Kwik-Save chicken that's going cheap,
And we'll make it last right through the week,
And some sausages and eggs and things and some streaky bacon,

We'll be alright tonight.

I know you work hard for next to no pay,
And your life's all work and not much play,
And sometimes it's hard just getting through the day,
But we'll be alright tonight.

And I know it's been hard since I got the sack,
But you'll see, I'll get our lives back on track,
And I'll show those bastards who's coming back!
And we'll be alright tonight.

It doesn't really matter how sparse the flat is,
It doesn't really matter that our life's in tatters,
It's that we've got each other and that's what really matters,
So we'll be alright tonight.

Things are really hard yeh but we're not gonna die,
So come and rest your head down now and just lie
Right here in mi arms and.... don't cry...
We'll be alright tonight.

It's Easy Dying Now.

I'm crying now,
I'm hiding nothing now,
In this strange land,
Even mi palms are in other people's hands,
Even under mi arms where no one ever sees,
Is exposed
Now these people've crucified me.
Hanging naked,
Nailed to a tree
Is not what I expected life to be.
I know why I'm here
And I know how it's got to be,
But sometimes, I can't see,
Is it really necessary?
I keep thinking you've forsaken me...
Dying's pretty easy,
The pain's crazy!...
But the dying's easy.
It had to be this way, you see,
I've walked a road of martyrdom
So your kingdom will come
To earth
As it is in heaven,
And I understand that, even
Though I feel so saddened,
So sad,
But at the same time I'm glad
That all these people here,

Who you say have been really bad,
Won't need to get mad with each other
Anymore,
Won't need to be sad about what's
Gone on before,
Because I know that when I'm gone,
This act of dying
Will linger on
In their minds
And spur them on
To be kind to each other,
Forever,
To stop lying to each other
Forever,
To stop fighting each other
Forever,
And ever,
Amen.
So no crying now,
Yeh, I'll stop crying now,
It's easy dying now.

Spy.

A goblin peeped in through mi window,
And saw me sitting there,
He saw me in mi chair,
He studied me there,
He saw the shape of mi head,
He watched while I read mi book,
And saw how i held mi hand,
Waiting to turn the page,
He saw mi age
He saw mi grey hair,
He observed me there,
He saw me stare into the mirror,
And saw me expression change
From serene to deranged
Then back again,
He saw me walk around
And get another book
And then sit back down,
And he saw how long it took to cross mi legs,
He saw the dregs in mi tea cup,
He could see I'd eaten a sandwich
And left some crumbs and crust,
He watched as I put mi hand down mi trousers,
.......To readjust,
He saw the poor quality of mi clothes,
He saw me press mi nose
The way I do,
He could see the newspaper I'd just bought,

He saw me grimace at some bad internal thought,
He saw me rub mi eyes,
He saw the lies I tell miself,
The whys and wherefores
That get me through,
He could see the crimes I've committed
That no one else knew about,
And he could see that nobody cares,
But the thing that scares me the most
Is that he can see me climb the stairs,
So he can see me everywhere,
He can see that I'm a misfit,
He watches me when I'm having a shit,
And sees the faces I pull when I'm doing it,
He can see me in my bed,
And knows that I sleep at an angle instead of straight,
He sees inside mi head....
He watches me get up late,
He sees me deliberate
Over what clothes to wear,
Then hesitantly go down the stairs
Because of mi limpy leg,
He watches me boil mi egg and eat mi toast,
Some days it seems mi only purpose
Is to host
This nosey bastard!

New Woman.

Winnie made croquette potatoes,
When everyone else had mash.
Everyone else made a meal of the housework,
But Winnie went round in a flash.
She had the edge,
She used Pledge
She was the first in the street to make kedgeree,
She used a whisk
To stir the cake mix,
Not an old wooden spoon like it used to be.

Her husband Ronnie,had a Vauxhall Viva,
It was green and keen and streamlined,
Hardly anyone else had a car at that time,
No one was that way inclined,
He was a rep,
A step ahead,
He always had a pocket of peppermints.
He had a tash,
And a splash
Of Old Spice around his silky chin.

They were the first in the street to have a telly
And a gas fire with a switch to turn it on,
And they had a telephone that no one could ring,
Because nobody else had one,
It was class,
They were working class
With middle class aspirations,
It was a sign,
Of the times,
Things were changing all over the nation.

Winnie worked days in a lightbulb factory,
She was the eyes of the quality control,

And everyone could see how good she was,
Because the eyes were the windows of the soul.
But making bulbs,
It was dull,
So she needed something light to ease the load,
She couldn't wait
Till Friday late,
To clock out and do her shopping on the way home.

And Winnie knew how to do the shopping,
Get the big things all at the Co-op,
Leave the fresh stuff till Saturday market,
Friday treats from the corner shop,
And a cake,
And a piece of hake,
For Sunday smelled of sweetness and success,
It added spice
And it was nice,
To close her eyes and dream of nothing less.

On Saturday it was the market,
It was a good place to go and meet,
Folk from all over the Valley,
Not just people from her street,
A cup of tea,
A cig or three,
And find out about all the goings on,
Across the town,
The ups and downs,
Of all the people from where she belonged.

And Sunday was always for resting,
The Lord's day it was called,
Nobody seemed really to know what to do,
Because the Lord had done nothing at all,
They went to church,
It didn't hurt,
It's the place you've got to go to beg for pardon,

For your sins,
Then put out the bins,
While Ronnie washed the car and did the garden.

Sunday afternoon was always sunny,
Jesus guaranteed it that way,
But Winnie always felt a bit funny,
About the singing and the kneeling and the praying.
But soon,
Her friend June,
Would come round for Something Simple on the radio,
And at night
If it's still light,
A walk to Coronation Park to where the flowers grow.

Winnie was making casseroles,
When everyone else had stew,
She was always on time at the clocking in line
And always the first in the bus queue,
It was her way,
Everyday,
To be up there with them knowing what was what,
It was a good way,
Instead of every day,
Moaning about what you hadn't got.

Winnie was the first to make pasties,
When others couldnt see further than a pie,
But it's true that other women can be nasty,
And blow out another woman's pilot light,
It's a curse,
There's nothing worse,
Than a woman who's got trouble on her mind,
It's just a shame,
No one's to blame,
But some women are just the trouble kind.

Ivy Rowbottom was one of those,
"Ivy the Terrible" they called her,
She smelled like a chip pan, had a tongue like a whip
And a face like a bulldog had mauled her.
She was feared,
And she just appeared,
And slapped Winnie round the face with a sheet of tripe,
"Let that be enough,
Of your snobby stuff,
We'll have no more parsley sauce while I'm alive."

Winnie was shocked for a second,
What would Lord Jesus do?
But Jesus had never been tripe-slapped,
As far as Winnie knew,
Blessed are the meek?
Turn the other cheek?
But a tripe slap could not be forgotten,
So make a stand,
The future's in your hands!
It's time to confront this Rowbottom.

A rolling pin to the abdomen,
Had Ivy reeling about,
And a baking tray across the head,
All but knocked her out.
She stood
Like a pudding,
And wobbled just a bit from side to side,
Then she dithered,
And then withered,
And the poison Ivy spouted upped and died.

There was no longer any trouble from Ivy,
And Winnie continued to cook

Experimenting with ingredients,
There was more to life than Mrs Beeton's book.
There was rice,
And Kraft cheese slices,
And baked potatoes with fillings instead of chips,
And fried steak
And milk shakes,
Stuff that made everybody lick their lips.

The sixties were just round the corner
And a new sense of freedom was here,
The age of the tyrant was over,
The path of the new woman was clear,
Then on TV,
On the BBC,
Fanny Craddock first presented the quiche,
And so it goes,
Who could know,
What would happen once Fanny was unleashed.

The Fortune Teller.

She lived up mysterious Sion Street,
In a hocus pocus hut,
With a consecrated iron roof,
She used desecrated coconut.
She was evil,
She was mean,
She chased kids with a switch,
They called her Jinny Greenteeth,
She was a witch.
Her doors and windows were all unhinged,
Curtains cobwebbed and moth-winged,
Copper rings had turned her fingers green,
She was skinny and she was lean.
A wizened old thing, all stitches and patches,
Tea leaves read and spent matches,
Abscesses bled, she had a crystal ball and
Messages from beyond the shawl
Came flooding with the silver moon,
We went there one afternoon.
She told fat Mrs Bates she'd eaten too much cake,
She told Mrs Rowbottom that her ring was a fake,
She told Aunty Alice that it wasn't tripe
But hake that'd killed our Jack
And sent him to the grave,
But he might come back
If the moon was right and the silver stacked.
As a clairvoyant, she seemed to have the knack
Of seeing what went on in the past!
Oh, just how long would this afternoon last?
When suddenly...
"Bring the child to me!"
Oh no, the crone was pointing at me!
They sat me on her boney knee,
I was about thirteen.
She smelled of lavender and dried urine.

Her teeth were green,
Her eyes were violets,
"Cross my palm with silver an' I'll see whats
On the cards for him."
She closed her eyes and became serene,
Then, with the dirtiest thumb I'd ever seen
Crossed my brow with grease
Then gasped...
And keened...
"This is a goblin child, a halfling!
Cuckoo-born, crow's spawn,
Caul-clad on a snowy morn,
A moon-calf, calf-licked,
Flibberty gibberty
Leg-limping-swapling,
A switched,
Shape-shifting
Milk thief!
There's no use he'll bring
To any living thing,
Born in the cold.
You should've left him in the snow,
There's nothing he can possibly ever know,
Except Poetry!

It was like a bomb had dropped!
Aunty Alice was in shock!
The Rowbottom was choking!
This was no joke!
A Poet?
No!!!!!

Witch.

There's a witch standing beside me......
Can you see her?
She's not the same as she used to be,
She's changed,
More deranged
If anything
Because she died
And she died in pain,
I've always thought it strange
That she came to stay with me!
She just stands there quietly,
And mostly, thats how it's always been.
But, sometimes, she interferes,
Whispers mad things in mi ears,
Things that can't possibly be,
Like that old lady wants to take me home for tea,
And sit me on her knee
And feed me cream cakes.
Sometimes she'll take me off
Where I shouldn't be,
And, it's like she abuses me...
Over and over till I'm sore...
And then she abuses me some more!
Can you see her....
She's usually grinning, it's like smiling
It doesn't make me happy,
But it's alright by me,
It's fine by me,
But if I sing,
Or just say the wrong thing,
Then it happens, Ping!
She goes right off on a broomstick,
Giving me shit.
A whirlwind of this and that,
Treats me like a black cat,

Way over familiar
An' I can't think of anything sillier than that
But that's that!
Shit happens!
Crooked twat!
Can you see her?
She'll say there's someone behind me when there's not,
She'll tell me to take apples from the shop
And not pay for them
She'll say it's just the day for them
When it's not,
It's not always a day for apples!
She'll look in the mirror when I shave
And then there's not enough room for my face.
She displaces me
Makes me more.... all over the place!
Sometimes she'll take time away
And three weeks'll only last a minute
Then she'll take a minute
And spin it into three weeks
It's scary innit
Can you see her?
Sometimes she'll cry,
She says she died in fire,
She was tortured with devices,
By wise men and their lies,
And found guilty at the Assizes,
She protested her innocence all along,
But I've done nothing wrong either!
So why's she mithering me?
She says she came because she can,
And I'm just some random mad man
She says she's come home,
She says she's mi mother, maiden and crone.
I just wish she'd leave me alone!
But she says she's always going to be here.
A witch standing beside me....
Can you see her?....

Tell me you can see her!

Notes…

Where Beggars can Be Choosers: I was in Lancaster town centre just before Xmas and I'd got two pasties from Pound Bakery. I couldn't manage both so went to give one, in a Pound Bakery bag, to a young homeless person I'd seen sitting in a doorway. As I gave it him he said "God bless you mate." Then he looked in the bag and said "You usually get two for a pound in there!"

Little Tommy Tittlemouse: I came across the word "Murine" which means "Mouselike" and it immediately reminded me of a bloke I used to work for in a factory when I first left school.

Thief: A goblin poem and a true story!

Pity the Lune: when I moved to Lancaster I spent some time walking along the course of the River Lune from where it rises in the Cumbrian hills, down through Cumbria and Lancashire to the City of Lancaster and its estuary into the Irish Sea. I realised along the way that all our beautiful rivers have born witness historically to all the horrible things that humans do to each other.

Pie Tin: this started as a poem about my mate's grandma's enamel pie tin but developed into a rant about the plight of women in a pre and post war patriarchy.

Solstice: I wrote and first read this on the Winter Solstice 2016 at Long Meg and her Daughters, a stone circle in North Cumbria.

Alice Taylor's Wood: About a wood near where I grew up in Radcliffe, Lancs.

Light My Fire: the healing plant commonly known as St. John's Wort has been around a lot longer than St. John! I prefer to call it Solstice Wort as it flowers on the Summer Solstice.

March of the Hobgoblins: the word "gay" in this poem is used in its original meaning of "happy and carefree."

Dog Shit Valley: The town of Radcliffe is known, by people of the surrounding areas as "Dog Shit Valley." The town, always in Lancashire was subsumed under Greater Manchester, as M26, under the 1972 Local Government Act and proceeded to decline under the ensuing Thatcher years.

Sitting: "Dukha" is a Sanskrit word meaning "suffering."

Sambo's Grave: where the River Lune estuaries into the Irish Sea lies Sunderland Point a former outport of Lancaster where slave ships docked in the 18th and 19th centuries. At one time, a young black slave who had died mysteriously was buried, by a ship's crew, in a rabbit warren, without explanation and without ceremony. It is a very desolate place known locally as Sambo's Grave.

Oystercatchers: I first saw Oystercatchers on a school trip to the Welsh coast. I wrote the poem many years later whilst watching them on Morecambe Bay.

In the Shadow of the Church: About the first church I went to, St John's in Radcliffe.

M and M Schafter Ltd.: Many companies these days seem to attach meaningless adages to their names in the bizarre belief that it convinces the unsuspecting public of the quality of their service. This is the most meaningless I've come across.

The Ballad of Billy Openshaw: this poem is for my uncle Harry who has always told this tale and made it last for hours!

Charlie Peace: Charlie Peace was a character in the Buster comic based on the notorious thief Charles Peace who was hanged for his crimes in 1879. I was intrigued by him and wondered what he'd been like in his youth.

Jimmy Nipples: I once worked in a Paper Mill labouring for a machine engineer. We had to maintain huge machines in which blades would reduce waste paper into pulp which was then subjected to some chemical process and then compressed by giant rollers to emerge as paper for the newspaper industry. Jimmy was a bit of a local legend. He used to tell me that one day he'd make the headlines! Bolton Nevada was a roller skating rink frequented by people for the purpose of enjoyment.

Raggy Trousers: this poem is for Robert Tressell who wrote "the Ragged Trousered Philanthropist." Hest is a nice district of Lancaster.

Tip Man: I seem to have spent an inordinate amount of time using Local Authority Tips and have always been impressed with the friendly service provided by their employees, until...

We'll Be Alright Tonight: when I met my wife Ann in 1978 we were both student nurses in a mental hospital. This entailed very hard work for very little money but we managed to save enough to get a flat together. Then, just before xmas, I got the sack!

His Eyes Watch The Nations

Ps 66;7 (NIV)

By

Bob Dunnett

Published by New Generation Publishing in 2024

First Edition

ISBN   978-1-83563-133-1

www.newgeneration-publishing.com

New Generation Publishing

CONTENTS

"THE LION HAS ROARED"
Amos and Judgement

1. GOD and JUDGEMENT
"The lion has roared- Who will not fear?" Amos 1:2 NIV

The roar of the lion was not unknown to Amos- he was, after all, a shepherd. It seems, however, that at least on one occasion such a roar was the vehicle of a profound prophetic revelation, one that epitomised in an intense and startling way the message he had to convey to Israel (1:2; 3:4, 8, 12). The lion does not roar without intent: he is out to devour. There was now a roar from God, and with similar intent. The roar of God was his word of warning to Israel in the mouth of his prophet. It was not to be ignored or laughed off! Its import is made plain in 2:12; "As a shepherd saves from the lion's mouth only two leg bones or a piece of an ear, so will the Israelites be saved". God was about to devour Israel. Thus Amos presented a God who was threatening judgement.

1. The Divine Dynamic of Amos' Prophecies

It is very clear that Amos was deeply aware that in speaking as he did he was under a prophetic compulsion. He was not giving his own opinions on the fate of Israel and invoking God as some form of psychological pressure to reinforce his opinions. As a shepherd he was no scholar or intellectual or political observer (though clearly thoughtful and perceptive), and he never presents himself as such. He clearly operated in the conviction that "the Sovereign LORD does nothing without revealing his plans to his servants the prophets" (3:7), and that he was one of those prophets. Everything about his message conveys the fact that he knew that it was actually God who was speaking through him. For example we find that the statement, "The lion has roared - who will not fear" is followed immediately by the words, "The Sovereign LORD has spoken - who can but prophesy". This means that he spoke because he had heard

God speak, and therefore could do no other but speak. His whole ministry in fact was under girded by a profound recollection of his calling to be a prophet: "I was neither a prophet nor a prophet's son, but I was a shepherd, and I also took care of sycamore-fig trees. But the LORD took me from tending the flock and said to me, 'Go, prophesy to my people Israel'." (7:14) Thus spiritually he was always fully aware of God himself speaking through him. He came to his nation with a word of disaster because he was divinely impelled.

2. God Revealed as a God of Judgement

What he had to speak, therefore, was not a human prognosis of the situation in his nation, but a divine revelation – and that revelation must therefore be not only a revelation from God but also a revelation of God. The God who speaks out judgement must by that fact be a God of judgement. The very language which Amos employs testifies to this, for it directly represents God as actually speaking out his judgement.

In 2:6, Amos uses the formula, "This is what the LORD says" followed by the words, "Now then I will crush you as a cart crushes when loaded with grain" (2:13). It was not Amos who was threatening to crush Israel, but God. Later (3:14-15) we read "On the day I punish Israel for her sins ... I will tear down the winter house and the summer house, declares the LORD". Again God is responsible: it is he who is going to do the punishing, the tearing down and the demolishing. God even speaks openly of his anger: "This is what the LORD says, 'I will not turn back my wrath'" (2:6). This is the consistent pattern all through his prophecies: God speaks personally in the language of punishing, crushing and wrath. If Amos is inspired of God we do not have the option of discounting God as a God of judgement or of divesting him of personal responsibility for it.

Furthermore we need to recognise that when God speaks judgement, he speaks of appalling and horrific events. What he is presenting through Amos is not a mildly painful rebuke, but rather a lacerating scourge. The language of destruction is never only symbolic imagery. What his judgement was going to mean to the Jews was also portrayed in more prosaic and precise terms, but equally horrific: "An enemy will overrun the land; he will pull down

your strongholds and plunder your fortresses." (3:11); "I abhor the pride of Jacob and detest his fortresses; I will deliver up the city and everything in it." (6:8) ;"In that day," declares the Sovereign LORD, "the songs in the temple will turn to wailing. Many, many bodies— flung everywhere! Silence! (8:3). These words amount to a total destruction of Israel as the Jews knew it. Only the event itself, when the nation was devastated by the merciless Assyrian war machine, would bring a full realization of the unspeakable human horror and agony that lay in this judgement. It would be something that overtook the whole nation, men, women, and children. Where there was not death, there would be unspeakable hardship.

3. Amos' Revelations are Borne out by all Contemporary Prophets

Amos does not come across as an extreme exception among the biblical prophets in this depiction of judgement. His are not the "outlandish" bits in a collection of prophetic writings that are otherwise more "reasonable". Everything he says is abundantly borne out by his fellow prophets. The fact is that wherever God speaks of judgement he speaks of something for which he is responsible, and which is devastating and painful for humanity. Jeremiah says, for example,
    "But I am full of the wrath of the LORD, and I cannot hold it in. "Pour it out on the children in the street and on the young men gathered together; both husband and wife will be caught in it, and the old, those weighed down with years. Their houses will be turned over to others, together with their fields and their wives, when I stretch out my hand against those who live in the land," declares the LORD. (Jer. 6:11-12 NIV)
    Like Amos (though over 150 years later, and to Judah, not Israel) he speaks out of huge prophetic conviction and is deeply aware of being simply a mouthpiece.

4. The Rejection of a God of Judgement - Then and Now

The sheer horror and weight of what the judgement of God meant is something that Amos' generation had lost. It was no longer a real threat in their thinking. The Israelites of Amos' day came to grief because in their complacency they were not able to engage with such a prophetic message. They did not disbelieve in prophets of course

3

– they had lots of them. Nor did they disbelieve in "God", or even that he would judge. It was simply that they were so deeply involved in a lifestyle that put a total focus on self-indulgence that they were unable to discern any longer when a message truly came from God. Nor could they receive a message which was so hard. They were spiritually blind. What theology they did have led them to believe that as a nation they could not be destroyed for they were God's people. Amos and his kind were therefore to be dismissed as a nuisance. It was only a later generation, purged in exile, that, having taken due stock of what the prophets had said, and comparing it with what had actually happened in the national history, was forced to acknowledge the validity of the prophetic message, and was obliged to re-instate its divine origin.

If Amos' generation was reluctant to receive such prophetic words, our own is, of course, much more so. Our generation has lost any concept of prophetic activity which has its source in God, simply because it has lost any living concept of God. If there is any "prophetic" strain in the world at all, it is purely a human instinct, the wisdom of a knowledgeable person who has a high degree of insight into the affairs of men and can make educated assessments that appear far sighted. The modern world of rational enlightenment is not in the least likely to respond to divine prophetic insights. In simply responds with contempt.

Unfortunately, this attitude is not just to be found in the secular world. It is also present to a very large extent among those who profess faith in God, even among those who in other respects would call themselves of Christian Evangelical persuasion. Much of modern Christian thinking would like to put God at a convenient distance from any activity of judgement. An "enlightened" view of God cannot accommodate the idea of such appalling visitations as are depicted by the prophets. It is a view which would acknowledge that men and women might well do things which bring their own punishment, but God would not get actively involved in any process of "judgement". The very idea of God becoming involved in a retribution that had elements of cruelty or pain would seem somehow to lessen any appropriate image of God, who must be epitomised as "Love". Even less would such modern thinking feel that "anger" was an appropriate term to describe the motivations of God. It would be better to speak of "the consequences of man's

folly" or "the inevitable working out of wrongdoing" and leave God at a respectable distance from the outcome.

This sort of thinking seems attractive and satisfying to the modern mind, but it certainly does not fit with the prophetic witness - nor, indeed, with the whole biblical witness. At bottom it calls into question the prophetic experience. The prophets are seen fundamentally as men of their own age, speaking of values which belonged to their own age. They may have been useful to their generation but require reinterpretation today. When Christians take this viewpoint they move away from any concept of genuine revelation, and from any firm ground for ascertaining the nature of God. For the re-interpretation that is sought is inevitably based on purely human thinking and concepts. The nature of God, however, can only be found by revelation, never by human wisdom. God has his own double test for the genuineness of a prophetic revelation: if it upholds behaviour endorsing the moral law, and if it comes to pass, then it will be known to be the voice of truth. On both counts Amos abundantly passes the test. His was patently a message to re-instate the moral law and it was a message that came true, and with deadly accuracy, against all the seeming odds. When prophetic words have been so vindicated as those of Amos have, it is the height of folly to act as though they had no stamp of God upon them or to think that God has ceased to act on the principles which such words enshrine. He spoke judgement then, and he remains the God of judgement now.

At another level altogether it is, of course, possible, and rightly so, to see wars, and the cruelty and destruction associated with them, as an expression of Satan's hatred of humanity. There is something demonic about the lust for power and booty that launched the Assyrians on their path to empire, causing them to overrun Israel. There is something equally demonic in the appalling cruelty and oppression they brought to the nations they conquered. That having been said, however, the prophets still insist on the sovereign action of God in judgements (Assyria was the rod of God's anger!). Whatever Satan's part may be in such scourging, ultimately God is orchestrating the events. Moreover, it is clear that God does not condone the behaviour of the oppressing powers: the Assyrian cruelty would itself be judged in due course.

5. Why God must be A God of Judgement

On what basis can the concept of a God of Judgement be defended? The answer to this lies fundamentally in the fact that the God who has been revealed to us through the biblical writings is a God of righteousness – he is a holy God. He is a God who must therefore by nature react against evil when it appears. Certainly he is a God of love, but a love that is pure. Genuine love cannot coexist with injustice, or any other evil, but must ultimately banish it. Love is very patient; something that was very evident in the way God had, over a long period, warned the Israelites of their shortcomings. Love is very faithful and is full of explicit warnings; witness the prolific nature of the prophetic word to Israel. Love is never weak, however, and does not turn a blind eye to everything that happens, nor does it forgive everything that may happen. The reason for this is that real consequential love cannot but be holy and righteous. We cannot, therefore, have a God of love who is not at the same time righteous; and we cannot have a righteous God who does not act against evil. The biblical witness is clear: God does act against evil, both at individual and national levels. That action is judgement.

The understanding of God as one who will judge evil in nations (the clear testimony of Amos) is critical for our generation and for our current situation. Amos' prime testimony is that when God's patience is exhausted then a very painful, destructive reckoning is bound to come. Failure to give this the weight it demands is a great failure. We are in the gravest danger of being in precisely that position.

2.GOD and THE NATIONS
"His eyes watch the nations". Ps. 66.7 NIV

God's involvement with the nations is evident throughout Scripture. God told Abraham that he had been chosen in order that the nations of the world might be blessed through him. God has never been concerned for anything less than the whole world. The reason is simple: "I made the earth and its people" (Jer. 27:5) He is never pictured as allowing history (which is all about nations) to be something in which he has no concern or control. The revelation of

the Old Testament comes out of an historical narrative which involves nations, especially the Jewish nation, and, as far as the nations are concerned, in that narrative of events God can only be seen as a "hands on" God. "His eyes watch the nations" is what we learn from the Psalmist (Ps 66:7). Job records that "He makes nations great, and destroys them; he enlarges nations and disperses them" (Job 12:23 NIV). Everywhere he "rules" the nations, and they are exhorted to "Be still and know that I am God". This personal God is concerned for all people everywhere.

1. God Speaks to the Nations of the World

The prophetic writings of the Old Testament leave us in no doubt about the fact that God has dealings with the nations of the world. Though Amos has such a devastating word to bring to Israel, the collection of his prophecies that have come down to us actually begin with a series of prophetic statements concerning the nations which surround Israel: the Syrians, the Philistines, Tyre, Edom, Ammon and Moab all feature in these statements (Amos 1-2). It is very evident from what Amos had to say about these nations that his "eyes were watching" them. In this respect Amos is followed by very many of the other prophets. For example, Jeremiah was told right at the outset of his ministry, "See, I have made you a prophet to the nations" (Jer. 1:15 NIV) The prophetic voice for him was to nations, not just to individuals or even one nation. Whilst the main weight of the writings of the prophets falls, naturally, upon the two kingdoms of Israel and Judah, bringing severe warnings about their behaviour, the same kind of warnings are very clearly being given to the surrounding nations. These nations actually included three superpowers, Egypt, Assyria and Babylon, all of whom featured in the prophets as well as the smaller nations which bordered on Israel and Judah.

Isaiah, Jeremiah and Ezekiel, the three largest of these prophetic books, have a total of no less than twenty three chapters devoted entirely to nations other than Israel and Judah. Of the smaller prophetic books Jonah, Nahum and Obadiah do not mention Israel or Judah at all, the first two dealing exclusively with Assyria and the last with Edom. Habakkuk's writing is mainly concerned with how God will first use Babylon in judgement on Judah and what God will then do to Babylon. Amos and Zephaniah speak prophetically about

God's dealings with a number of different nations. All the "major" prophets, therefore, and six, at least, out of the twelve "minor" prophets address the destinies of the nations and the part God plays in ordering those destinies.

Thus the word of God among his prophets is by no means exclusive to his "own nation", even if he has a special purpose for them in the world. God rules among the nations, speaks to the nations, has an active concern for the nations and decides their destinies.

2. The Prophetic Words were made known to the Nations Concerned.

In some instances reference is made to nations other than Israel or Judah in order to reinforce the message to those nations. Isaiah's pronouncements of coming destruction to Egypt are meant to stop Judah trying to look to Egypt for help when they were oppressed by Assyria. It may be that Amos' pronouncements on Israel's neighbours were meant to similarly reinforce the devastation that was to come to Israel itself. However, it is clear that God does not always make prophetic announcements over the nations simply for the sake of letting Israel know his intentions. His concern is directly with those nations, even if his prophets belong to the Jews, and in a number of instances he insists that his word to the nations is actually heard by those nations. The reason for this is simply that he has a concern for those nations.

An obvious example of this is found in Jonah. He was sent to Nineveh, the capital of Assyria, with a message to preach against its wickedness. God's desire was to let Nineveh know its danger, and he looked for repentance. Jonah knew this, of course, but could not bear the thought that, after he proclaimed destruction, God would show him up by having mercy on Nineveh. So God had to fight his own prophet to make him speak to Nineveh. God's final word to Jonah about that city was, "Nineveh has more than a hundred and twenty thousand people who cannot tell their right hand from their left, and many cattle as well. Should I not be concerned about that great city?" (Jonah 4:11 NIV). Jonah did not want to receive it. The truth is, however, that God was concerned for that nation, and he remains concerned for every nation of the world. He shows it by being ready to speak to them.

8

Jeremiah also made the word of the LORD known to the nations of his day but in a different manner, as the following passage indicates:

"This is what the LORD said to me: "Make a yoke out of straps and crossbars and put it on your neck. Then send word to the kings of Edom, Moab, Ammon, Tyre and Sidon through the envoys who have come to Jerusalem to Zedekiah king of Judah. Give them a message for their masters and say, `This is what the LORD Almighty, the God of Israel, says: "Tell this to your masters: With my great power and outstretched arm I made the earth and its people and the animals that are on it and I give it to anyone I please. Now I will hand all your countries over to my servant Nebuchadnezzar king of Babylon; I will make even the wild animals subject to him. All nations will serve him and his son and his grandson until the time for his land comes; then many nations and great kings will subjugate him." (Jer. 27:2-7 NIV)

Thus, Jeremiah had the position and profile in Judah to be able speak to all the envoys of the surrounding nations and declare to them the mind of God. Jer. 25:17 sums up his work in his own words, "So I took the cup from the LORD's hand and made all the nations to whom he sent me drink it". God did actually cause his word to the nations to be heard by those nations, and at the highest level of government. The failure of those nations to respond does not invalidate God's concern for them.

3. God weighs and judges the moral behaviour of nations.

The major work of the prophets whose writings we have in the Old Testament was to warn the two kingdoms of Israel and Judah that their ways were not right before God and that severe judgements were likely to fall on them as a consequence. In other words, they brought a call to repentance - a repentance that meant a turning back to the godly ways to which God had called them when he formed them as a nation in the wilderness. It was this same theme of warning that God sounded to the other nations: as with his own people their ways were not right. Though they were not in a covenant relationship with God, as were the Israelites, there was an expectation on God's part that they would behave in ways that were just and righteous. Thus, whilst the prophets did not accuse the other nations of spiritual "adultery" and "prostitution" as they did the

Jewish people on account of their turning from Jehovah, they warned them severely about the inhuman behaviour they were perpetrating.

The first two chapters of the book of Amos provide a terse summary of the kind of thing that God found unacceptable among the nations which bordered Israel and Judah. Damascus (Syria) had "threshed Gilead" - probably some kind of genocide; Gaza (Philistia) "took captive whole communities and sold them" - they were into slave trading; Tyre likewise sold whole communities as slaves despite treaties to the contrary; Edom indulged in the vindictive killing of Jews, "stifling all compassion"; Ammon killed pregnant women in a policy of genocide designed to gain more land; Moab desecrated the dead. These were not isolated instances but were continual offences by these nations (as is indicated by the expression, "for three sins, even four"). God, in pronouncing judgement through the prophet Amos, was warning those nations against behaviour that they knew only too well was beyond the bounds of acceptability. He expected from them some demonstration of conscience.

Amos was not the only voice speaking for God and warning these neighbouring lands. Moab's pride and its hatred of the people of God were condemned by Isaiah, Zephaniah, Obadiah and Jeremiah. Isaiah spoke against the overweening pride of Tyre in its wealth and worldly political influence. Ezekiel spoke against the bitter revenge that Edom and Philistia had inflicted on Judah. These nations were arraigned by God through numerous prophets for their acts of inhumanity, and he held them guilty, for such acts were self-evidently evil.

4. The Charge against the Super-powers

The charge against the super-powers was much stronger still. Assyria dominated the Middle Eastern countries for a hundred years from 722 BC to 612 BC. The prophet Nahum spelt out graphically its criminal course of empire and listed the crimes of Nineveh (Assyria's capital): "The city of blood, full of lies, full of plunder, never without victims! .... charging cavalry, flashing swords, many casualties, piles of dead, bodies without number, all because of the wanton lust of a harlot who enslaved nations". Assyria was an empire built on violence, cruelty, death and wanton destruction. Its

objective was to gain as much booty as possible from subject peoples. It knew neither mercy nor compassion. Its behaviour was unspeakably brutal. It sought only power and prestige. The Assyrians were ultimately destroyed by the Babylonians who succeeded them as the premier super-power. Babylon held sway from c. 612 BC to 539 BC, and God's charge against her was the same as that against Assyria, namely wanton lust for power and wealth. Habakkuk speaks out God's charge against the Babylonians with great force: they were, "ruthless and impetuous people .... they are a law to themselves and promote their own honour ... they come bent on violence ... guilty men whose own strength is their god ...... destroying nations without mercy ... wealthy by extortion ... plotting the ruin of many peoples, shaming your own house and forfeiting your life" (Hab. 2:6 NIV).

Egypt, though dominated by Assyria and Babylon for two centuries was always a potential threat to them and of potential super-power status. Its general outlook was never very different from the other two super-powers. The same conquest and prestige were its aim, and the same cruelty and oppression were its methods. In addition, both Isaiah and Jeremiah speak of God's distaste at the idols of Egypt. Whilst not having the same guilt as the Jews with their rejection of their betrothal to Yahweh in favour of idols, Egypt's idolatry was none the less obnoxious in the sight of God and for this it was called to account.

The selfish exploitation that superpowers are tempted to exercise is always on God's agenda. Superpowers (or empires) always come and go, stricken down after great prestige, for none ever seems able to escape the temptation to oppress and control in ways that lack justice and righteousness.

5. Judgement on the Nations.

The whole purpose of the prophetic writings was to point out the sin of the nations and to call them to repentance. The desire of God was that repentance should forestall the inevitability of judgement on their sin. We have a God who, in his grace and compassion, is always seeking to bring blessing to nations. Where this is rejected, however, the outcome is death, destruction, pain, agony, exile and the like, all being described as his judgement.

It is equally clear from the prophetic writings that the nations themselves, in their wanton rejection of God's ways, were to be the instruments of God's judgement in their destruction of each other. Whilst famine and plague are amongst God's armoury of judgement, so also is the sword. In the two hundred years or so that were spanned by the prophetic writings, two superpowers wielded "the sword". The first was Assyria, and the second was Babylon. Each of these in turn devastated the smaller nations of Israel and Judah and their neighbours. Their power and lust for empire became a "day of the LORD" for many nations - that is, a day of reckoning and judgement. However, when Assyria had wielded the sword with great devastation and effected the judgement of God on smaller nations, Assyria itself came under the sword in the form of a newly emergent Babylon, and in its turn Babylon, as Habakkuk was to learn, itself was to come under the sword wielded by yet another emergent superpower, Persia.

The sovereignty of God is never surrendered in all these huge movements of the nations. God called Assyria, "the rod of my anger in whose hand is the club of my wrath" (Is. 10:5 NIV). God spoke of Cyrus the Mede (a Persian) as "his anointed, whose right hand I take hold of to subdue nations...." (Is. 45:1 NIV). Habakkuk has to acknowledge before God, that the Babylonians were "appointed to execute judgement", "ordained to punish" (Hab. 1:12). Thus were all the super-powers fulfilling the purpose of God in his very dealings with the nations of the world. It still happens today!

3. GOD'S JUDGEMENT and "NATURAL DISASTERS"

"I gave you empty stomachs" Amos 4:6 NIV

1. The Prophets and Human Catastrophes

Despite the clear biblical evidence to the contrary, many people are reluctant to accept the idea of God acting in judgement. A great many more are reluctant to accept that judgement involves any notion of natural catastrophe, widespread diseases, economic failures, war and the like.

The reason for this is that in our enlightened age we understand the nature of natural catastrophes much better than people once did. They are no longer fearful mysteries, but simply natural occurrences. They can even be, to some extent controlled or kept at bay, and there is no reason to find any sort of god lurking behind them. Thus the prevailing attitude to such events as foot and mouth disease, or AIDS is to give them entirely a natural explanation. Even events over which we have absolutely no control, like a Tsunami, can be explained and, if not prevented, at least their damaging effects can be lessened.

Thus, to think of God being involved in such events is to be obscurantist, and guilty of turning back the clock. The major problem of this "enlightened naturalism" is that unfortunately, it stands in stark contrast to the witness of the prophets for whom the varied disasters of life were at times only too evidently a mark of the displeasure of God. Thus we are either driven to pursue our enlightened attitude further, and say that the prophets were creatures of their own age, merely reflecting ideas which we have now outgrown, or take the view that "all scripture is profitable for doctrine" and that the words the prophets enunciated have a timeless authority. If we opt for the latter, then we have to face the challenge of the prophets concerning the way we live, and what God is likely to do if we fall short of his demands. If we do not, we cease to live under the prophetic word That has immense dangers.

What, then, exactly, did the prophets say?

2. The Verdict of Amos.

A key passage to start the enquiry is found in Amos 4:6-11. In this passage God reminds Israel of a series of disasters which he has already brought upon the nation, and he rebukes the people for failing to see the disasters as judgements and warnings, and for not repenting of their evil ways.

The first of these disasters is starkly described:- "I gave you empty stomachs (lit. cleanness of teeth) in every city and lack of bread in every town, yet you have not returned to me, declares the LORD". "Empty stomachs" obviously refers to a time of famine or food shortage, and two things are immediately apparent. First, God was responsible for the food shortage in whatever way it came! The text says simply, "I gave you empty stomachs", and the "I" is

unmistakable. The shortage could not be dismissed as "one of those things that just happen"! Second, God expected the people to recognise why the drought had come and to respond by amending their ways and returning to him. Quite clearly they did not respond, and God, speaking through Amos, was trying to impress on them again why he had sent the drought.

Amos goes on to record a number of other "natural" disasters. He speaks of a failure of rain at a critical time for harvest (vv7-8), of blight and mildew in the gardens and vineyards (v9), of locusts devouring fig and olive trees, of plagues (v10), of the death of elite troops in battle (v10), and of an earthquake (v11). A number of lessons are all too apparent. First God was just as responsible for these events as he had been for the food shortage. There is a repetition of the first person pronoun "I" referring to God as each disaster is recalled. Second, they constitute a wide range of disasters. They involve the weather, crop diseases, insects, epidemics, defeat in war, even large scale natural disasters like earthquakes. Anything that brings about shortage and distress might well have been part of the list. Third, God expects each "judgement" to be recognised as a warning from him. Fourth, the patience of God is apparent in the way that he persistently brought so many different judgements over a period of time, none of them being totally destructive, but destructive enough to warn the people of the danger of their lifestyle. In other words the process of judgement was measured and had a remedial intent. However, as Amos elsewhere makes clear, where there is no adequate response there is no remedy and the cup of destruction is eventually filled up.

It is not difficult to see from this passage that Amos was aware of an ongoing "movement" of judgement initiated by God on Israel. It was shouting at him. God was at work in all these happenings. It was all too much for his contemporaries, however, who bitterly, angrily and contemptuously rejected his words. To them he was not speaking from God. He was a traitor and misguided. He was ordered out of Israel by Amaziah the priest of Bethel (7:10-13), and there was an adamant refusal to heed his warnings about past judgements as well as about his warnings of future (and worse) judgements.

3. The Verdict of other Prophets.

Though Amos provides a good starting point, it would be possible to start from almost any of the prophetic writings and see precisely the same conclusions. Perhaps the outstanding thing about the prophetic witness (which forms quite a large part of the Old Testament) is its total unanimity in making the link between natural disasters and the judgement of God. For example, Hosea, a contemporary of Amos, declares the following:-

"Hear the word of the LORD, you Israelites, There is no faithfulness, no love, no acknowledgement of God in the land. There is only cursing, lying and murder, stealing and adultery; They break all bounds, and bloodshed follows bloodshed. Because of this the land mourns (dries up), and all who live in it waste the beasts of the field and the birds of the air, and the fish of the sea are dying."
(Hosea 4:1-3 NIV)

It is evident from this "word of the LORD" that the sin in the land had been the cause of the land "drying up" with widespread loss of animals, birds and fish. It is all highly reminiscent of Elijah's rebuke to Ahab many years before when Elijah called for a devastating drought on Israel which lasted three years, and which only came to an end with the destruction of the priests of Baal and a return to Jehovah.

Jeremiah faced drought in Judah a century and a half after Amos faced it in Israel. He described the devastating nature of it:

"This is the word of the LORD to Jeremiah concerning the drought: Judah mourns, her cities languish; they wail for the land, and a cry goes up from Jerusalem. The nobles send their servants for water; they go to the cisterns but find no water." (Jer. 14 1-4 NIV)

He recognises it as a judgement of God and immediately goes on to pray for relief. He knows perfectly well the connection between event and judgement.

Jeremiah also notes the general lack of understanding about connecting these things:

"They do not say to themselves, Let us fear the LORD our God, who gives autumn and spring rains in season, who assures us of the regular weeks of harvest. Your wrong doings have kept these away; your sins have deprived you of good." Jer. 5:24 NIV

15

A further example might be taken from Haggai, who spoke God's word to Judah after the return from exile, when once more they were forgetful of him:

"You expected much, but see, it turned out to be little. What you brought home, I blew away. Why?" declares the LORD Almighty. "Because of my house, which remains a ruin, while each of you is busy with his own house. Therefore, because of you the heavens have withheld their dew and the earth its crops. I called for a drought on the fields and the mountains, on the grain, the new wine, the oil and whatever the ground produces, on men and cattle, and on the labour of your hands." (Haggai 1:9-11 NIV)

The expression, *"What you brought home, I blew away"* is very graphic. It means that in one way or another, in a variety of "natural" causes and afflictions, God was acting in sovereign power and quite deliberately causing warning judgements in the shape of disappointing shortages.

The overall picture is plain. There is a consistent "word of the LORD" from numerous prophets in which the judgements of God are to be found in all sorts of calamities. One of the major prophets, Ezekiel, sums up the issue. Ezekiel, himself in exile, felt very bitterly and personally the meaning of God's judgement. Moved by God he spoke of the coming destruction of Jerusalem in the following terms: ""For this is what the Sovereign LORD says: How much worse will it be when I send against Jerusalem my four dreadful judgements--sword and famine and wild beasts and plague--to kill its men and their animals! (Ez. 14:21). He had learned only too well the dreadful truth of God's judgements in natural and man-made disasters.

4. The Prophets' Words Reflect God's Covenant with His People.

It is by no means the case that the concept of judgement by "natural" disaster was something peculiar to the prophets. It is to be found in the very covenant that God made with the Israelites in the wilderness. The blessings and curses written out in such detail in Deuteronomy 28 epitomised that covenant. Blessings were to follow obedience to God and curses were to follow disobedience. The curses meant that disobedience by the nation would spell out disaster. Deuteronomy makes it very plain that such disaster would be found in the field, among the animals, in drought, in locusts and

other plagues, diseases (for both humans and animals), defeat in battle, rule by aliens, loss of children and possessions to invaders, and, finally captivity and deportation. Thus the prophets in one sense were not receiving new revelation from God, but a quickening of old revelation. It had always been the case that judgement would come when the nation moved away from God, and that such judgement would take many forms and include natural disasters.

5. Conclusion.

There are at least three very good reasons for accepting this unanimous message from the prophets. First is the fact that it survived and proved wrong the bitter criticism with which it was first received by its contemporary generation. It was rejected on the grounds that it was dubious theology. The prophets' contemporaries took the view that God could not be speaking to them through natural catastrophe because, as everyone knew, God's promises of blessing rested over the land. After all, the Israelites were the chosen people of God, Jerusalem was his chosen dwelling, the land was his gift. None of these blessings could be removed, and those who said that God had been warning, through droughts and the like, of his intention to do so, were simply out of step; the prophets must have a wrong theology. Such people were simply peddling doom and gloom, and were demoralising. Time was to show, of course, how bankrupt was this theology of those who opposed the prophets, for history vindicated the prophets. The contemporary and accepted view is not necessarily right.

Second, as the course of history began so clearly to vindicate the prophets, the Jews came to accept their writings as oracles of God; they treasured them as God's truth. That was sensible. What the prophets said would happen, actually did happen, and they took the lesson to heart. When God vindicates his prophets, we also need to be careful not to reject their basic message of judgement, even if it does involve natural catastrophes. The fulfilled prophetic word is a very powerful argument, and was intended by God to be so.

Third, our generation needs to remember that, though we may be able to give a natural explanation to such events, there are always factors in those events that are beyond our knowledge. The size and timing of them can be notoriously unpredictable. Their disturbing feature is their unexpectedness. Given that God does judge, there is

no good reason to think that he cannot judge through "natural events" which, despite all our science still remain very largely in his own hands. He is still the God of "Providence", and a "hands on" God in his own world! If he moves through the "natural" events of our own personal lives, it is illogical to deny him any connection with other kinds of "natural" events.

4. THE TSUNAMI of 2004
A Contemporary Reflection

1. The Headlines and the Comment

The 9/11 event in America was one which could be ascribed to (and was ascribed to) "the force of evil in the world". It was the work of madmen bent on obscene objectives, the fruit of hatred and anger. For a great number of people, it was possible to leave out any reference to God, and simply assume he was not involved in that event. A great many churchmen, particularly in America, took that view: by looking at man's inhumanity to man it was possible to excuse the Almighty. It was a view which prevailed despite the presence of some who felt there was an issue with the nature of God that had to be addressed. The Tsunami waves, however, are clearly in a different category. They simply cannot be explained away in terms of human hatred or madmen. They cannot even be explained as the consequence of thoughtless human ecological behaviour: they were not, for instance, the result of humanly generated global warming. On the contrary, the origins of those waves lay in the very depths of the ocean, at a point of known geological friction between tectonic plates, way beyond any human influence. As a leader in a daily national said at the time, "a sudden unprecedented surge by the Indian Ocean is as near to a pure "event" as one can get". It was very easy for some such phrase as "the hand of God" to spring into the mind. Another newspaper leader went so far as to explain it as "the wrath of nature" but would never have dared to go as far as using the words "the wrath of God". Under the circumstances that seemed, of course, too outrageous to consider, let alone take seriously. It was insulting to the victims, and involved a concept that belonged, as yet another leader put it, only to "loonies" at the fringe. Yet the question

plague of locusts, which is quite clearly portrayed as an affliction from God on a godless people. Hosea states that "the land mourns, and the people waste away (drought and famine)" because of the "cursing, lying and murder in the land" (4:1-3). Amos puts the case very clearly when speaking for God he says God gave drought and famine, blight and mildew, locusts and plague and still could not get the people to acknowledge him. Jeremiah (30 times) and Ezekiel (12 times) make frequent use of the triple nature of judgement, "sword, famine, and plague".

When nations do not have the prophets of God, God still speaks, therefore. His language is that of disasters, for that alone seems able to penetrate the heart.

5. Epilogue.

An Irishman who had spent his life as a labourer gave me his verdict on the Tsunami: "it's meant as a warning to us all". He did not judge the victims; he felt we are all just like them. He would not stand aloof to say, "It was a judgement on them", but he knew that God was speaking, and that the message was directed to him and to us. It could justly happen to us. That was an exemplary attitude to adopt. Instinctively, he knew that what had happened had meaning. He was not without compassion for the sufferers, but neither was he blind to our lack of innocence. Our predicament, like the Jews prior to their exile, is much worse than we have reckoned with in the sight of God. We unconcernedly walk in evil ways, as though it were of no consequence to the God of this world. When we cease to listen to our conscience, the warnings about those consequences can come in no other form than episodes that horrify us, and even make us curse.

The Tsunami has spoken to the world, however, not just to a part of it. The world knows, the world has seen it, not just one nation. It is a prophetic marker at the beginning of the new century. It was a judgement in itself, but, more sobering, it was in the nature of a judgement to warn of what could yet come on nations if they continued to "defile the earth".

"I LED THEM WITH TIES OF LOVE"
Lessons in Love and Judgement

PURPOSE and BACKGROUND

This study shows how clearly the prophets came to understand that, though they had to speak of the judgement of God, there was in the heart of God a great love for his people. The study shows how they came to reconcile love with the prospect of the appalling destruction and devastation that was to be visited on Israel and Judah. Today many still wrestle with the same need to reconcile love and judgement.

The study is not written simply for bible study, though it may hopefully lead to that. It is written out a deep sense of the need of the Christian church to understand the times in which we live, and particularly to understand that these are times in which the judgements of God are increasingly threatening. Though there has been much prayer for revivals and outpourings of the Spirit, and such revivals will undoubtedly come, indeed are with us worldwide, they will come against a very dark background of persistent and increasing judgement everywhere.

The pamphlets are offered, therefore, primarily in a prophetic vein though they are also studies of the prophets in a teaching sense. Application has been minimised, but it is hoped that readers will see the application only too clearly for our own times.

The object of such writing is to forewarn and to forearm. It is to clarify the nature of the judgements of God, and to indicate how we may best respond and face up to them.

the God of the prophets – a God of love, a God who feels deeply - but who, nonetheless, has to speak judgement!

Love Destroys Evil

How does this love of God relate to God's threats of appalling judgement, and all the pain and cruelty that belonged to it?

In seeking to answer that question, the essential fact we have to recognise is that love cannot ultimately co-exist with evil. The very nature of love is such that it abhors evil and must destroy it, just as light must dispel darkness. The two are utterly opposite and irreconcilable. It is part of our understanding of God that in the final analysis he will not be reconciled to evil but will utterly remove it from the place it has usurped in his creation. If there is no removal of evil there is no "heaven" of any consequence, for the difference between heaven and earth is the removal of evil and the consequent full presence of the peace and joy of God. The destruction of evil (but the sparing of us who have been touched by it) is the quintessential hope that God brings to us, and is totally in keeping with his nature as a God of love.

Love is irreconcilable with evil because love seeks the genuine happiness and peace of humanity, whereas evil is inherently destructive of humanity. Love, therefore, can never say, "do what you like; anything goes; you are free to express yourself in whatever way you like", because it is precisely at those points that evil lurks to draw people into wrong actions that only destroy. Love is bound to put up barriers to evil. Love is aware that all actions have consequences both for the person who does them and for those who are affected by them. Love involves wisdom, and wisdom knows what will bring happiness and peace, or distress and anguish. This means that love inevitably has a moral aspect, and to some degree can be expressed in clear statements about acceptable behaviour, such as the 10 Commandments. But love is so much more than a few rules. The love of God is something that has a consummate, burning sense of morality, something that is described as "holiness". God is holy, he is not touched at all by anything that is evil – it is totally foreign to his nature, and cannot come anywhere near his immediate presence without being burned up. He abhors evil. This burning holiness is part of his love, bent on blessing but implacably destructive of evil. This is the essence of what elsewhere is called by the prophets the "wrath of God".

Humanity is always in grave danger, therefore, when it is caught up in sin and deliberately persists in it. For to be caught up in sin, is to be exposed to that burning holiness, utterly destructive of sin. This is a real and serious danger in this world, but infinitely more real and serious in eternity. This is the point that needs grasping fully, and our generation is again lamentably slow to grasp it. It is the fundamental lesson of the prophets. The Israelites had deliberately rejected God and his call "to be holy", and they were contemptuous of his righteous commands, going after pagan gods whose worship involved doing the opposite of those commands. They were, therefore, in grave danger. Instead of accepting his love, the Israelites were constantly frustrating it. Hosea cries out, *"Whenever I would restore the fortunes of my people, whenever I would heal Israel, the sins of Ephraim are exposed and the crimes of Samaria revealed. They practise deceit, thieves break into houses, bandits rob in the streets; but they do not realise that I remember all their evil deeds. (6:11-7:2 NIV).*

The Pleadings and Patience of Love
How does God in his love react to this rejection? He certainly does not compromise or move to middle ground, for love, thankfully, does not compromise with evil. Neither does God immediately react in judgement, for love is "slow to anger". Love starts by stating with acid clarity firstly, what it sees to be wrong, and secondly, what wrongdoing is bound to lead to. So Hosea typically exposes evil in unmistakable tones: *"There is no acknowledgement of God in the land. There is only cursing lying and murder, stealing and adultery; they break all bounds and bloodshed follows bloodshed"* (Hos.1:3 NIV). Equally clearly he states the consequence of evil: *"Swords will flash in their cities, will destroy the bars of their gates and put an end to their plans."* (11:6). Warnings like this, of course, are not idle warnings. God means what he says, but love speaks the truth in an endeavour to turn the beloved from a path of disaster.

It is important to remember also that love allows choice, indeed demands choice. Love cannot make others love, but it can plead with them and reason with them. It is simply because of God's desire that his people should make the right choices that the pronouncements of the prophets are so searching and uncompromising, so graphic and realistic in their description of judgement. Nothing but the plainest of speaking would help the Israelites, for their corruption

was endemic – *"a spirit of prostitution is in their heart; they do not acknowledge the LORD"*. (5:4). Moreover love persists, and so the prophecies come out in a constant stream, using every kind of imagery in an attempt to persuade.

Love also offers forgiveness. There is no greater manifestation of the love of God offered to mankind than the offer of mercy and forgiveness, for that is mankind's greatest need in the light of its sin. But forgiveness can only be effective where the offer is received and repentance is evident. The offer of forgiveness is abundantly present in the prophets: *"Return, O Israel, to the LORD your God ... say to him, 'forgive us our sins and receive us graciously."* (14:1-2); *"I long to redeem them but they speak lies against me"* (7:13). This is an offer through his prophets which, in the grace of God, went on for years, even decades, right to the very last moment before judgement fell.

The Horrors of Judgement
Love cannot allow sin to go on indefinitely, however, and God's judgement has to come eventually. When it comes it takes the form of allowing what is evil to destroy evil. The Assyrians (and later the Babylonians) were the rod of God's judgement and they were evil, even more evil than Israel or Judah. They were cruel beyond belief; merciless, sadistic and endlessly destructive (see Nahum). It can never be said that God has not warned that this is the nature of his judgement. In his love he pleads and pleads simply because he knows judgement spells an onrush of appalling evil. God does not unveil the origin of evil, but he certainly warns of the horrors of it, and offers a refuge for those who will listen to him. On the other hand, God allows those who wilfully choose to be associated with evil to be caught up in its destruction, for evil has to be destroyed.

2. GRACE and JUDGEMENT

Judah - a Nation that Despised the Grace of God

"For 23yrs the word of the Lord has come to me, and I have spoken to you again and again, but you have not listened". Jer.25:2. NIV

"Though grace is shown to the wicked, they do not learn righteousness; even in a land of uprightness they go on doing evil". Isa. 26:10

The long "Years of Grace"
Hosea reveals once and for all the depth of the love of God for Israel, despite the fact that God had to judge that nation. A hundred years afterwards, God's love for Judah, Israel's sister nation, became equally evident despite Judah's rejection of God. This love was nowhere more evident than in the 23 years that Jeremiah referred to in the text above. Those years can only be described as amazing "years of grace", because they were years in which God made a huge final effort to bring back Judah to himself before his ultimate judgement was released on it. The sheer patience of God and the depth of his pleading with Judah which characterized those years were profound expressions of genuine love in action. They constituted a huge offer of mercy and forgiveness over a long period of time.

Those 23 years were in fact the brightest years in the last and darkest century of Judah's existence. They followed 50 years of unrestrained paganism in which King Manasseh, along with his priests and court prophets, was responsible for encouraging every degenerate kind of behaviour. That behaviour was so vile that even before those years had ended God's had already pronounced that the nation would suffer severely and bitterly because of them. Yet, despite that word of judgement, God still visited the nation with a time of grace and gave it over twenty years to come to its senses.

This time of grace began after Manasseh died and when Josiah took over the kingdom. Josiah was quite simply a great gift from God to Judah (God's best gifts are so frequently seen in godly people and leaders). He was energetic, resourceful, and godly, utterly

dedicated to the abolition of paganism. The grace of God did not end, however, with Josiah. Not only did God give the nation a godly ruler to provide a surge back to true moral religion; he also gave it an extremely powerful group of prophets, most notably Jeremiah, who faithfully spelt out the disaster that lay ahead and powerfully preached repentance. Josiah ruled for 30 years and actively reformed for some 20 years. Jeremiah spoke out to the nation during those same 20 years (and beyond). God's grace to the nation was, therefore, manifest in powerful political and spiritual leadership which operated for two full decades, giving a great opportunity for it to change its ways. Tragically the time of grace was rejected, and less than 20 years after Josiah died Jerusalem was in ruins and Judah was in exile. Jeremiah summed up the rejection of those years of grace in a great cry of distress and warning: *"For 23 years the word of the Lord has come to me and I have spoken to you again and again, but you have not listened"* (Jer.25:2 NIV). And even as Jeremiah recognized the rejection of the prophetic voice, he also knew that Josiah's work was already being undone by his godless successor, Zedekiah.

The Disaster of Godless Leadership
There could hardly have been a greater contrast between King Manasseh, under whose rule paganism flourished so rapidly for half a century, and the Yahweh-centered King Josiah, who did all he could to eradicate it. Manasseh deliberately turned his back on the godly outlook of his father Hezekiah, mistakenly assuming that it was because of Hezekiah's adherence to Yahweh that the Assyrians had come to oppress Judah. (This is, of course, by no means the only time that influential and powerful rulers have seen godly religion as more of a source of trouble than of blessing.) Manasseh really wanted a religion that the surrounding nations would appreciate, not one which seemed to set Judah apart. It was also particularly important for Manasseh to have a good relationship with Assyria the "superpower", and that meant religion needed to be subservient to politics: it was politically wise to flow with the tide. So he deliberately embraced everything contrary to the godly heritage of the nation; *"He sacrificed his sons in the fire, practiced sorcery, divination and witchcraft and consulted mediums and spiritists"* (2 Chron.33:6 NIV). He even infested the temple with pagan altars. In this way, whoever came to Jerusalem, no matter what brand of

paganism they followed, they were sure of a welcome for their practices. This was a very acceptable stance to them, all embracing and "enlightened". Prophets from God never ceased to warn him of the danger of what he was doing, but only when he found himself being taken by a hook in his nose as a prisoner to the King of Assyria did he show any repentance (2 Chron. 33:10ff). Though, to his credit, he actually lived his later years as a worshipper of Yahweh, the nation did not follow his repentant example, persisting in their pagan ways, and when Manasseh died, his son, Amon, actively opened the door again to a flood of paganism for two further years before he was assassinated by the palace officials. Godless leadership had been utterly disastrous for the nation.

The Grace of a Godly Ruler.
It was very different with Josiah. Coming to the throne when he was a mere eight years old, this grandson of Manasseh was diligently seeking the Lord by the time he was sixteen. He rapidly embarked on a purge of paganism as thorough as his grandfather's promotion of it. It was a staggering change of direction in the family, and clearly a work of sovereign intervention by God. The new king was an incalculable gift of grace to the nation, a divine opportunity for the nation to come back to God, something for which the nation ought to have been profoundly grateful. Josiah scoured Judah tearing down every pagan altar and smashing every idol he could find (2 Chron. 34:3ff). He did what the kings of Israel were always intended to do, backing up the commandments that God had given to the nation with his royal authority. The king alone had the position and power to make the secular agenda a genuine spiritual and moral agenda. Even so, it was an act of tremendous courage for so young a king to challenge the widespread popularity of paganism and its entrenched priesthoods. When, ten years into his reform, and during the process of a major restoration of the Temple itself, the Book of the Law of Moses was found, the king realized just how far Judah had left the ways of God, and he ceremonially tore his clothes in shame and distress. That the Law of Moses had been "lost" for so long was an appalling measure of how far the paganism of those days had gone, and how much the basic knowledge of God's word had been obliterated in the national life. Such spiritual ignorance in Judah at one time would have been inconceivable. Deeply troubled by all this neglect, Josiah called a great public meeting with leaders,

people, priests, and Levites. He then solemnly renewed the Covenant to follow the Lord and the Book, and *"made all who were present in Israel serve the LORD their God"* (2 Chron. 34:33 NIV).

Josiah stands, therefore, as the epitome of the ideal ruler who legislates and enforces what is godly in the nation: the force of the law was used to remove shrines at which immorality and violent human sacrifice took place. His rule was a return to the boundaries of civilized behaviour after Manasseh's liberalized but degenerate policy of "anything goes". Josiah's was a reign which God honoured, and as long as he remained king, the judgements previously pronounced on the paganism of the nation under Manasseh were held back (2 Chron. 34:27-28). Indeed, the nation actually gained respite, even some independence, from Assyrian domination. Godly rulers (in all walks of life) have always been vitally important gifts to a society, and their godly exercise of whatever power and influence they have always brought benefits to that society. It was tragic for Judah, therefore, when after 20 years of courageous work, Josiah was killed in battle against Egypt.

The Grace of the Prophetic Gift.
There is, however, a limit to what a godly ruler and godly legislation can achieve, no matter how thorough or desirable such legislation may be, for legislation may secure some degree of obedience but it does not necessarily change the hearts or desires of the people. To achieve that a prophet was needed. God's gift, therefore, of Jeremiah (and Jeremiah's fellow prophets) was a crucial addition to Josiah. It was in resisting Jeremiah as well as Josiah that Judah's stubbornness reached its height of folly. When Jeremiah cried out that he had been speaking to the nation for 23 years and they had not listened, 20 of those years had coincided with the reign of Josiah. The nation that had had to accept Josiah's enforced reforms had evidently held out against Jeremiah's call to repentance. Its heart had remained untouched.

Though only a youth, Jeremiah was true to his calling. His preaching was very strong and very sharp. He faced a nation that had gone over to paganism to a degree beyond anything it had ever embraced before, and nothing less than a very stern message would produce any change. The atmosphere of his preaching was, therefore, heavy with judgement. No other warning note would be loud enough for the nation to hear. Such strong preaching was, of

course, in itself an act of grace. Only if Judah realized that it really was in imminent danger of the most appalling judgement would there be any hope of a return to godly ways. This severe note was never to leave his prophesying. It was the only effective medicine but proved too strong for most. It is still proving too strong in our own contemporary situation.

In Jeremiah's prophecies we hear God not just making hard threats, but also arguing a cogent case against Judah. First, he made it clear that Judah had done the unthinkable among the nations in changing its God: *"Has a nation ever changed its gods? But my people have exchanged their Glory for worthless idols"* (2:11). Second, he spelt out the absurdity of idolatry (worshipping sticks and stones). Third, Judah had actually witnessed what God had done in destroying her faithless sister Israel for her idolatry, and yet was still persisting with her own idolatries (3:6-10). Nothing of this availed, however, despite the frequency of the message and the variety of its presentation. Neither legitimate threat or reasoning prevailed. What Isaiah uttered, over a century before Jeremiah, was shown to be devastatingly true: *"though grace is shown to the wicked, they do not learn righteousness; even in a land of uprightness they go on doing evil"* Isa. 26:10. NIV

The Grace of Revival
Some have described these twenty years as revival years. This is not an inaccurate description. It is highly likely there were people in Judah apart from the prophets who had longed for a return to godliness and prayed diligently for it. It seems equally likely that there would have been some response to Josiah's work and Jeremiah's preaching, and doubtless many turned to the ways of God with a genuine heart. Those years must have seemed to such people as being wonderfully fruitful and a great answer to prayer. For those who wanted it, this really was a rich outpouring of grace, not only providing a refreshing but also something that would enable them to face the evil that was to come on the nation later. But, as with so many revivals, the nation as a whole simply turned its back on the opportunity God was affording. This meant that the revival became a forerunner to judgement, merely highlighting the rejection of the majority and hastening the evil day. For within twenty years of the national rejection of those years of "revival" judgement had

Fourth, Habakkuk had little concept of how imminent the coming disaster was. Babylon was only just appearing on the world stage again, and most people's eyes were still on Assyria. But within 20 yrs Babylon had shot to power, destroyed Assyria and was a world threat. The time before God's judgement proved to be short. To-day the time is short.

God's Final Answer
God's reply to Habakkuk's question was simple, yet unanswerable: Babylon would be the agent of his judgement, but the day would come when Babylon itself would feel the wrath of God's judgement on its own sins. God was not unjust, simply letting Babylon do what it liked. God made it abundantly clear to Habakkuk that he knew the sins of Babylon. He was not blind to their behaviour. He surveys Babylon's huge evils. It was *"puffed up" (proud) (v.4), "greedy as the grave" (v.5),* and it *"piled up stolen goods" (v.6), "built its cities with bloodshed" (v.12), "destroyed lands and cities and everyone in them" (v.17).* It indulged in the most inhuman of behaviour. Habakkuk learned afresh that God's eyes were always on the nations, weighing them, using them, judging them and always acting towards them with righteousness. So the destroyer would be destroyed. God wanted Habakkuk to be quite clear about this, and wanted him to make sure Judah heard of this final outcome for Babylon. Thus right at the start of this answering revelation, (2:2-20), God told Habakkuk to write it down plainly on tablets. It lay in the future (*"the revelation awaits an appointed time"*), and a permanent record must be kept, one which anyone could read. We need to remember that at the point when Habakkuk received this revelation Judah had no idea what Babylon would do to it, much less any idea about what God might do to Babylon. But the day would come when the revelation of Babylon's demise would be food and drink to the hopes of Judah in exile.

Accepting the Unthinkable.
It is highly fitting that the last chapter of Habakkuk should record his prayer of response to what he had heard. The first two chapters are an invaluable insight to a prophet's prayerful wrestling with God, trying to grasp new horizons. Now he shows an extraordinary composure as, before God, he accepts the unthinkable.

Taking first the latter part of the third chapter (vv. 16-19) we find that what he has heard has set up a feeling of horror, even fear: *"I heard and my heart pounded, my lips quivered at the sound; decay crept into my bones, and my legs trembled" 3:26* NIV. He feels precisely the dreadful fear of a people under siege. It is this profound feeling of what was to happen that indicates just how deeply the prophetic word had entered his consciousness. It was not just a matter of words and warning about judgement – it was as if he were already in the midst of it. This is an experience typical of the prophets of that era – they both heard and felt what God was saying, and that put massive weight into their proclamation of what was to happen.

In the light of what he felt for the horrors that lay ahead, the attitude he adopted toward the future is remarkable (vv.17-19): he would wait patiently for the judgement to pass and for calamity to come on Babylon (v.16). Despite the horror of what lay ahead, he was fortified by the thought that it would have an end. It was perhaps as well that he did not realise that it would be seventy years before the slavery of exile would end, and that he would not in fact see it. An ignorance of the future is not always a bad thing, indeed is sometimes a mercy! Supported, however, by the prospect of an end to judgement, he was determined to rejoice in the Lord (v.18), no matter what shortages and devastations might come. God would be his strength and help him to rise *"on the heights"* above it all (v.19). Whether this positive attitude was ever tested in Habakkuk's life we do not know, but it was certainly the right one to adopt to bring composure in the face of such a dark future.

In the earlier part of the third chapter (vv.2-15) he in fact was rejoicing in his God. His mind surveyed the greatness and majesty of the God of Israel, and the mighty deeds he had done in the past history of the nation. He thought about the power exhibited in the exodus (vv.3-6), and he thought about the deliverances that had been wrought against Israel's enemies (7-13). The coming judgement could not change any of this. His God was still *"in his holy temple"* (2:20), still in control, and had not lost his sovereign power over either nations or nature. He could still rejoice in this God, and plead that though he had to judge his people, he might none the less show his power and *"remember mercy"* (v.2)

NOT ONE STONE WILL BE LEFT ON ANOTHER

PURPOSE and BACKGROUND

This study sets out to show that the issues of national judgement which are raised by the Old Testament prophets are underlined in the New Testament, and that, far from there being a difference, the New Testament strongly affirms the Old Testament approach. This study looks at the ministry of both John the Baptist and Jesus, showing in particular how Jesus himself stood where Amos and his contemporaries stood on the question of judgement. If we find ourselves a little nervous with applications of judgement from the Old Testament this booklet, we hope, will bring some reassurance. As a generation that has departed from the prophetic understanding of judgement, we need to hear afresh what Jesus and John were saying to their generation.

The booklet is not written simply for bible study, though it may hopefully lead to that. It is written out a deep sense of the need of the Christian church to understand the times in which we live, and particularly to understand that they are times in which the judgements of God are increasingly threatening for the nation. There has been much prayer for revivals and outpourings of the Spirit, and such revivals will undoubtedly come, indeed they are with us and world-wide. But they will come to us against a very dark background of persistent and increasing world-wide judgement.

For our own nation (and the West) the word of judgement hangs very heavy. This is nothing less than a word of cataclysmic judgement, and time is now short. The indicators are that the cataclysms will be both the result of mankind's own violence, hatred and warmongering, and also of natural disasters.

CONTENTS

1. NATIONAL JUDGEMENT

Facing the Facts

"Not one stone will be left on another" - Jesus at the Temple

Some Christians are rather nervous about expositions of judgement that are taken from the Old Testament. There is a general tendency to feel that all that sort of thinking must have been somehow superseded by the New Testament. Questions are raised such as, "Now that Jesus has come, aren't things rather different?" or "Are the Old Testament prophetic statements on judgement really valid today?" It is highly important that these questions are answered lest they should prevent us from fully grasping and accepting any word of judgement that God may be bringing from the Old Testament for our own nation today. The best way to answer such doubts is obviously to move into the New Testament itself and see whether anything like the lessons concerning judgement that come to us out of Amos and his fellow prophets can be found there. And when we do we find that such lessons are very definitely there. Moreover, they are to be found in no less a place than the ministry of John the Baptist, and, even more significantly, in the ministry of Jesus himself.

Jesus the Prophet of Judgement

Jesus was known generally among the people of his day as "a prophet"; *"A great prophet has appeared among us"* they said (Lk. 7:16 NIV). Even his disciples referred to him by that title: *"He was a prophet, powerful in word and deed"* (Lk. 24:19). We know, of course, that he was much more than a prophet, but unquestionably he did have a very powerful prophetic ministry: he was not one bit less a prophet than Amos or Isaiah. Now while it may be true that what marked him out as a "prophet" in the minds of the people was primarily his mighty works, it is equally true that the latter part of his ministry was marked by persistent and strong prophetic proclamations about the disastrous fate that awaited Jerusalem and its leaders. Jesus spoke of a disaster coming to the Jews in ways that bear a very marked resemblance with the prophets of Amos' era.

Those great "prophetic" proclamations of judgement began on the Sunday before his crucifixion (Palm Sunday) as he made his triumphal entry into Jerusalem. He paused on that journey at a point on the Mount of Olives where he could see Jerusalem spread out before him and he uttered the following word over the city:

"If you, even you, had only known on this day what would bring you peace—but now it is hidden from your eyes. The days will come upon you when your enemies will build an embankment against you and encircle you and hem you in on every side. They will dash you to the ground, you and the children within your walls. They will not leave one stone on another, because you did not recognize the time of God's coming to you." Lk 19:41ff

This was, to say the least, a very strong word indeed: he was prophesying that the city would be surrounded, destroyed, and taken apart stone by stone; the people, children included, would be dashed to pieces. The reason for this would be that it had rejected God's call to repent and accept him as Messiah.
Jesus re-iterated the pronouncement later on in that week:

"Some of his disciples were remarking about how the temple was adorned with beautiful stones and with gifts dedicated to God. But Jesus said, "As for what you see here, the time will come when not one stone will be left on another; every one of them will be thrown down." Lk 21:5-6 NIV

These words were only an introduction, however, to a major "apocalyptic" prophecy in which Jesus went on to reiterate once again that Jerusalem would be surrounded by armies and become desolate; people would fall by the sword and any taken prisoner would be dispersed among the nations (Lk. 21:20ff). There is a huge resonance in these words with those that were spoken centuries before by Amos, Isaiah Jeremiah etc. They constitute a clear, specific, and devastating prophecy of judgement in exactly the same manner.
This word of judgement was not just for the ears of those who were close to him, his friends and disciples. Teaching openly in the Temple Courts, the public arena, he related before all the people the

Parable of the Tenants in which the tenants of the vineyard felt the full wrath of the owner because they would not receive either his servants or indeed his son. The chief priests and the scribes heard this and knew full well he was directing the parable at them and the nation, warning them with the wrath of God. Very much like Jeremiah's generation of old, they reacted by seeking more eagerly to kill him. Jesus, unperturbed, pursued the same theme in the parable of the Wedding Banquet (Matt 22). Later, discarding the use of parable, he directly addressed the crowds with a full and lengthy condemnation of the behaviour of the Scribes and Pharisees, a condemnation which he couched in seven "woes", a formula pregnant with a coming wrath (Matt 23). Significantly, however, this condemnation concluded with a note of deep lament (so reminiscent of Hosea and Jeremiah):

"O Jerusalem, Jerusalem, you who kill the prophets and stone those sent to you, how often I have longed to gather your children together, as a hen gathers her chicks under her wings, but you were not willing. Look, your house is left to you desolate. For I tell you, you will not see me again until you say, 'Blessed is he who comes in the name of the Lord.'' Matt 23:37ff NIV

Here, then, at the end of his ministry was a strong, loud, and uncompromising prophetic statement of a coming judgement. He had been with them for two or three years, and, despite all the response of the crowds to his mighty works, the city and its leaders had rejected his teaching. Such rejection would mean that the "Owner of the Vineyard" "would bring those leaders to a wretched end" (Lk. 21:41). God's wrath on sin was as plain to him as to any Old Testament figure. The nation would have to pay the penalty, and that meant an appalling catastrophe for humanity, young and old.

John the Baptist Sounds the Alarm

Though it was Jesus himself who uttered the final pronouncement of judgement on his generation, it was John the Baptist who had uttered the first warnings about such a judgement. Luke records the strident words that John sounded from the very start of his ministry: *"You brood of vipers! Who warned you to flee from the coming*

wrath?" (Lk 3:7) and *"The axe is already laid at the root of the trees, and every tree that does not bear good fruit will be cut down and burned"* (Lk. 3:9). These statements constituted a direct threat of imminent judgement. The figure of an axe laid to the root of a tree refers to the process whereby a tree which had proved to be no good for fruit was finally on the point of being cut down: all waiting time to see if it would bear fruit had gone; destruction was imminent. John was saying that the nation had reached precisely that point. In the grace of God in its extremity it was going to be offered its Messiah; but it was to have only a very short "now or never" moment to respond! This is the meaning of John's words in their context: what he was saying was not a generalized spiritual word about a future wrath for those who fail to respond to God, but a specific message to the nation of his day about imminent national judgement.

There is, of course, a huge similarity between John the Baptist and his Old Testament prophetic forebears, even if there were 600 years between him and Jeremiah. He is in the same mould, and the crowds knew it. That is why they flocked out to see him. After centuries of no prophet there was now a prophet in their midst: everyone, including the Scribes and Pharisees was stirred. He was dressed like an Elijah, he spoke with huge directness and authority, and he came out of the desert like an Elijah. Jesus was later to vindicate his ministry and message with the words, "a prophet, yes, and more than a prophet!" And like prophets of old he had a message of judgement for the nation.

The fact of the matter is, therefore, that with Jesus and John the Baptist we are watching, not the superseding of Old Testament prophetic activity and values, but an endorsement of them in the most affirmative way possible. Jesus and John expose the sin of the nation and its leaders, they call for repentance, they speak with great clarity and authority, they do it with tears, they warn of devastating consequences, and both of them pay for their honesty with their lives. They are clearly upholding an old tradition.

The Vindication of New Testament Prophecy
And just as history vindicated the Old Testament prophets, so history vindicated John and Jesus. John spoke of a coming wrath and Jesus of a destruction of the city and desolation in the land. Events fell out precisely as were prophesied, though, once again as

with the old prophets, not overnight. It was in fact some forty years, in AD 70, before the word of judgement was fulfilled. That compares with the 25 years or so between Amos' word to Israel and the destruction of Samaria.

The fulfillment, in AD 70, of Jesus' prophesying came when Jerusalem was besieged and destroyed by the Romans. In the mid-60s AD Jewish extremists gained political control of the city and raised a flag of rebellion. They actually had early success, routing a Roman army. But the ultimate end was never in doubt, and neither was the punishment that Rome would bring to such a wayward corner of its empire. Vespasian one of the empire's most formidable soldiers began a thorough and methodical campaign in which he reduced all the important cities of Galilee and Judah, before making a full-scale siege of Jerusalem. In the midst of it he became Emperor, but his equally capable son, Titus, took over. It took several months for the starving city to be taken, and taken it was, piece by piece with appalling slaughter. The extremists fought on, hoping to the very end for a divine intervention which never came. Finally, the temple itself was taken and smashed to pieces. The city was sacked and burned; its walls totally demolished. Thousands of Jews were then crucified around the city in a hideous manner. Any left were sold into slavery or taken off to die in the arenas of Rome. For the next sixty years Jerusalem was in ruins, simply providing a base for the Roman army. We have a detailed description of the process from the Jewish historian Josephus.

But not even the events of AD 70, however, completed Jesus' prophetic words. In AD130 the Emperor, Hadrian, started to rebuild Jerusalem intending to turn it into a modern Roman and pagan city with all traces of its Jewish history removed. The name "Jerusalem" was banned, and Hadrian renamed it "Aelia Capitolina" (a combination of Hadrian's family name and a place for Jupiter). He began to build a temple to Zeus on the Temple Mount. Widespread revolt ensued under the leadership of Bar Kokhba, but the end result was a complete repetition of the AD 70 disaster. The whole of Judea was laid waste, a thousand of the bigger villages were ruined and some 600,000 men killed. Jerusalem was taken in AD135 with great slaughter and all Jews were banned from the city as part of the renewed paganization of the city. In the words of one historian, "These two catastrophes of AD70 and AD 135 effectively ended Jewish state history in antiquity", "Judaism ceased to be a national

religion in any physical or visible sense". The long exile had begun. The outworking of Jesus' prophecy had proved to be much more devastating than anything Amos or Jeremiah or Isaiah had prophesied in their day. The Old Testament lessons of judgement had been indelibly underlined on a much greater scale in New Testament times.

If anything should make us very concerned about the relevance of God's judgement for our times it should be an appreciation of Jesus' words of judgement to his own nation and generation. He underlines precisely every attitude and understanding that are to be found on the pages of the Old Testament. He who brought such grace through his death can nonetheless speak of imminent catastrophe. We should have no illusions about the fact that God has been and remains a God who has to deal with the utmost severity with those nations who continue to spurn his demands.

2. CALLING A NATION TO REPENTANCE
What Repentance Involves

"What shall we do then?" - the crowds to John the Baptist

The prophetic message of judgement given by the Old Testament prophets was invariably accompanied by a strong call for repentance, since only repentance could avert judgement. Precisely such a call for repentance was very evident with John the Baptist, who in his generation also came with a message of "coming wrath". Like his Old Testament forebears, he too challenged the prevailing behaviour of his day and called for a radical change of lifestyle. When his demands are examined, they prove to be remarkably similar to the demands made by the Old Testament prophets many centuries before. They focus on possessions, money, violence, and sexual license. They fully underline the message of the Old Testament prophets and greatly strengthen the message they have for our times.

John engaged in a widespread ministry of baptizing people for the repentance of sin. He would not, however, baptize people lightly but demanded *"fruit in keeping with repentance"* (Lk.3:8). The crowd wanted to know exactly what he meant by this: *"What do you want us to do?"* was a constant question on people's lips. It was a realistic and important question, and fortunately we know enough about his preaching be able to put together a fairly comprehensive picture of his answers to that question.

Money and Possessions
His main thrust in calling for repentance had to do with money and possessions. When the crowds repeatedly asked him what they should do he had an extraordinarily simple word for them: *"The man who has two tunics should share with him who has none, and the one who has food should do the same"* (Lk. 3:11). There was no "social program" here, simply an incredibly penetrating personal demand to think more of the poor and less of themselves. Though so simple, it amounted to nothing less than an outright challenge to each person to re-appraise their outlook on their possessions. Contemporary society had become utterly selfish in its outlook and attitudes. It was this that John was rebuking; this was a matter of great importance to God.

This simple answer needs looking at in detail lest it be too easily brushed aside. The "tunic" to which John referred was an undergarment, not the indispensable outer tunic (there are precise words for both). It was common for a traveller to wear two of these undergarments, though one was sufficient. John did not imply there was anything wrong in having two, but he said that if a person came across someone without such an undergarment, he should give him one of his two. John was advocating, in other words, a readiness to share with others to the point where a person might be left with a bare but sufficient minimum for themselves. He is not advocating in general giving away something that is an absolute essential (like an outer tunic or one essential undergarment) so that the person is left destitute. Neither is he referring to sharing an excessive overflow of possessions (a third or fourth garment!). He is referring to giving something that will not leave a person destitute but will nonetheless call for a real sacrifice in terms of normal living. It will bring the person to a level of having simple necessities whilst providing for those who do not have those necessities. The same

implication is present in the call to share food with someone who has none.

The simplicity of this should not blind us to the fact that it amounted to an attempt to establish a completely new "benchmark" of behaviour concerning possessions. In modern parlance we might say it constituted an outright challenge to the mindset of the consumer society. There was no place for anything remotely connected with the amassing of excessive personal possessions or the pursuit of the latest luxuries. Selfish pleasures were not to be the main goal of life. Greed, selfishness, self-seeking, and the neglect of others in need was evidently the prevailing outlook of John's generation, and it was completely contrary to the outlook of the Kingdom of God which he was heralding. He wanted to make clear that unless his generation faced up to this and repented, the coming of the King would bring judgement, not life. **It is precisely this challenge of John's which is the challenge which God presents to our own generation, and not least to Christian people caught up in the prevailing standards of the consumer society. It is a challenge all too easy to fail to see, and it is a very difficult challenge to respond to when its implications are fully understood.**

Jesus himself picked up exactly the same theme in his own teaching: *"Sell your possessions and give to the poor. Provide purses for yourselves that will not wear out, a treasure in heaven that will not be exhausted, where no thief comes near, and no moth destroys". Lk* 12:38 NIV. And what he preached he practiced, for the disciples' money bag was frequently used to help the poor (Jn 13:29). It was a theme no less evident in the early church which was full of the Holy Spirit and saw people selling their second homes in order to give the proceeds to the poor. The prevailing attitude of that church was that what belonged to them was as much for the benefit of others as for themselves (Acts 2:44-45).

It may come as a surprise to us that John in his ministry should major on such a reply, rather than what might appear to be grosser sins. But the covetous, self-seeking spirit with its luxurious indulgence knows no bounds and leads ultimately to corruption, violence and gross injustice, all of which was prevalent in Judea. It was precisely this that Amos exposed in his day and for which his generation was judged. It was a key message for John's generation, and it **is a key message for our generation.**

Excessive Money Making and Violence

"What shall **we** do?" was also a question on the lips of tax collectors and soldiers. Both of these categories were almost certainly Jews, not Romans. The "tax collectors" were of lesser rank than the main tax "farmers" and did the actual collecting of the money. They were normally Jews, and such service for Rome brought them hatred from the people. Likewise, the soldiers were Jews who had a military function under the Romans and were similarly despised. In the nature of the case, therefore, these were people who were prepared to face criticism for the sake of getting rich. They were ready to use the ample opportunities that lay before them for substantial and dishonest gain. The tax collectors could set their own price and reap a profit beyond anything that could be considered fair, and the soldiers could extort money by the threat of false accusation. Dishonesty, greed and corruption marked out these two categories of people and such blatant self-seeking was actually protected by the very structures of Roman rule. The Jewish world of John and Jesus stands out as appallingly venal and corrupt. The modern world and our own nation present clear parallels.

To the tax gatherers John replied, *"Do not exact more than is due"* and to the soldiers, *" Be content with your wages.* They were a long way from a lifestyle in which they knew contentment with a reasonable return. They were just money orientated and unscrupulous. Again, it was an incredibly simple response, but an introduction to a profound and radical new lifestyle. The crowds would have consisted of a great many more people who, though not as blatantly avaricious as the tax collectors and soldiers, nonetheless were guilty of just the same discontented attitude. Violence and dishonest money making seemed to have been part of the way of life. Such a society is always under the threat of judgement; and violence is always both a judgement in itself and an invitation to greater judgement.

Religion without Morals and Politics without Principle

One particular phrase stands out vividly among the rebukes that John had for those who came for baptism; *"You brood of vipers! Who warned you to flee from the coming wrath?"* (Matt. 3:7). Matthew particularly sees this sharp description as primarily aimed at the Pharisees and Sadducees. It was to these that the call for *"fruit*

in keeping with repentance" was especially directed. Thus, rather than seeing the religious leaders as exempt from his demands, John saw them as those most needing the call to repent. This was strong language. But he was not simply being abusive: the fact was that the religious establishment, like snakes, was not to be trusted and was poisonous, both in behaviour and teaching. It was in fact language that Jesus himself used of the same people: at the end of his ministry in his great proclamation of woes on the Pharisees he referred to them not only as snakes but as whitewashed tombs! (Matt 23)

John knew that they were most unlikely to listen to the highly personal demands for moral uprightness he was making, for he knew that there hung over them an overweening spiritual pride that made any real heart attitude of compassion to the poor virtually impossible. He also knew that if they asked for baptism, it would be for motives other than repentance, most probably to keep their status with the crowds. The overriding concern of the Sadducees (the High Priestly families), moreover, was not simply religious but political. Their energies were taken up by making sure that they remained in favour with the Roman authorities but without seeming to be unpatriotic. They were intent on maintaining the religious observances of the Temple and enjoying its monetary benefits and the prestige it afforded because it brought them political status. They were particularly sensitive to any kind of extremist activity, political or religious, that might bring retribution from Rome and lose them their position. They were hopelessly enmeshed in a politico/religious framework.

John knew perfectly well that both Sadducees and Pharisees would have a theological answer for any moral castigations he might make, and he anticipates the classic form of defense that both were likely to make by saying to them, *"do not think you can say to yourselves, 'We have Abraham as our Father '"* (Matt. 3:9). The fact was that in the minds of both Sadducee and Pharisee their acceptance with God depended entirely on their birth as Jews, literal sons of Abraham – this was the rock of their religion. God was bound to approve of them because they were Jews, and Jews of high spiritual rank. The witness of their prophetic scriptures was completely lost on them: in no way could they see themselves as counterparts of the religious figures for which the Old Testament prophets had such strictures in their day, and there is nothing

stronger in the Old Testament prophets than their condemnation of their religious and political leaders. They were absolutely (and willfully) blind to the moral essence of the Jewish faith. Tragically right throughout John's ministry and Jesus' ministry this was exactly the position they clung to, even to the point, like their fathers, of destroying the prophetic witness. Thus, the religious and political establishment brought upon itself and the nation an appalling judgement.

Sex and Wrong Relationships
John's challenge to repentance was widespread, and dangerous. It was never more dangerous than when it touched on the many evils in Herod's life, and in particular his personal and sexual life. He rebuked openly Herod's adultery and incestuous marriage with Herodias (Lk. 3:19). Herod had been determined to have Herodias even though they were both married to other partners, and he persuaded Herodias to leave her husband and at the same time forced his own wife to flee. Two forced divorces, however, were made much worse by the fact that Herodias' husband was Herod's half-brother and therefore any union between Herod and Herodias was illegal and incestuous. Herod's behaviour brought its own nemesis: friendship with his divorced wife's father, Aretas (a ruler of Arabia), ceased and struggle broke out between their respective kingdoms, and eventually Herodias' brought about the downfall of Herod through her willful ambition.

There are indications in the ministry of Jesus that it was not just Herod but the whole generation that was sexually lax. Divorce was for the most part easy, being obtainable for anything that offended the husband. Even Jesus' disciples expressed surprise at Jesus' own strong statements curtailing divorce, wondering how people could possibly live without some real freedom in that area! (Matt. 19:10). We see Jesus being tested by the Pharisees over a woman taken in the very act of adultery, and more significantly, we see how a deep conviction of the sin of immorality came upon all those "righteous" people who accused her (Jn. 7:53ff). At a worse level still, Jesus own ministry to redeem prostitutes comes out very clearly in the gospels and suggests such women were not few in number. His was an immoral age and on that account ripe for judgement. Bad as it was, however, the sexual license of that generation was nothing like that of our own. At least the forms of marriage were in place, and

open promiscuity was frowned upon. If a lack of restraint brought the nation of John and Jesus under strong proclamation of judgement, how much more must our own. A more accurate comparison of our own would be with Sodom and Gomorrah, and the judgement on those cities is plain for all to see.

All this reveals John the Baptist, Jesus, Amos, and his fellow prophets as very much in the same mold in their prophetic activity with regard to judgement. Far from any contradiction there is mutual confirmation in what they demanded of their fellow countrymen. Their demands remain only too plain for us today.

3. JUDGEMENT and HOLY SPIRIT REVIVAL

The Grace of God in Judgement

"He will burn up the chaff" - "He will gather the wheat"
John the Baptist speaking of the work of Jesus

In AD 27 John the Baptist came to his nation with a stern word of warning about a "wrath to come", pronouncing that the "axe is already laid to the roots of the (national) tree". He called for repentance. Three years or so later Jesus himself confirmed that the cataclysmic judgement of which John warned would certainly come on the nation. It simply had not heeded John's call to repent and neither had it accepted him. At that point, therefore, AD 30, a heavy word of judgement hung over the nation and it was only a matter of time before it was fulfilled. The extraordinary fact is, however, that it was another 40 years before it came – a whole generation. And even more extraordinary was the fact that those intervening 40 years (and the 3 years preceding them) were to be paradoxically an era of amazing spiritual opportunity for the Jewish people, one in which large numbers of Jews found true faith in the God of their Fathers and in their Messiah. They represent unparalleled years of grace before an unparalleled plunge into centuries of national exile. Thus, whenever national judgement is a real threat, we should bear in mind the possibilities of the extended grace of God. It could be something of a lifeline for our own generation, though we can never afford the

luxury of easy presumption. We could, therefore, have much to learn from those years of grace which God permitted his people. They are very well worth examining.

Judgement and the Grace of God in John the Baptist

When we look at John's message as a whole it is obvious that he had a much greater message than a word of stern warning; he had a message about one who was coming who was infinitely superior to him and who would bring forgiveness of sin and a baptism in the Holy Spirit. It was a message that said, in fact, that the nation was about to be visited by the Messiah, it's Saviour. This was good news of the highest order. This was a message of grace. John was actually heralding an unprecedented visitation from God: he was pointing to a window of immense opportunity, even if it was a context of judgement. He was saying that even if this Messiah would "burn up the chaff with unquenchable fire", he would also "gather the wheat into his barn". Thus, the context of judgement was at the same time offering a window of great opportunity. Every time John proclaimed judgement, he proclaimed repentance and every time he called for repentance, he announced the coming of the King and his kingdom. But there was an intense urgency about his announcement of the good news of the kingdom, an urgency that came only from his own thorough grasp of the dark clouds of judgement that overshadowed the nation. It was this urgency which reached the hearts of people. The urgency was matched by the extraordinary boldness and authority of a man who had been filled with the Spirit since birth and trained in the desert where he had tuned in to God's word for his generation. He really knew the state of the nation and he really knew what God was offering. Undoubtedly his work had a deep effect on many. There was a widespread response to his call for a baptism of repentance (Lk.3:7); many ordinary people acknowledged that he was a prophet of God and much genuine response undoubtedly took place. His fiery talk of judgement and his plain and pertinent preaching hit home. God was in a sense in a threatening mood with the message of his prophet, but he was at the same time seeking to bring blessing through the message. He was offering an extraordinary opportunity for them to get right with him, and many were doing so. These were days of grace as well as judgement. Neither did John's work of pointing people to Jesus go unheeded. At least two of his own disciples followed Jesus after

John pointed him out to them, and they subsequently became disciples of Jesus (Jn. 1:35ff).

Judgement and the Grace of God in Jesus

With the beginning of Jesus' ministry, we move from what was a very powerful prophetic and preparatory ministry under John into something of a totally different order, a demonstration of the presence and power of the Kingdom of God, an expression of the love and grace of God in full measure. There had never been such a time of grace ever before among the people of Israel. As the disciples were later to declare, Jesus moved about "powerful in word and in deed before God and the people". And all this was to a generation that had come to such a point in its lack of genuine spirituality that it was under threat of severe judgement. There could not have been a greater demonstration of the patient and loving desire of God to bring them to a better frame of heart. For some three years everywhere, Jesus went there was healing, deliverance, a call to follow him and an offer of eternal life. There was the same note of uncompromising urgency that had been with John, and an even greater note of authority and depth of teaching.

There was also widespread response; people were not only coming to him for healing but also believing on him. Soldiers, tax collectors, synagogue rulers, prostitutes, widows, whole households and even Pharisees were all responding despite the growing antagonism of the rulers. Even if Jesus trusted himself to no man and can be seen sifting the crowds after the feeding of the 5,000, many like Martha, Mary, Lazarus, and Nicodemus remained. It was all far from a full national response but there was a widespread harvest for the Son of Man.

Jesus' ministry was a "Kingdom" ministry. He was a man "anointed of the Spirit", moving in the power of the Spirit, anointed to preach and to heal. He drew large crowds. The common people heard him gladly. He exposed hypocrisy, he demanded response of the heart, he majored in clear moral response and was utterly fearless in his presentation of the truth, especially in the presence of both religious and political leaders. He faced up to the inevitable consequences of such a ministry.

All this amounts to an extraordinary outbreak of Holy Spirit activity through an extraordinary person and ministry. What it underlines is the simple fact that though severe judgement is the

backcloth with a whole generation under threat, God is at the same time prepared to work in the most amazing way to bring people to a better frame of mind and to the "things that belong to peace". In more modern parlance we could say that judgement and Holy Spirit "revival" can be found operating together, the latter being a visitation of grace before the former has to arrive. For without question Jesus' own ministry was the prototype of Holy Spirit outpouring to which all subsequent outpourings point back. In his generation it was almost as though the darker the clouds of judgement the stronger became the outflow of grace.

Judgement and the Grace of God in the Early Church
Jesus said to his disciples, "Greater things will you do than I have done", and the years from AD 30 to 70 bear witness to the truth of that promise. They were years which were to see the growth of a Christian church in Israel numbering many thousands of Jews, a church which was in the same period to spread to the gentile world of the Eastern Mediterranean and bring in many more thousands on non-Jews. In fact, the very land which Jesus put under judgement by his proclamations during the last week of his ministry was to become the cradle for the birth of the church and was to exert a profound and lasting influence on the rest of the world. These were years of grace indeed! It was almost as if the word of judgement had been reversed!

To be even more pointed it was in the very city whose walls were to be torn apart, Jerusalem, that the greatest blessing the world had ever experienced was first seen, namely the gift of the Holy Spirit "on all flesh": and that within a few weeks of the Jesus' word of judgement. Shortly after Jesus rose from the dead, he had promised to his disciples a baptism in the Holy Spirit, an enduement of power that would make them witnesses to him first in Jerusalem and then progressively to the entire world. Fifty days later this was made good at Pentecost where, after the sheer supernatural happenings associated with the Holy Spirit as he fell on the disciples, the anointed preaching of Peter brought an immediate harvest of 3,000 Jews to faith in Jesus. Luke makes it plain to us that in the days that followed many thousands more accepted the Messiah and received the Spirit; so many indeed that they could not be counted. Even more significantly, perhaps, as time went on a great many priests became believers.

There was, however, no response among the ruling religious classes that had been responsible for the rejection and death of Jesus. On the contrary they embarked on a policy of persecution which, starting with a futile attempt to stop the disciples speaking of Jesus became increasingly violent, leading through the martyrdom of James and Stephen to a widespread attack on Christians which caused them to flee and saw many of them put to death. This, however, did not stop the outpouring of the grace of God; in fact, the very chief of the persecutors, Paul, was converted to Christ by a direct sovereign intervention of God. He was given a revelation of Jesus whilst in the very process of making a journey to facilitate more persecution and execution of Christians. Not only was he converted but he became an apostle whose work was foundational in the work of spreading the gospel to the gentiles and in formulating the newfound experience of God's salvation to Jew and Gentile alike. The grace of God was a fact indelibly stamped upon Paul's experience; he, a persecutor, was given a chance to make peace with his Saviour. His experience epitomizes what God was seeking to do to a nation which had turned its back on him and was under a profound word of judgement.

By the mid-60s, however, the period of grace began to draw to a close. James the leader of the powerful Jerusalem church was put to death by the Jews. Jewish extremists gained power, rebelled against Rome and within a few years brought Jerusalem to its destruction. Judgement had arrived. The cradle of the church was destroyed, but by then the church's centre of gravity had moved to the gentile world. It is astonishing, however, that the church began and came into prominence within a nation under judgement and took its most significant early leaders from among the very people under threat, the Jews.

This means that even with a nation under judgement a serious seeking of an outpouring of the Holy Spirit, and with it a large ingathering of believers, is not foolish or out of the question. Whether God grants such a visitation is for God to decide, but the possibility undoubtedly is there. If there was any historic situation in which an answer to the great prayer of Habakkuk, "In wrath remember mercy" was amply demonstrated it was in those first decades of the early church.

It would be a mistake to think that this lesson concerning the grace of God even at the point of judgement was one which was

absent from the Old Testament. This is simply not the case. One has only to consider the preaching of Jonah at Nineveh. Nineveh was the capital of an extremely cruel and warlike nation, Assyria. In no way did it deserve such a visitation that accompanied Jonah's preaching, but it was for that nation a time of great mercy. It did not last, but while it did, many undoubtedly found a netter way of life. More significantly, the combined and powerful ministry of Jeremiah the prophet and Josiah the king of Judah reveal God giving a huge window of opportunity for the Jews to return from their prolonged and flagrant indulgence in appalling paganism; one of Judah's greatest kings and one of Judah's greatest prophets appeared at one of Judah's worst moments of rejecting God and his ways. Whilst it is true that it is only the New Testament that gives us moments of great outpourings of the Spirit on people, both Testaments abundantly concur in the picture of an amazingly gracious God.

The Hope of Grace - a vision to work with
We may well be in a time in which a severe word of judgement lies over this nation, but it is crucial that the time in which we now live is seen as a period of grace, a window of opportunity. Ministries in the power of the Holy Spirit are vitally important for whatever time remains for us to gather many into the Kingdom and to make sure that re-planting takes place in many other parts of the world so that the gospel and its witness may continue in power. It is certainly not difficult to trace outpourings of grace and blessing in the life of our own nation when it has either been under judgement or when it was about to go through judgement. In response to the prospect of judgement we simply have to fix our eyes on this great propensity of God to remember his mercy even when judgement is inevitable.

THE NATION THAT LOST ITS SOUL

CONTENTS

1. THE NATION THAT LOST ITS SOUL

"They have forsaken the LORD" Isaiah 1:4 NIV

A nation's "soul" is determined by its beliefs. If it is true that "as a man thinks, so he is," it is also true that "as a nation thinks, so it is". Its values and belief system are primary because they determine its behaviour and its character, and, therefore, its soul.

It was God's plan for the Jewish nation that it should put him at the centre of its belief system. It was to know him and believe in him, and to this end he revealed himself to the nation, gave them a Law to follow, and prophets to speak his word. Because he was in his essential being a holy God and the source of true morality, believing in him meant obeying his call to righteous behaviour. Thus, the nation was to be characterized by the twin touches of faith and holiness, and these characteristics would prove to be the source of peace, joy, and prosperity. It would have a truly healthy soul with righteousness at its core. This was the privileged birthright of the Jewish nation.

The tragedy was that, after repeated disobedience the nation finally spurned its godly birthright and heritage and embraced instead the soul of the godless world around it. This happened at the time of the biblical prophets when the nation had already been split into the two parts of Israel and Judah. On such unbelievable folly, God was obliged to pronounce devastating judgement. Israel, the northern part of the nation was destroyed first. Judah, the southern part, totally ignoring what happened to Israel, and wantonly persisting in rejecting its heritage, in turn suffered Israel's fate. Judah truly lost its soul and with it everything else.

The process by which this happened in Judah holds a lesson for any nation spurning a godly heritage.

Early Struggles

From its very inception under Moses, it was a struggle for the Jewish nation to keep God central. Humanity and society find godliness difficult at any time, and the Jews were no exception. Even as Moses was receiving from God the commandments which were to be the rock of its moral life, Israel went after the Golden Calf and

succumbed to permissiveness and drunkenness. This tendency to backslide was never eradicated, and when, on the death of Solomon, Judah eventually emerged as a separate nation it was always ready to pick up the "easier" and less demanding gods of its neighbours, fighting shy of a religion (even if it was their own) which made moral demands. Fortunately, for some two centuries Judah was blessed by a number of godly kings whose hearts were for the Lord and who encouraged genuine faith. They managed on the whole, despite the people, to keep godly characteristics alive. If it had not been for such kings who sought to follow the ways of the Lord, Judah would almost certainly have gone into exile a good century or earlier than it did. By contrast, the northern tribes (Israel) had a succession of idolatrous, power-seeking rulers and they were eradicated from the map 130 years before Judah. That is the difference godly political leadership can make. Even if is true that ungodly and immoral leaders can still make good economists or show clever political skills, the fact is that they invariably kill the soul of a nation, deeply damage its most valuable characteristics, and bring disaster. The morality of a nation's leaders is crucial for the wellbeing of its soul. They are opinion formers, and all opinion formers have a huge responsibility in a nation: they are the leaders who guard or destroy the soul.

The Disastrous Effect of Wealth and Luxury
Even godly kings or leaders cannot always keep a population pure: there are always forces ready to overwhelm the best of legislation and example, and it was, in fact, under a godly king, Uzziah, that the rot in Judah really began to appear in a serious way. This was due in fact to a prolonged 50 year period of extraordinary prosperity which unfortunately proved to be also a period when the gods of mammon and hedonism reared their heads high and came to rule the behaviour of the whole nation, especially its leaders. It was a period which provides a perfect example of Jesus' own comment that "the love of money is the root of all evil". Prosperity, pleasure, and power became the nation's goals and also became its deadly enemies, effectively undermining its moral and religious heritage. The heartbeat of the nation changed for the worse: selfishness and greed, pleasure, and personal indulgence, even debauchery and robbery became the dominant characteristics. The whole nation, rich and poor, priest and people, rulers, and subjects, became deeply infected

during those 50 years. It is evident from Isaiah and Micah just how much this change affected the nation's leaders; instead of being a bulwark against the new tide, they themselves were carried along with the self-interest and greed, becoming even worse than those they ruled. It is astonishing how deeply the prosperous age of Uzziah corrupted Judah's soul. **It clearly demonstrates that there is something in human nature that finds it virtually impossible to resist the temptations that affluence brings.** Rather than bring contentment it whets the appetite for more riches. It does not satiate the desire for pleasure but, if anything, increases it; neither does it reduce robbery, violence and corruption but causes them to escalate. It heralds decadence in the moral sphere.

Dangerous prosperity was not an entirely new experience for Judah: it had been an Achilles heel for Solomon himself during his great and prosperous rule in Jerusalem some 300 years before. The oppression and injustice which had grown up then in the midst of all his riches had been a root cause of the breakup of the kingdom into two parts. On a wider front secular history is full of examples of the debilitating effect that great prosperity can have on even the most powerful of nations, the Roman Empire being a notorious example. Justice, principle, and honesty are rapidly neglected where money and pleasure begin to rule, though, of course, justice, principle and honesty are loudly and hypocritically trumpeted when convenient for corrupt leadership.

The Corrupting Influence of Idolatry
A second phase in the loss of the nation's soul began after Uzziah's death, when Ahaz (preceded briefly by Jotham) took over the throne and deliberately opened wide the nation to every pagan religion and influence. He himself even indulged in child sacrifice with his own son. This flood of paganism effectively nullified any attempt to bring the nation back to any moral discipline: it cemented the damage already inflicted by the prosperity. In fact, the prosperity and trade under Uzziah had made it all too easy (and economically even necessary) to become accustomed to the idolatry of other nations and imitate its corrupt and barbaric ways. Thus, it opened the way and encouraged the idolatrous policy of Ahaz. Where money and profits were demanded the old moral religion was pushed into second place. **It was much more convenient to have religions which offered no moral restraints or asked no**

awkward moral questions, but rather had a focus on personal comfort and could even be perceived as a boost to economic success, as for example in case of the Baal fertility rites. Idolatrous religion was no real barrier to the hedonistic lifestyle but was easily accommodated.

Ahaz was further pushed in the direction of paganism by the fact that shortly after Uzziah's death the Assyrians had become a dire threat to the nation's existence (as Isaiah and Micah had warned). Ahaz was forced to swear allegiance to Assyria, and thereby inevitably had to allow altars to her gods in the Temple at Jerusalem. Thus, paganism became politically necessary. It was the political correctness of its day. In this way pagan barbarism was rapidly and widely adopted by a population already pre-disposed in their prosperity to worship many gods, and now openly encouraged to do so by the highest authority in the land. For twenty years under Ahaz, Judah went downhill rapidly. A whole generation grew up to know little other than religious confusion: there was no "one God", a true God whose moral absolutes were at the core of belief, but a plethora of gods, most of whom were there to make sure life simply ran smoothly and pleasurably, and who were to be coaxed into helpful action by sacrifice. All had to be found a place, but each could be ignored when convenient for the business of wealth and pleasure. If affluence had whittled away the moral restraints of Judah's God, paganism blurred them completely in a fashionable syncretistic religious system that reduced Judah's God to something existing only in ritual.

It is conceivable that Judah might have recovered from this downward trend if a succession of godly kings had followed Ahaz, and if they had had time to bring things back on course. However, this was not to be. Though Hezekiah, who followed him, was indeed a godly king and reigned for almost thirty years (and supported throughout by Isaiah), his successor Manasseh once again opened the door to paganism and practiced it even more blatantly than Ahaz. Moreover, he did so for over 50 yrs.

It was this long period of 50 years under Manasseh that did irreparable damage to Judah. It meant that a generation which, even under Hezekiah, had not really thrown off the paganism of his predecessor, Ahaz, passed on its idolatrous beliefs and behaviour to two succeeding generations. It meant that children grew up who not only saw nothing wrong in the paganism of their parents but, even

every suggestion of "sincerity" about the religious devotions, but "sincerity" is an insufficient guide. In a remarkable passage God speaks to Isaiah and says, *"do not hold back ... declare to my people their sins. For day after day, they seek me out; they seem eager to know my ways, as if they were a nation that does what is right and has not forsaken the command of its God. They ask me for just decisions and seem eager for God to come near them. 'Why have we fasted', they say 'and you have not seen it? Why have we humbled ourselves and you have not noticed?'* Here is a religious nation pleading its prayers and even its fasting. It all looks desperately sincere. But God rebukes with the words, *"is not this the kind of fasting I have chosen: to loose the chains of injustice ... to set the oppressed free .... to do away with pointing finger and malicious talk .... to spend yourself on the hungry"* (Is. 58:1-6 NIV). The reality of religion is in its ethical behaviour. No one faced this issue of empty religious practices more sharply than Jesus in his generation, and he firmly underlined the lesson God had made plain through his prophets.

The Israelites were not without their theology, of course. They had a very clear doctrine of Yahweh as the God who had made a covenant with David and promised that his line would endure forever. The sacrifices, and the temple in Jerusalem (and those at Dan and Bethel), were the assurance and token of this. God indwelt his temple and land, and any suggestion that he was not in their midst was simply not acceptable to them. The notion that the sacrifices they offered were void was nonsense. But it was deficient theology: it had completely lost touch with the covenant at Sinai with Moses with its moral demands. Theology can be very inadequate at times!

God was not, of course, advocating a purely ethical religion devoid of any prescribed rites or any worship of him. The rites and offerings he had given the Israelites epitomized what he had done for the nation, and they expressed the terms on which he had brought his deliverance and forgiveness. They were full of important instruction about God and were an integral and necessary part of genuine religion. They were a proper basis for theology. They were not optional, but the very seat of corporate worship. But they epitomized God's love to the nation, his forgiveness, his grace, and his righteousness. Hearts involved in such rites must first mirror the

heart of this God of love if they were to use those rites to come close to God.

The Problem of Perverted Religion

Because it had lost its own moral dimension, the religion of Jahweh saw no harm in tolerating other amoral religions. It was wide open to syncretism. God, therefore, had another quarrel with the Israelites over their religion. This had to do, not with "empty" religion, but with the tolerance and practice of "perverted" religion. Amos draws attention to the fact that the land was littered with altars and rituals to gods other than Yahweh. He singled out the shrine to Sakkuth, the Assyrian war god, who was also worshipped as a star (Amos 5:26 NIV). Hosea declared that the Israelites *"consult a wooden idol and are answered by a stick of wood" (4:12), "they sacrifice on the mountain tops and burn offerings on the hills, under oak, poplar and terebinth" (4:13).*

A cursory look at the worship of such gods might pose the question of why such cultural deviations should warrant such condemnation. It's the sort of question the modern secular world poses as a matter of course. Why not a Pantheon of different gods? Would that not make for harmony among "faith communities"? That was quite evidently the prevailing outlook at the time of the prophets. It could be argued that some such syncretism of religion enabled marriages between rulers of different nations to take place with the consequent possibility of peace. After all that was the example that even Solomon had set, one whereby he had built up a vast and peaceful empire. Unfortunately, however, a closer look at the gods that the prophets denounced shows that there was not the innocence about them that might at first appear.

The chief influence which led to the presence of idolatrous shrines on every hill throughout Israel and Judah, along with idolatrous sacred stones and sacred trees, came from Canaanite Phoenicia. The main feature of that religion lay in its fertility cult. Ashtoreth, a mother goddess was worshipped in the form of Asherah poles erected in every town and high place. The rituals which surrounded her worship were sexual in nature, and her shrines were attended by temple prostitutes, whose services were offered as part of the rites intended to ensure agricultural fertility. Her consort was Baal and again the emphasis was on sex and fertility, male prostitutes being part of his rituals. **The consequence of this**

religion was to bring about widespread prostitution and adultery. The whole moral tone of the nation was polluted with promiscuity. God's perspective is given in Hosea; *"I have seen a horrible thing in the house of Israel. There Ephraim is given to prostitution and Israel is defiled"* (Hos. 6:10 NIV). Amos notes that as a consequence of temple prostitution, *"Father and son use the same girl and so profane my holy name"* (Am. 2:7 NIV). This sexual licence is a constant theme in the prophets, and it is this gross degradation that makes the idolatry of Israel so detestable to God. Ashtoreth, the goddess, was not only grotesquely sexual but violent, a goddess of war who also encouraged cruelty and violence.

The polluting effect of pagan religion did not end with the Asherah pole. Israel boasted altars to Chemosh, the god of Moab, and to Molech the god of Ammon. These were no innocent idols, for they demanded human sacrifices. Violence, fear, dehumanization, cruelty were all involved in the religious practices encouraged by such gods. Kings as well as subjects were involved in those practices. The fact is that there never was any essential underlying moral basis in pagan religion; it was religion that expressed and played to the baser human instincts. The encouragement of it was a heavy price to pay for political alliances, and it was never the case that the mutual sharing of such gods always secured peace.

Conclusion - The Ultimate Yardstick for Religion
The condemnation of the pagan religions lies ultimately in the same place as the condemnation of empty Israelite religion; they both allow the breaking of the moral law, empty religion by neglect, paganism by active encouragement. They are both an affront to a God who puts righteousness, holiness, love and justice at the heart of what he seeks to do for humanity. Such is his nature, and true religion and its practices must reflect that nature.

The severity with which God dealt both with the empty institutions of his own religion and the obscenities of the idolatrous religion may seem offensive to some. But both, in different ways, were leading to abhorrent human behaviour which could not be tolerated forever. Failure to reform meant only one thing; they had to be destroyed so that humanity might be driven to re-appraise and learn an essential lesson. There is a warning here for traditional Christian institutions: empty profession of faith is an affront to God

and invites judgement. With regard to pagan religion, in proportion to its obscene behaviour patterns so will it bring its own nemesis. Righteousness alone will prevail.

3. THE PROPHETS IN JEWISH HISTORY

Their Place and Purpose

God Speaks through History.
God has spoken through history, revealing himself and his nature through actual historical events. More specifically, he has revealed himself primarily through the history of the Jews. Speaking through Abraham, he called them to be his people, and through Moses he demonstrated his power by delivering them from Egypt and fashioning them into a nation. Through Moses he also gave them covenants and a law, making it quite clear that he was a holy God with moral demands and that he required the obedience of his people. His power, holiness, forgiveness, guidance and love were all revealed through the actual historical events of that era. The people learned that God is a God who entered into the happenings of their lives, and in those happenings showed himself for what he is.

The times of the prophets (that is, the prophets whose writings we have in the Old Testament) belong to a later historical period in which the Jewish people had to learn a particularly hard lesson about the nature of God. It was an period when their disobedience to God reached such a peak that, despite his desire to bless them, he had to bring upon them devastating judgements to make clear his intense hatred of evil and sin. He was holy and they could not be allowed to hold that holiness in contempt. It was a lesson they should have learned much earlier in their history, but persistently failed to do so.

Since this lesson was worked out on a canvas of historical events it is very important to have some grasp of what those events were. Without this historical background the study of these prophets can be difficult, vague, even meaningless. True, we can always pick up a few choice encouraging texts without knowing the background, but we will gain no revelation of the main themes of the prophets.

The Tale of Two Kingdoms.

A good starting point for this historical context is the death of Solomon in 922 BC. In his final years Solomon was overcome by his lavish wealth, his wives and his extortions. The result was that he lost his way with God, and on his death, God caused his kingdom to split into two parts. The northern part became known as Israel (made up of most of the tribes, including Ephraim), with its capital (ultimately) at Samaria. The southern part was known as Judah, with its capital at Jerusalem. These kingdoms never got together again. Israel lasted until 722 BC when it was destroyed by Assyria. It showed nothing but a constant disobedience to God's ways. Judah lasted for a further century or more, when the same fate overtook her in 587 BC, being destroyed by Babylon. She had been somewhat more faithful overall to Jehovah than Israel, but the last century of her existence saw her degenerate into the same disobedience as her sister state, and share her fate.

At no time during those 200 yrs of Israel's existence and 300 years of Judah's existence did God cease to speak to either of these nations through his prophets. The prophetic voice had been there right from the time of Abraham and was the essential way in which God guided and warned the Jews throughout their history. The prophets, therefore, were familiar figures to all the kings of Israel and their office had national recognition, even if individual prophets were often persecuted. From 922 (after the split) to 750 their warnings were frequent, and divine visitations of war, drought and plague followed when they were ignored (e.g. with Elijah).

A major watershed in prophetic activity appeared, however, with the arrival of Amos and Hosea prophesying to Israel in c. 750 BC. By 750 BC the degradations and apostasy of the northern kingdom, Israel, had reached such a peak that God's warnings through his prophets began to take a much more severe and destructive note: the nation was not just to be punished with war etc. for its sin, but was now to be destroyed completely and even removed from its "promised land". This sharper word ("I will spare them no longer") that they brought to Israel was also brought also to Judah by Isaiah and Micah. Both nations were under severe threat, and in a manner that they had not been before. Not only was the prophetic word sharper but there was a new and extraordinary release in the amount of prophetic activity, all designed to make both nations sit up, take notice and repent before they were destroyed. The Jews were to find

such a message very difficult indeed to accept. They had been in "their" land now for some 500 years (since approx. 1200 BC), and to them it was unthinkable that God would go back on his promise and remove them. This, however, was the word God was pronouncing, and pronouncing with his full weight through some of the greatest prophets the Jews had ever heard.

Which Prophet Fits Where, and When?

It helps our understanding of these prophets if we look at each and see where they fit into the overall picture of this period. We can distinguish for most of them which kingdom they were sent to and the period of time when they were sent.

There are two major catastrophes which form the epicentres of this historical period: the destruction of Samaria in 722 BC and the destruction of Jerusalem in 587 BC. There is, in other words, a double catastrophe among the Jewish people, a dreadful duplication of destruction, when first Israel rejects the prophets and then Judah, not heeding Israel's fate, also rejects them. Not surprisingly we find that the prophets are most active at the peak of the two crisis points, and some prophets focus on the first destruction, and some on the second. Israel's destruction in 722 BC and Judah's in 587 BC means that the historical period of these prophets is quite lengthy, and the gap between the first group of prophets and the second group is considerable (a good sixty years). The story is all of a piece, however, and forms a double witness to God's attitude to persistent sin.

Amos and Hosea are essentially prophets to the northern kingdom, and are, therefore, early, though Hosea continued to prophesy until the Israelite debacle. **Micah**, a contemporary of Hosea speaks both to the north and the south. **Isaiah** is also a contemporary of Hosea, receiving his call in 742 BC, and, though having words for Israel, was primarily sent to steer Judah through the period of Israel's collapse and the Assyrian threat. Isaiah had a prophetic career of some forty years, continuing to speak to Judah long after Israel fell. He was responsible for saving Jerusalem from destruction by the Assyrians.

Just as Amos and Hosea gave a generation's warning to Israel, so **Habakkuk and Jeremiah** gave the same to Judah. Like Isaiah, Jeremiah had a prophetic career which lasted some 40 years. For the

first 18 years he prophesied alongside a reforming young king, Josiah. Josiah legislated to bring back true religion whilst Jeremiah preached to turn the hearts of the people back to the Lord. Both king and prophet eventually failed, but Jeremiah survived and was actually present at the final capture and destruction of Jerusalem. **Zephaniah** prophesied against Judah and was a contemporary both of Jeremiah and Habakkuk. His message to Judah is in the context of a huge scenario of a general "Day of the Lord" involving all the nations in a judgement from God. **Nahum** prophesied the downfall of Assyria, which took place in 612 BC with the fall of Nineveh, its capital, to the Babylonians. **Jonah** is an undated prophecy of warning to a rampant and cruel Assyria. **Obadiah,** likewise, undated, is a short but devastating prophecy against Edom, one of Judah's bitter enemies.

Ezekiel was one of the Jewish people taken into Babylon as hostage during a preliminary deportation in 597. As a prophet in exile, he was called to strengthen the exiles but to pronounce unqualified destruction on those still left in Jerusalem, witnessing a fulfillment in 587. **Daniel,** taken into Babylon during the first deportation (609), spoke no word about the fall of Jerusalem, but became in old age the spokesman and intercessor of the return of Judah.

What the prophets had to say.
1. Quite obviously, then, **their main (and united) theme was one of devastating judgement**. They brought, so to speak, God's final word after centuries of disobedience. They demonstrate the awful truth that no matter how patient God may be with sin and disobedience there has to come a day of reckoning. Sin, whether in nations or individuals, will always bring pain and distress, but the blatant persistence in sin which ignores all warnings brings something much more devastating – a terrifying day of final judgement. That is what these prophets are really saying. It's a lesson we all need to understand.

    At the same time the grace and patience of God is to be seen in the very fact that he sounded the warning to Israel and Judah so loudly, so clearly and so persistently. He showed himself to be always "slow to anger". On the other hand, the "wrath" of God is seen in a manner which is very frightening. Death and destruction with unimaginable pain both to young and old is painted in vivid

colours, but with the purpose not merely of genuine warning but of attempting to bring repentance. God's judgement on sin was a theme all through Jewish history, but the biblical prophets speak of it with a force that is not found elsewhere. Their lesson is not one to write off as the product of undisciplined and uncouth prophetic figures, for they were not that at all: they were thinking, godly men, some of whom ranked high in society (as Isaiah and Ezekiel), and all had a very clear grasp of national and world affairs. They also heard God.

Their message is spoken out on a very big stage, the stage of national and international history. They have an understanding of history, and they have a philosophy of history which is divine in origin. They recognized that the nations are not their own masters but are weighed in the balance by God himself. He determines their destinies, and he determines them on the just basis of their moral and humane behaviour. Wherever injustice, immorality, cruelty, wanton ambition are to be found there is sure to be judgement. Thus, we even find that many chapters of these prophets, and indeed some complete books, are devoted not to the Jews at all but to the nations involved with them at this time in history. That is why their message is so important for us today.

2. The main target of the theme of judgement is of course Israel and Judah. The threat is total destruction. **Yet constantly breaking out is the promise of God that he will not make a complete end of either nation,** no matter what agonies they go through and how much destruction they suffer. Prophet after prophet refers to a restoration, a reuniting of Israel and Judah in a new way, purified of idolatry. In this we see something of the love and faithfulness of God that somehow even transcends his wrath. This was partly fulfilled when the Jews came back out of exile in Babylon some 70 years after the first deportation took place. There is a dimension, however, in those prophecies about restoration (some of which are detailed and extensive) which clearly goes beyond a return from Babylon. There is, in fact, an "end time" dimension to these prophecies about the Jewish nation, indicating that God has not yet finished with the Jewish people. This is a critically important dimension of their prophetic work, even if the implications of it are not as clear as we would like. It remains a guide for our own times.

3. Alongside the pointer to a restoration are **prophecies about Jesus himself**. This is remarkably clear in Isaiah, where a whole string of prophecies about the Shoot of Jesse and the Servant of the Lord provide an incredibly comprehensive picture not merely of the birth, death, and resurrection of Jesus but also of his divine/human nature and his ministry among the gentile world until "the latter days". These pointers to Jesus come out of the appalling distresses and failures that constitute the history of a nation that was intended to bring blessing to the world. These promises of a Saviour, so expressive of the love of God, provide more than anything the greatest balance in these prophets to the appalling word of wrath that is their primary mandate to the nations of their day.

4. THE PROPHET and OPPOSITION

The Experience of Jeremiah

The Prophet as God's "Hatchet Man".

The prophet is the mouthpiece of God. He is expected to hear and to speak what God wants to say, when God wants him to say it. Unfortunately much of what God has to say is in the form of warning and correction. The tenor of Scripture is that the prophet is likely to function most at times when warnings are required. It has to be that way simply because of the waywardness of humanity. Warning and correction are, of course, to be seen as an expression of the love of God, but the need to convey them, nonetheless, make the ministry of the prophet at times very unpleasant, for whilst no one minds giving words of affirmation (which, of course, the prophets frequently do) giving words of warning and correction can be a very different matter. Those are much less likely to be received with grace, if indeed they are received at all. But the true prophet is hardly likely to avoid commissions of reproof. He will not relish them, and if he has any human sensitivity, he will not go looking for them.

Thus the prophet becomes God's "hatchet man", trying to cut through a pattern of behaviour which is contrary to God's way and dangerous for those following it. It can be at a personal level or at a national level. So Samuel had to call Saul to order in his

disobedience, and Nathan had to face up to David at David's moment of adultery. These were unpleasant and dangerous moments for those prophets, even if in those two instances the prophetic correction was received. Not all prophetic corrections are received with such grace; indeed the vast majority are not and they are likely to arouse an unpleasant and even violent response.

This latter sort of negative experience was precisely that which the prophets experienced in the two kingdoms of Israel and Judah. For 200 years in the case of Israel and over 300 years in the case of Judah their calling was almost entirely a calling to warn those nations severely about their rejection of God and their evil behaviour. As the years passed the message of correction and condemnation became stronger and stronger until, as the imminent destruction of each kingdom approached, they reached a climax in the pronouncements of the Major Prophets (Isaiah, Jeremiah, and Ezekiel) and most of the so-called Minor Prophets. Page after page of these prophecies speak against what the people are doing, and even if the prophecies convey the love of God for his people and speak occasionally of the hope of restoration or a coming Messiah, the overall thrust of the message was an unpleasant exposure of the sins of the people. Such ministry required extraordinary conviction, courage and persistency.

Jeremiah Demonstrates What Such Ministry Demanded.
Jeremiah's prophetic work began in Jerusalem in 627 BC, and he was still pursuing it forty years later in 587 AD when Jerusalem was captured by the Babylonians. From the very start his message had to be one of strong warning for he was called to prophesy after 50 years of blatant paganism in the nation under King Manasseh and his son, Amon. God had already pronounced dire judgement on Judah on account of the Manasseh years, but he wanted remind Judah of exactly where she stood so that she might have an opportunity to repent. This was Jeremiah's essential task as God's spokesman.

It was obvious that speaking correction to a nation which had been following the ways of paganism for two generations would be extremely difficult. Priests and people alike were set in their ways, and they were bound to react against any strong moral interpretation of religion which forbade them the pleasures of paganism. Their personal interests, especially the financial interests of the rich and the political interests of the national leadership, were intertwined

with the status quo. Moreover their paganism had now become so intermingled with the religion of Yahweh that they were spiritually confused. They would doubtless see Jeremiah as one who was just causing trouble and an outlandish radical. Small wonder, therefore, that at the very outset of his ministry Jeremiah should have received a stern reminder from the God for whom he spoke that *"they shall fight against you"* (Jer 1:19).

The Call for Plain Speaking.
There could be no half measures or innuendoes. A bold statement of undiluted truth was what was called for: Jeremiah had to tell the nation simply and directly that it was bound for a catastrophe in which Jerusalem and its Temple would be destroyed and the nation dispossessed of its promised land – unless there was repentance and a turning back to Yahweh. Thus the imagery of his prophetic words and his prophetic actions were inevitably vivid and unmistakeable. He was told, for example, to bury a belt in Babylon and then to retrieve it after many days, ruined and useless. With the belt in his hand, he was to proclaim that *"these wicked people ... ... who worship other gods will be like this belt – completely useless"* (13:1ff). It is true that his imagery could be very beautiful and persuasive at times: *"I remember the devotion of your youth, how as a bride you loved me .... What fault did your fathers find in me that they strayed so far from me?"* (Jer. 2:1, 5 NIV) but more often it was very earthy and blunt: *"under every tree you lay down as a prostitute .... You are a swift she-camel running here and there ... ... sniffing the wind in her craving – in her heat who can restrain her?"* (Jer. 2:20, 23). The image of spiritual prostitution used here was very frequent, and in the light of the fact that so much actual prostitution was taking place in Judah it was a most appropriate image. The very offensiveness of the language was designed to shock those who heard, for polite language was not always heard. Not that it was Jeremiah who chose to use such jagged and brutal words. Left to his own devices he would no doubt have watered down the directness and the abruptness of the message. But both the imagery of Jeremiah's prophecies and the force of the language was a direct function of the Spirit who was propelling his mind and his tongue. As Jeremiah confessed the word was *"like a fire"* inside him", and it simply had to come out.

Nor was Jeremiah allowed to give such plain speaking in a corner to a group of sympathisers. Judah's "prostitution" was proclaimed "*in the hearing of Jerusalem*" (2:1). He was told to "*stand at the gate of the Lord's House and there proclaim this message*". He was told to collect and send his messages to the king himself. God had a message and he wanted it heard, especially by the nation's leaders.

Thus Jeremiah embarked on a ministry of incredible difficulty, the sort of ministry that any prophet would seek to avoid. But the call of the prophet is not to glamour and popularity. There will always be something in his calling that will take him to stand against the tide, to speak out against the familiar and comfortable. The people of God are always wont to stray, always likely to become complacent. The prophet is the instrument to disturb such slumbers. Jeremiah could not have imagined, however, despite the warning God gave him, just how virulent the opposition would be to what he had to say. He was devastated to find that the people of his own hometown of Anathoth were actually planning to kill him even though he was one of their own priests , so incensed were they at his preaching (Jer. 11:18ff). The result of his preaching in the Temple court was that the son of the chief officer of the Temple, Pashhur, had him beaten and put in the stocks. A further proclamation from Jeremiah in the courtyard of the Temple court of the destruction of the Temple finished with the priests, the prophets and the people all seizing him and saying, "you must die" (26:8). Fortunately some officials took his side and he was spared, but the threat had been real and thereafter he was more a marked man than ever. He battled bitterly against the arrogant court "prophets" (Jer. 28 & 29). King Jehoiakim systematically burned his collected prophecies and sought his death (36:20ff). His enemies among the officials eventually threw him into a cistern to die (38:6), though thankfully he was rescued by a friendly official. In all this he learned at depth what God had meant by "*they will fight against you*"!

A very distressing feature was that these moments of great danger, which increased as his work went on, were merely the peaks of **a never ending background of constant and bitter rejection.** This persistent, ever present hardness was as wearing in its way as the high profile danger moments, and took greater toll on Jeremiah's heart and emotions. It went on for forty years. Even after working with the reforming King Josiah for two decades, he cried out "*For twenty three years the word of the LORD has come to me and I have*

spoken to you again and again, but you have not listened." (25:3 NIV). Over the next two decades it got worse. The temptation to bitterness of heart is very evident at times. He cried out on one occasion, *"Alas my mother that you gave me birth, a man with whom the whole land strives and contends! I have neither lent nor borrowed, yet everyone curses me"* (15:10 NIV); *"You understand, O LORD; remember me ... ... avenge me on my persecutors ... ... think of how I suffer reproach for your sake ... ... Why is my pain unending and my wound grievous and incurable?"* (15:15-18). God met him with a rebuke and a call to re-iterate his message. Self pity was never allowed to get the better of him. When he complained bitterly about the way the wicked prospered God again rebuked him saying that worse was to come and he must face that and keep preaching (Ch.12). This seemed a hard response, but it was the firmness of love. It was the prophet's call.

Jeremiah was never, however, entirely alone, even if must have felt like that at times. Part of the strengthening that God promised him came by way of human support. Though he doesn't mention him by name, King Josiah in his work of legislating against paganism must have been a great support to Jeremiah. Jeremiah was not alone in his prophetic activity either: we hear of Uriah (who eventually paid for his prophetic words with his life 26:20ff) and the faithful Baruch, his scribe. There were always individual officials and elders who supported him against the implacable priests and prophets. Such people were few, but they were there, and they proved to be sufficient for his preservation.

What are the requirements for such a daunting ministry?
What were Jeremiah's resources? How did he keep going? These are questions worth asking, and not just for prophets. Without question, t**he most important factor in this was Jeremiah's deep sense of call**. Unfortunately we do not have the details of his call in the same way that we have for Isaiah. What we do know, however, is that he was given a profound sense of being set apart as a prophet and *"a prophet to the nations"* before he was even conceived (1:5). There is a suggestion that he may in fact have had some visual experience like Isaiah for he recollects that *"the LORD reached out his hand and touched my mouth and said to me, 'Now I have put my words into your mouth'"* (1:9). This was evidently the moment of his anointing and his commissioning, as was the coal on Isaiah's

lips. Whatever took place, his sense of commission by Yahweh himself, Israel's God, was unshakeable – like Isaiah it was burned into him – and this in his 'teens. The depth of this meeting with God meant that he never doubted that he was acting for God or that he really heard from God. Not in his worse moments of despair and pain do we hear him voice in his prophetic writings any doubt about God – complain he might, and bitterly, about his lot, but he could not doubt the genuine hand of God in it. Nothing but this sort of conviction could hold him firm in the face of violent opposition from the acknowledged "prophets" of his day. This was the essential root of a powerful and prolonged ministry against bitter opposition. It was precisely the same with Paul the Apostle, whose whole life was informed and built on his Damascus road experience and call.

One aspect of the prophetic calling and commission is to be found in what might be described as "prophetic compulsion". This is an inner urge to speak out, and to speak out with the heart of God. Such compulsion is part of the anointing on the prophet. Jeremiah clearly refers to this on more than one occasion: *"But if I say,' I will not mention him or speak any more in his name,' his word is in my heart like a fire, a fire shut up in my bones. I am weary of holding it in; indeed, I cannot"* (20:9 *NIV); "The word of the LORD is offensive to them ... but I am full of the wrath of the LORD and I cannot hold it in" (6:11 NIV); I never sat in the company of revellers, never made merry with them; I sat alone because your hand was on me and you had filled me with indignation.* (15:17 *NIV*). This compulsion was also part of the reality of the continual dialogue that he maintained with God (or that God maintained with him!). It was a persistent reminder that he had not had a one-off visionary experience

A further aspect of the prophetic call was that the word of judgement that God had entrusted to him was constantly refreshed in Jeremiah's heart by a variety of prophetic inspiration: it was never allowed to get dull or become tired. These fresh injections were crucial in keeping alive his ministry. His favourite expression is the "The Lord said to me", but the word would come to him visually as well as audibly. He clearly saw pictures (as in the almond tree 1:13), and God spoke to him through the things he saw around him (like an earthen pot); he saw prophetic parables (like the ruined belt and the purchase of a plot of land in a Jerusalem about to be destroyed),

and he heard the inner voice. In all ways the word of the Lord came to him.

Prophets pay a high price for a singularly important ministry but their reward is a vivid awareness of God and his ways. Rejection is part of their life - it is the same today when an unpleasant word has to be spoken.

SIGNS OF THE TIMES

among

JEW and GENTILE

CONTENTS

Introduction

During the last week of his earthly ministry Jesus was asked by his disciples the question, *"What will be the sign of your coming and of the end of the age?"* (Matt. 24:3 NIV). He responded by giving a full prophetic statement about the future of the world and the signs that were to be looked for before his coming. This statement is sometimes referred to as his "apocalyptic discourse", and there are three accounts of it; Matt.24:1-35, Mark 13:1-31 and Lk. 21:1-33.

The four sections that make up this study are not intended to be a full commentary on the discourse, but point to some fundamental statements which Jesus made about the future and which seem particularly relevant to our times.

Trying to interpret the meaning of prophecy is never something to be undertaken dogmatically, but with an open mind and heart. Nonetheless there is a clear expectation that we will watch out for the signs of his coming, since one day he will come.

These signs will not necessarily come over night. On the contrary they will become more and more evident over many years. Two such

signs, the ingathering of the Gentiles and the restoration of the Jews have become very evident over the course of the last century, and we do well to take note of them. These two signs form the bulk of the material in this booklet.

1.SIGN OF THE TIMES: THE GENTILES

"This gospel will be preached in all the world, and then the end will come" Matt. 24:14 NIV

Jesus was very much aware of the great prophecies which spoke of him in the writings of the prophet Isaiah. He knew from those prophecies that Galilee would see a great "Light" which would be a source of much joy among the Jewish people - *"the people who walked in great darkness have seen a great light"* (Is. 9:2), and he knew that the same "Light" would eventually shine across the gentile world, *"I will also make you a light for the Gentles, that you may bring my salvation to the ends of the earth"* (Is. 49:6). His last words to his disciples were, *"Go and make disciples of all nations"*, (Matt. 28:19). Very early on in the apostolic church the gospel was in fact being preached among the Gentiles, and the witness rapidly increased with Paul who had a specific and direct commission from Jesus to go to the Gentiles. In the centuries that followed, Christianity spread across the whole of the Roman Empire and became the accepted faith of the emperors. It also spread across the Middle East and even into parts of India and China. It remained very much, however, essentially a European expansion until European nations began the process of empire building across the world from the 15th century onwards. There was a marked impact on the Americas from the Roman Catholic Church, and particularly on South America through the Spanish explorers. It was in the earlier part of the 19th C that Protestant missionaries began to make an impact in the world with an evangelical witness, very largely as a consequence of British conquests. By the end of the 19th Century there were some 14,000 missionaries across the world and a marked impact had been made notably in Africa, China, Canada and the United States. It was the 20th century, however, which saw the

greatest impact with some 200,000 missionaries at work and a witness established across most parts of the world.

In the light of Matt. 24:14 such an extraordinary global development demands attention and explanation. It implies we are getting close to a fulfilment of the "end time" sign that Jesus announced. It is a massive vindication of his words. It calls for careful watching of 21st century development, and much prayer. How has this happened? There are 4 major features that can be seen in this world-wide spread of the gospel, and they are crucial pointers for us as we look for its future completion.

1. Prophetic Vision - The Root Factor

When we see how small the evangelical world was and see how besieged the early 18thC evangelical witness was we may well ask what gave that witness the dynamic to spread across the world like it did. The answer to that question is simply that prophetic vision was germinating in that small Northern seed bed. The word of God had been released by the Reformation in the 16th century, and this allowed a biblical vision of God's purposes for the nations to grow. In the 18thC it was ready to bear fruit.

This vision was more deeply based than just a recognition of the "Great Commission" of Jesus. It was born out of a discovery of the widespread promises in the prophetic scriptures about the vast blessing that was the come to the Gentiles. These promises came alive and were hugely motivating. A representative selection would be: *"All the ends of the earth will remember and turn to the Lord, and all the families of the nations will bow down before him, for dominion belongs to the Lord and he reigns over the nations"* Ps 22:27 NIV; *"God will bless us, and all the ends of the earth will fear him"* Ps 67:7 NIV; *"They will neither harm nor destroy on all my holy mountain, for the earth will full of the knowledge of the Lord as the waters cover the sea"* Is. 11:9 NIV; *"In that day the Root of Jesse will stand as a banner for the peoples; the nations will rally to him, and his place of rest will be glorious"* Is 11;10 NIV.

The prophets were full of such statements, and it was the inspiration of these that sent out the early missionaries with such extraordinary vigour and purpose. These were the staple texts that were preached at the inaugural meetings of the great new missionary societies that sprang up at the end of the 18th century and the middle of the 19th century. This was a movement essentially of prophetic

vision which came alive and was acted on. The depth of the grasp of the idea of all the nations coming to the Lord was astonishing. Nineteenth century missionaries were ready to die on the field with little to show yet none the less spoke with enormous faith that the harvests would undoubtedly come.

It is imperative that we keep alive and foster world vision for Jesus in the life of the churches. Christians must think deeper than their own spiritual consumer needs. We need to regain a new depth of prophetic vision for God's ultimate purposes. It would not be wrong to say that such prophetic vision was the consequence of illumination by the Spirit through revival among Puritans and their German counterparts. That is one of the reasons why we constantly need revival. Revival is critical in other ways as well.

2. Revival - The Crucial Dynamic

The 18thC was to show how Holy Spirit revival would be the agent of world-wide growth, the dynamic of prophetic vision. Jonathan Edwards in New England was deeply immersed in the prophetic vision for the nations. He himself became involved in widespread revival in 1734 with large growth in the numbers of Christians (The Great Awakening). He also witnessed through his friend and missionary David Brainerd widespread revival among the American Indians. He was convinced such revival was the way forward to growth - God himself at work through the Spirit in awesome power. At the same time Zinzendorf in Moravia learned the same lesson. He, also deeply moved by missionary vision, became involved with revival among religious refugees on his estate at Herrnhut. After three days of intense prayer and confession the Spirit descended on them. The ensuing fellowship became the vehicle of Zinzendorf's vision, sending missionaries into numerous coastal areas across the world, even as far as the Pacific Islands. The Moravians became the trailblazers of later missionary activity. They were also the catalyst for the revivals under Wesley and Whitefield which further increased missionary work later in the 18th century.

This "vision + revival" pattern is equally evident in the 19thC when for example the early missionary societies sprang up owing both their dynamic and manpower to the 2nd Evangelical Revival. Later in the mid-19thC a second wave of societies sprang up fuelled by the great "Prayer Revivals" of 1857-59 in America and Britain. The earlier societies established widespread stations on seacoasts

and the second wave took the witness inland, notably in Africa, India and China. The 19thC, with its huge gains, has been called the "Great Century" of mission. This is evident in the fact that whereas the 18thC had finished with some 120 missionaries, the 19thC finished with some 14,000 of whom 6,000 came from Britain and 4,000 from N. America. It was a huge privilege for Britain to spearhead such great endeavour.

It is when we come to the 20thC, however, that the full force of revival as the dynamic of world mission properly comes into focus. This is the century in which converts were numbered in the millions, something that Jonathan Edwards could only dream of in faith (and did!). Perhaps the most outstanding was the Pentecostal revival which began in an inauspicious Azusa Street of Los Angeles in 1906. Marked in particular with speaking in tongues, but also characterised by healings and other gifts of the Spirit, it spread rapidly as a great many people went to and from the meetings. Its most spectacular advance was into the Hispanic areas of America (Mexico, the Caribbean Islands) and then into South America proper. In S. America there were some 2 million converts in 1940, there were 5 million by 1950, 10 million by 1960, 20 million by 1970 and 90 million by 2000, 30 million in Brazil alone. It was very largely a grass roots movement among the poor with working pastors. There was massive evangelism with the likes of Tommy Hicks, Billy Graham, and Annacondia.

It spread all over the world, not least in Britain, and the Pentecostal missionary arm was very strong right from the start. By the end of the century there were some 200 million denominational Pentecostals. In addition the Pentecostal revival had, in the latter part of the century, a huge impact in refreshing other mainline denominations, even the Roman Catholics. By 1985 Catholic Charismatics numbered 7.5 million in 80 countries, and by 2000 there were 50 million.

20thC China has been the scene of repeated revivals. There were revivals in 1908 in Manchuria under Jonathan Goforth and in 1927 under Watchman nee and John Sung, but the great outpouring of the Spirit came in the latter half of the century after all mission agencies had been ejected in 1949-50 and when the church numbered some 1.5 million. By the end of the century it numbered an estimated 50-70 million, very probably more.

Why "tongues"? This is important. Given on the day of Pentecost, the "tongues" sign has from the start primarily signified the fact that we are in the time when the gentiles would praise God in all their different languages. No wonder such a sign re-surfaced early in the 20thC when so many millions were to become members of the Kingdom, and no wonder it continues!

There were so many more revivals: the Welsh Revival was international in impact, the East African revival of the mid-century had profound repercussions in Europe and elsewhere. The Nepalese revival has taken the church in Nepal from no known Christians in 1960 to over 400,000 by the year 2000 and is still growing. Large revivals in Indonesia, India and Nigeria could be added. Significantly as the 20thC has progressed the numbers of converts have increased. It has been a remarkable fulfilment of God's words to Zerubbabel, "Not by power, not by might, but by my Spirit, says the Lord". It was clearly a work of God through Holy Spirit revival.

3. Prayer - The Spiritual Trigger
Prayer forms the essential link between vision and dynamic. It is prayer that brings revival into being. At the same time it is revival that sustains prayer. That is the clear lesson of the last three centuries. The Puritans, the Pietists and the Moravians, the evangelical missionary visionaries who set the advance in motion were profoundly prayerful people. The 18thC witnessed many prayer groups at work, a trans-Atlantic prayer network with its origins in Scotland, and a 100 year Moravian prayer gathering to back up its missionaries. Their burden of prayer was clear: that the nations might be visited by outpourings of the Spirit. Every revival throughout those 300 years can be shown to have been preceded by strong, directed and united prayer. The prayer testimony is astonishing. None more so than the prayer focus on China both from within and from the rest of the world during the great Communist clamp down after 1950. The prayer was desperate and prolonged, and the result was the conversion of tens of millions of Chinese. Prayer remains our greatest challenge.

4. The Catastrophic Background.
The historical background against which this huge world-wide move has been made has been dark and very unpromising. For example in the 18thC Britain and France were in conflict over the

control N. America, and the French Revolution and the Napoleonic wars later threatened Britain at the very time the first missionary societies were getting under way. The American civil war with its huge loss of life, was the background to the great mid 19thC prayer revival in the U.S.A.

The 20thC, however, provides the clearest examples of the dark background. It was supremely a century of revivals but at the same time by general consent of historians a century of endless human cataclysms. These can easily be listed: World War 1 and the even more lethal world flu pandemic which followed; inter-war economic depression; World War 2 which literally convulsed the whole globe; the demise of Western empires; cold war dislocation and the threat of nuclear war; a world AIDS epidemic; the rise of militant terror; widespread national tyrannies. In all this tens of millions died in warfare or through disease, far more were displaced, and whole nations suffered under vicious oppression.

2.SIGN OF THE TIMES: THE JEWS

"Jerusalem will be trampled by the Gentiles until the time of the Gentiles are fulfilled"

Lk. 21:24 NIV

In our times there is a bitter impasse in the theological battle between those who consider the Jews have yet a significant role as a nation in the ultimate purposes of God and those who do not. The battle, of course, centres on prophetic interpretation. Unfortunately such a conflict is not likely to be resolved by more theological debate. That will only increase the contention and bitterness. Since the battle is over prophetic outcome, it is much more likely to be resolved by the emergence of historical facts which either demonstrate the validity of a purpose for the Jews or the opposite. It is worth remembering that the controversy between Peter and the Judaizers over whether all Christians must be circumcised was resolved in the Council of Jerusalem by facts, and not by theories: what God had actually done to Cornelius (and other Gentiles) in

filling him with the Spirit without him being circumcised was the deciding factor. Likewise the theological battle over the validity of tongues in our own generation has been decided by the extraordinary way God caused that gift to spread amongst so many of his saints over the course of the 20th C. Facts are critical.

Accordingly there is a real call, not to revisit interpretive arguments, but to recognise and properly assess historical facts which speak directly into the discussion about the Jews. That is what this pamphlet seeks to do. Such facts are numerous and important.

1. The Fact of the State of Israel.

We live in a time when a Jewish nation has re-emerged after some 2,000 years of painful exile. By any reckoning that is an astonishing fact. It is a fact which can find no better description than the prophetic utterance given by Ezekiel: *"I will assemble you out of all the countries where you have been scattered, and I will give you the land of Israel"* Ez. 11:17 NIV:. Many other such texts provide a similar description.

In the last 60 years Jews have come to Israel from over 80 different countries where they have lived for centuries. The population of the State of Israel is now over 5,000,000 and has become a focal point of world Jewry. Starting from a very gradual settling of Jews in the Holy Land during the mid 19thC onwards, the flow gradually increased over the years up to 1939, and then in 1948 burst into a veritable torrent. By 1968 a nation had been thoroughly established. The fact astonished and amazed the Jews themselves, and for a great many of them the word "miracle" seemed a very appropriate description. We are, therefore, no longer in the realm of theory when thinking of a return of the Jews, but in the realm of fact and actuality. It demands an explanation commensurate with its astonishing happening. It cannot simply be brushed off because it does not fit some interpretive theory that has no place for a restoration.

To maintain the view that this return is of no consequence and is not a fulfilment of prophecy it would be necessary to demonstrate there was something in this return that was contrary to prophetic scripture, something that would rule it out of consideration. For example, would the fact that it was a return which had little spiritual motivation in it constitute such an objection? Is there reason to suppose it is a man-made thing that will be like the brief century

interlude of the Jewish nationalist Maccabean kingdom which held brief sway shortly before the Romans took over the Holy Land? Is it a purely secular happening which in due course will simply end in some historical national disaster? The short answer to that is, of course, that only time will tell. But the sheer magnitude of the new state compels one to think otherwise. Certainly the State of Israel is certainly of much greater historical magnitude than the Maccabean kingdom.

There is, however, nothing in it essentially contrary to prophetic scripture. On the other hand there are clear indications there that a return to Zion is foreseen for "the last days" and such a return will be the fruit not of spiritual thinking by the Jews but of strong action by God himself to bring it about.

2. The State of Israel as a Secular Achievement.

The movement back to Israel by the Jews has only in very small part been a religious or spiritual phenomenon. Two forward looking Rabbis, Alkalai and Kalischer, affected by the enlightenment broke ranks with the general body of orthodox rabbis and argued that some human effort at colonising Israel should be made in preparation for the Messiah. That led to the mid 19thC "Lovers of Israel" movement, the first colonising settlers. But the main protagonists of a true political Zionism were very much enlightened secularists. The outstanding figure in Zionism, Theodore Herzl, whose book *The Jewish State* became the major catalyst of the movement toward the state of Israel, epitomised this secularism. The main concern of such figures was to find a home for Jews where they would be free of the appalling anti-Semitism that surrounded them. Herzl did not envisage a theocracy but a liberal democracy on the European model. Many of the early thinkers and settlers found their "spirituality" in socialism. They could, of course, never escape the concepts of messianic destiny and the lure of the "Land" which were so deeply embedded in Jewish thought, but their interpretations of such concepts were thoroughly secularised: the reign of the Messiah, for example, would be one where they were free to live in enlightenment and peace, without any oppression from antiquated strictures from the Talmud.

Does this non-religious motivation nullify any prophetic significance being applied to the 20thC return? Not necessarily. God did many things with the Jews in their early history to achieve his

purposes with and without their "spiritual" co-operation. Even the exodus from Egypt was an enterprise God undertook for his people without any real spiritual intent on their part. The plagues of Egypt not only moved the Egyptians out of the way, but moved the Israelites on their way: God brought them out with his "strong arm". Indeed the Israelites insisted on bringing their idols with them out of Egypt and were very reluctant followers of Yahweh..

There are some important indications in the Prophets that God would make the restoration of the last days equally the consequence of this same "strong arm": *"Not for your sakes do I do this, says the Lord God, "let it be known to you. Be ashamed and confounded for your own ways"* Ez.36:32 NIV. *"I will bring you from the nations and gather you from the countries where you have been scattered ... With a mighty hand and an outstretched arm and with outpoured wrath"* Ez.20:34. There is abundant space in the prophetic scriptures for a return of the Jews in unbelief.

3. The Prayer Factor
It is a profound and important principle that in working out his purposes God seems invariably to draw out from his people a heartfelt cry for those purposes. Prayer is always the first stage of his activity. Luke carefully noted a crucial example of this in revealing the intercession of Simeon and Anna who were praying earnestly for the Messiah just before Jesus was born. In similar fashion, before the exodus from Egypt took place a great cry went up from the Israelites in their bondage, and God heard it and answered it in the birth of Moses. What evidence do we have of intercession for the Jews and their return prior to or alongside their 20thC return? Such evidence would be an important fact to reckon with, and it is in fact available.

The Reformation brought about a great re-discovery of fundamental biblical truth. One such truth was that God was intent on spreading the gospel across the world and converting people from all nations. This revelation released a very powerful stream of intercession from the evangelical world for the conversion of the "heathen". Over the last three centuries that stream has grown enormously and, more significantly, so has the spread of the gospel. The prayer and the answer are there for all to see. However, the stream of prayer included within it an element which had a focus on the Jews. It grew commensurate with the prayer for the nations, and

a great prayer concern for the conversion of the Jews is very discernible in the last three centuries. As time has gone on that prayer has included very specific request for the restoration of Jewry to its land. As with the nations generally prayer for the Jews is stronger than it has been at any other time.

The people involved in such praying have not been people on the fringe but those who have been again and again at the heart of the major revival movements that have brought so much advance to the church. It is to be noted that a very great deal of this has taken place in Britain from the Puritans onwards.

The Jewish people have always for centuries kept up their prayer for restoration. Whilst doubtless these were perfunctory for many; it is equally certain that for others it was deep and earnest. We have no way of measuring the great cry that went up from Jews during the anti-Semitic oppressions of the 20th C., and especially just prior to and during the horrific years of the Holocaust., but we know such a cry certainly existed and was very profound. It very much echoed the cry in Egypt just before the exodus under Moses.

4. The State of Israel and the Holocaust.

Perhaps the most startling fact concerning the Jews' return to Israel is the extraordinary juxtaposition of that event with the Holocaust. The "final solution" began in 1942 and was to destroy 6,000,000 Jews. In the same year the German army was poised to overrun Palestine, which would have brought obliteration of the embryonic Jewish state. Even in 1945 the situation hardly seemed much better with Jewry devastated and Britain adamantly opposed to Jewish settlement in Israel. But within 6 years of the start of the final solution and within 3 years of the end of the war the State of Israel had come into being. Within a further 20 years some 2-3 million Jews were settled in the land as Israeli citizens. The move from national genocide to national state in so short a time is simply stunning and seems to compel recognition of a divine hand. This nature of this juxtaposition was certainly not lost on many Jews, for whom the impact was that of a resurrection.

The whole episode has an awesome note, and it compels comparison with the equally awesome and parallel pattern of events that made up the exodus from Egypt. In that exodus a real threat of destruction was the prelude to deliverance, and God was certainly author of that deliverance.

5. The Concurrent Global Spread of the Gospel and the Return of the Jews.

The 20thC is notable for the widespread advance of the gospel into virtually every nation. It was a century of major revivals in every continent and hundreds of millions of converts. The century was quite unique in its impact. It was also the century in which increasing settlement was made by Jews in Israel, and in which finally the State of Israel emerged. That also was unique. Those are the facts. Is there any significance in that concurrent Jewish and Gentile development in the one century?

We certainly have to take that possibility into account when looking at some of the most debated prophecies about the Jews. Jesus said, *"Jerusalem will be trampled by the Gentiles until the time of the Gentiles is come"* Lk. 21:24 NIV, and Paul said, *"Israel has experienced a hardening in part until the full number of the Gentiles has come in."* Rom. 11:26 NIV. Both of these statements seem to point clearly to the fact that a time of release for the Jews is directly connected with the gathering in of the Gentiles. Isaiah's great prophetic statement about the work of the Messiah also bears this out: *"And now the Lord says - he who formed me in the womb to be his servant to bring Jacob back to himself - he says, 'It is too small a thing for you to be my servant to restore the tribes of Jacob and bring back Israel I have kept. I will also make you a light for the Gentiles, that you may bring my salvation to the ends of the earth"* Is. 49:5ff NIV. There is a dual work for the ascended Jesus: the gathering in from the nations and the restoring of Jacob. When we see real evidence of the former getting much closer and the latter physically appearing we are bound to take note. These are signs of the times.

6. The Providences of History

The Old Testament is full of descriptions of the acts of providence that God worked for Israel. There is a strong emphasis on calling the Jews to recognise them and remember them. Their God is found in their history. That lesson should not be ignored today, even if our modern assessments cannot be of the same order as those in scripture. Note the following pointers:

(i). The defeat of the massive German onslaught ideologically and physically on the Jewish nation, with the consequent utter

97

destruction of Germany, bears comparison with the biblical episodes of the exodus and later of Haman and all other genocidal attempts. The unassailable lesson of scripture is that God keeps a watch on his people.

(ii). Note the removal of Britain's mandate over Israel together with post war British opposition to the return of the Jews. At the same time the proposal of partition with the unique agreement of the two mutually antagonistic superpowers of Russia and America, and the recognition of the legal right of the new state by both superpowers gave totally unexpected status to Israel.

(iii). Note the deliverance from concerted military attack from the vastly more numerous Arab world at a point of extreme vulnerability both in 1948 and 1967. Note also the extraordinary acquisition of arms from the Czechs and later the French at those crisis points.

(iv). The settlement of several million Jews from all parts in a very short period after 1948 defied all reasonable expectations considering the utter lack of Israeli economic and financial resources, and the huge drain of constant military demands on money and manpower. It was as much a miracle as success in defence.

(v). The providential formation of very strong and numerous American Jewry from 1881 onwards gave critical support for the Israeli State many decades later.

3. SIGNS IN THE SKY

"There will be signs in the sun, moon and stars. On the earth, nations will be in anguish and perplexity at the roaring and tossing of the sea. Men will faint from terror, apprehensive of what is coming on the world, for the heavenly bodies will be shaken. At that time they will see the Son of Man coming in a cloud with power and great glory. When these things begin to take place, stand up and lift up your heads, because your redemption is drawing near." Lk. 21:25-28 NIV

"Immediately after the distress of those days the sun will be darkened, and the moon will not give its light; the stars will fall from the sky, and the heavenly bodies will be shaken." Matt. 24:29 NIV

In the words quoted above Jesus speaks of the most striking of the end time signs; there will come a time when the very heavenly bodies will be shaken, when the sea will roar with violent and destructive activity, and when humanity world-wide will be terrified at what they see. All this has yet to come. It will actually be "***at that time***" that the inhabitants of the world will see the Son of Man coming. It will be the time of his return in glory. This has to be truly the final sign. None will miss it. The other great end time signs, namely the preaching of the gospel in all the world along with the return of the Jews may be overlooked by many, but this will not be overlooked.

The warnings of such cosmic events have an awesome literalness about them. They are clearly not intended to be taken in a purely symbolic manner; things will actually happen to the sun, moon and stars, and the very stability of the earth will be shaken. This, of course, takes us to the very brink of the unthinkable and the unbelievable; the most secure things in human experience, the heavenly bodies, are to be "shaken". In a sense there is little more to say on the issue, since time alone will tell whether this is crass "doom watching" or not. It is, of course, very easy to put it in the pigeon-hole called "apocalyptic "and quietly and cynically ignore it.

Perhaps, therefore, it is worth reflecting on one or two factors in connection with such heavenly "disturbances".

Science itself has taught us that our solar system and galaxy are not quite as stable or safe as our daily perspective from earth might indicate. In fact they are a very uncertain and dangerous places. We now know only too well that the heavenly bodies have been battered and torn apart right from their inception. The universe itself is not static; stars come and go. It may appear static on account of the vast time spans involved, but the more we know of it the more frightening it becomes.

We do not necessarily have to postulate actual catastrophe for the sun, however, to imagine the fulfilment of Jesus' prophecy. The earth itself is now known to have been the scene of numerous cataclysms of world-wide proportions. Those cataclysms have not infrequently involved a "darkening of the sun", a darkening that is not of the sun itself but of its appearance from the earth, a darkening caused by vast clouds of ash and the like blotting out its light. This has happened not only from asteroid collision, but from earthquake and volcanic activity and other gaseous effects in the atmosphere. And of course a darkening of the sun involves a darkening of the moon. We also know that our climate and the oceans are very susceptible to happenings in the sun and the moon, and the seas are very likely to roar if there is any disturbance in what has been for us the natural order. Without any question, events in the heavenly bodies inevitably have portentous effects on the seas, and the seas have been both immensely formative and destructive of land formations and peoples in our planet's history. We would be foolish, therefore, to dismiss the notion of *"stars falling from the sky and heavenly bodies being shaken"* as being a primitive concept. That might well be exactly how disturbances on earth might make the heavenly bodies appear. Though, on the other hand, we may actually see real stellar disturbances.

All this amounts to the simple fact that modern scientific knowledge does not militate against the prophecy, but on the contrary makes such a prophecy a much more likely possibility. Catastrophe of this nature cannot be relegated to a primitive past.

The Prelude to the Signs in the Sky

These celestial happenings are said to come to pass *"immediately after the distress of those days"*. This gives us some indication of

the context, though it is necessarily vague. They will follow a period of great distress. This distress is something greater than *"wars and rumours of war"* and of *"nation fighting against nation"*, it is something greater than *"earthquakes and famines in different places"*, for all these are said to be *"but the beginnings of sorrow"* and are not to cause us alarm since they do not mark *"the end"* (see Matt 24:6-8 NIV). *"The distress of those days"* points to something much more calamitous, something that is *"unequalled from the beginning of the world until now"* and something that if not cut short *"would not allow anyone to survive"* Matt 24:21-22 NIV. They might indeed include wars and earthquakes but on a scale that vastly exceeds the normal historical experience of these things which have gone on through the ages.

In looking at this context of distress we should do well to keep in mind the prophecy in Zechariah of the nations of the world coming up against Jerusalem in the end times, destroying it with great carnage and then being faced with the direct intervention of the Messiah accompanied with seismic movements around Jerusalem (Zech.14).

If there is uncertainty in our understanding of such events at the point of history at which we stand, unfolding events as they approach will bring a devastating certainty.

4. PERSECUTION

"Then you will be handed over to be persecuted and put to death, and you will be hated of all nations because of me" Matt. 24:9 NIV

Persecution is not strictly speaking an "end time" sign in the same way as the full ingathering of the Gentiles, the restoration of Jerusalem and the "catastrophic signs in the sky". It is something that has been part of Christian history since Jesus' own times. It is placed alongside the prophecy about the continual presence of wars and earthquakes and famines, with the implication that it will always go on It is made to point to the beginnings of sorrows rather than the "end".

It is important to mention, however, on two counts:-

First the accuracy of this prophetic statement about the continual presence of persecution (alongside the truth of his statements about earthquakes and wars) has been utterly vindicated over a 2,000 year period since it was first made. Jesus' words have more than stood the test of time. Persecution is as real today as it was in the early church in Jerusalem. One might have thought that the Christian ethic alone would have by now secured the acceptance of the gospel by humanity, but such has not been the case. This 2000 year accuracy of Jesus' prophecies of persecution means that we should be assured that those prophetic happenings we have not yet seen will come to pass. Equally one might have thought humanity might have learned the futility of war, and that wars might have ceased by now despite Jesus' words. Again this is very far from the case and Jesus remains vindicated yet again.

Second we have got to an age in which such persecution seems to have reached a greater peak than ever before. Persecution of Christians is a marked feature of our age, and reveals the world-wide intensity of the struggle to gather in the *"fullness of the Gentiles"*, thus indirectly pointing towards the end. No Christian, therefore, should be unaware of the extent and nature of current persecution. Its sheer intensity is a sign for our times, and a challenge to prayer and action. It represents a fundamental "front line" in world evangelisation.

Persecution has political, religious and cultural roots. The very worst persecution area in the world - North Korea - is politically driven. The Christian ethic of respect for all men and the accountability of all men are propositions totally contrary to the basis and ideology of an absolute tyranny such as the North Korean rule. The same is true in Burma, it is present in China though not quite as viciously as it once was, and persecution remains a problem in parts of the old USSR communist empire. Religious persecution is evident in large parts of the Muslim world where some extreme and violent religious persecution and murder of Christians is by no means uncommon. Hinduism, as well as Buddhism, has shown a violent face in India and the Far East. Culturally, at the family level, religious differences have placed an enormous pressure against people moving from other faiths to follow Jesus. This cultural barrier is huge and is evident as much in the Western world as in

other parts. The more the gospel spreads the bigger the incidence of persecution.

We need to remember, therefore, that as we get closer to the end the obligation toward those of the world-wide church who are suffering such persecution will increase. The determination to spread the gospel and the determination to care for the oppressed church will be the two defining calls of the years ahead.

THE JEWS

and

THE TESTIMONY OF HISTORY

CONTENTS

Introduction

Herbert Butterfield, an acclaimed Professor of History at Cambridge University, wrote quite forcefully about God being a God of history. He stated firmly that God was at work in history over and above human decisions, and he was of the opinion that if God was not to be found in history then for us as human beings he would not be of much help or concern to us. He made this opinion clear in the ferment of a debate over God's part in history during the Second World War.

God certainly is a God of history -that fact shouts at us from the pages of Scripture. We must be bold enough therefore to seek out his acts of Providence in history, albeit with much deference and care. One thing is certain; if we are to see the Providence of God in history, he will be nowhere more clearly seen than in the history of the Jewish people for with the Jews we have the sure word of prophecy.

1. THE CHASTISEMENT OF THE NATION

"If you do not follow carefully all the words of this law .... the Lord will scatter you among the nations, from one end of the earth to the other" Deut. 28:64 NIV

"I will bring you into the desert of the nations and there, face to face, I will execute judgment upon you" Ez. 20:35 NIV

Prophetic Warnings Fulfilled
The history of the Jews has been remarkable for a number of features, and none more so than its dispersion or exile amongst the other nations of the world for over two and half millennia. The fact that prophetic warnings of such an exile were given at the very inception of the nation make that exile more remarkable still. Deuteronomy relates that God entered into a covenant with the Israelites just before they entered their "promised land". He covenanted to bless the nation and its land, but the condition was obedience to his laws. Righteousness and godliness were to mark the nation, otherwise it would be oppressed and, even worse, lose its land and be dispersed: *"The Lord will scatter you among the nations, from one end of the earth to the other"*.

Unfortunately the nation's history from the start was one of constant disobedience, and at Solomon's death God caused it to break into two halves. The northern half then descended into complete idolatry and was wiped off the map in 722 BC by Assyria, its people seemingly irretrievably lost in exile. The southern

kingdom suffered a similar fate in 586 BC with destruction followed by exile in Babylon. But the Babylonian exiles survived, and came to acknowledge that it was their disobedience that had brought such chastisement. Since that time there has always been a part of Jewish orthodox thinking which has associated the dispersion or exile with the chastisement of God.

After seventy years in Babylon some Jews came back to Jerusalem, eager for the promised land and determined on restoration. However, they represented only a small fraction of those exiled in Babylon, they occupied a very limited area around Jerusalem and they faced bitter opposition from foreign settlers. Moreover, apart for four brief decades in the 1stC BC, the restored nation was destined to be dominated and oppressed in turn by the great powers of Babylon, Persia, Greece and finally Rome, all of whom for a total of 600 years were to act as God's continued chastisement on the nation. From the exile of 586 BC onwards the greater part of the nation remained in exile and would remain so right up to our own times, a nation under severe discipline.

It was, however, with the double destruction of Jerusalem and Judea first in AD 70 and then again in 135 AD that the national home once more totally disintegrated, and an even greater episode in Jewish exile began. Jewish Rabbis see AD 70 as the start of the great exile. The Rabbinical schools and the office of Patriarch kept up a presence in Galilee for some time but eventually disappeared. The national life in Israel went into increasing decline until virtually nothing was left for nearly 1800 years. During the course of those two millennia the Jewish dispersion spread throughout the whole world. Though acknowledging this as divine displeasure the Rabbis, of course, never associated it with any rejection of Jesus whose claims they continued to oppose.

The Sufferings of the Jewish Exile
Deuteronomy graphically describes the distressing nature of that Jewish scattering:-

"Among those nations you will find no repose, no resting place for the sole of your foot. There the Lord will give you an anxious mind, eyes weary with longing, and a despairing heart. You will live in constant suspense, filled with dread both night and day, never sure of your life. In the morning you will say, "If only it were

the evening!" and in the evening, "If only it were the morning!"
– because of the terror that will fill your hearts and the sights that
you will see". **Deut. 28:65-68 NIV**

These words underline the dimension of suffering which is an integral part of the judgement of the dispersion. The Jews were not simply going to find themselves living quietly in different countries; their experience of being in exile would be full of fear, terror, anxiety and despair. They were going to meet an antagonism that would always be present and bring extreme distress. In the event they would be afflicted by what we today have come to describe as anti-Semitism. That word describes an historic hatred of the Jews simply because they are Jews, a hatred which has a great variety of causes; racial, religious, economic, social and political. Its sheer virulence and persistence throughout the centuries, no matter where the Jews were dispersed, has always been baffling. Only the divine pronouncement of chastisement can really provide a satisfactory explanation.

It would take untold volumes to catalogue the appalling accuracy of this warning statement as it was fulfilled in the lives of Jews who lived in exile over those last two and a half millennia. Only snap shots of the forces oppressing the Jews are possible.

Up to the 1stC AD
This anti-Semitism was apparent well before the Christian era began. For example, the Egyptians, amongst whom great numbers of Jews were dispersed, found the separatism of Jewish religious culture offensive and were unusually hostile to the Jews living in their midst. Manetho, an Egyptian priest (3rdC BC) incensed at the negative depiction of Pharaoh in the book of Exodus, even rewrote the account, making Egypt expel the Jews for leprosy. This degrading libel, like the very many other religious libels that followed in succeeding centuries, never died out. Karl Marx even used it.

In the later stages of the Greek Empire (2ndC BC) Antiochus Ephiphanes forcibly sought to destroy Judaism because it was an implacable barrier to his intense desire to spread Greek culture. This led to oppression, war and many deaths. The Greeks were the first to utter the great accusation that the Jews engaged in "ritual murder"; another libel still heard in the 20thC. Later, the Romans

made the Jewish religion legal and gave them privileges. None the less their foremost historian, Tacitus, accused them of "an implacable hatred for the rest of mankind", and throughout the first century the Jews found themselves under constant attack from Romans of all ranks. Their religious separatism and proud independent spirit caused them to be seen as particularly dangerous politically. It was Rome which finally destroyed Jerusalem and expelled the Jews, at the same time killing hundreds of thousands of the Jews in North Africa.

From the 2ndC to the 20thC AD
It is a huge tragedy that, the Christian church, as it gained political power after the conversion of the Roman emperor, Constantine (312AD), rapidly built up through its theologians, its councils and its popes an oppressive body of dehumanising regulations against what it perceived as its greatest enemy, the Jews. In 315 AD under penalty of being buried alive they were forbidden to proselytise Christians, or, later, even heathens. In 339 AD marriage between Jews and Christians was forbidden on pain of death. Next, Jews were forbidden to buy, sell or own slaves on pain of having all their goods confiscated. Since the entire economic life of the time was founded on slave labour this meant Jews were precluded from the major employments of agriculture, shipbuilding and many other trades and faced ruin. In the 5thC the building of new synagogues was forbidden, and mob violence against existing synagogues was frequently overlooked. Jewish soldiers were dismissed from the Roman army without benefit or compensation, and Jews were barred from gaining redress in the law courts and from holding office in municipal administration. Thus Jews were reduced to the status of a merely "tolerated group" outside the society of other Roman citizens.

All this was accompanied by virulent preaching from some church "Fathers" who worked up a violent response among ordinary Christians. John Chrysostom, Bishop of Constantinople, a notorious attacker of Jews, insulted the synagogue with such words, as "Let anyone call it a brothel, home of vice, citadel of Satan, abyss of all corruption - whatever he may say, it will be less that it deserved". Ambrose, Jerome and even Augustine, who was the most formative of the church Fathers, all used inflammatory language. Here, then, in the 4thC and 5thC aggressive rules and attitudes against Jews

were engraved in the church culture and were to become the cause of so much of the distress experienced over many centuries by the European dispersion. The Reformation and Luther did not relieve but rather strengthened them.

It was this underlying and growing sense of hatred for the Jews that turned a call for Jerusalem to be freed from the Muslims in the 11thC (the Crusades) into a blood bath for Jews across France and Germany. Seeing Jews as a enemy of the cross just as much as the Muslims, fanatical friars worked on ignorant peasants and soldiery to butcher Jews systematically in the towns all along the routes to the Holy Land. This same "crusading" spirit was responsible for the expulsion of the Jews from Germany in the 11thC and 12thC, from England in the 13thC and France in the 14thC. Such expulsions were accompanied with massacres (as in Norwich and York), loss of property and appalling privations. In the Catholic Spain and Portugal of the 15thC a particularly virulent anti-Judaist thrust brought the expulsion of tens of thousands of Jews from an area where they had lived since 500 BC.

Many took refuge providentially in Poland and Russia, but were none the less caught up in the violent 17thC Cossack attacks under Chmielnicki's leadership against oppressive landlords for whom the Jews were agents. Town after town right across Poland saw massacre after massacre of Jews. An eyewitness recorded, "they stripped the skin off one man ... others were buried alive .... they stabbed infants in the arms of their mothers .... heaps of Jewish children were thrown into the water to improve fords.....". The number of murdered Jews is estimated at 300,000 to 500,000, and some 700 Jewish communities vanished totally. Life thereafter remained one of abject poverty in the East for the Jews.

Nothing, perhaps, typifies the social stigma under which Jews lived during these centuries more than the "ghetto". These were walled areas of cities in which the Jews were forced to live separated from other citizens. There were penalties (e.g. whipping through the streets) if Jews were found elsewhere at night. The poverty, squalor, ill health and physically deforming effect of the Ghettos were notorious. Though in most areas the ghetto practice was abolished by 1870, in Russia the Jews continued to live in great poverty in the massive "ghetto" of the Western borderlands designated the "Pale of Settlement", which also became "killing fields" for Jews in the 20thC World Wars.

Despite all that could be written about Jewish suffering over the centuries, however, the worst episode of that history undoubtedly belongs to the 20thC. There is nothing at all comparable to the event of the Holocaust either in its size or in its unimaginable cruelty and cynicism. Here every root of anti-Semitism is to be found, every imaginable fear and terror is felt, every kind of distress and dehumanisation is endured, with genocide perpetrated on an industrial scale leaving 6 million dead. To the Jews it seemed beyond God, beyond chastisement; the stench was one of unmitigated evil. It was the most sobering moment ever in considering the judgement of God.

The Dispersion in Muslim lands (7thC. AD onwards)
"Christian" Europe is often compared unfavourably to the Muslim world in its treatment of the exiled Jews, the latter being seen as more tolerant. This was not altogether true. An oppressive religious apparatus very similar to the Christian version operated in the Muslim world; uncertainty, fear, death were always present. In the modern world Islamism provides a particularly virulent strain of hatred. It would not be out of place to say that it threatens to force even the State of Israel into a fortress/ghetto situation. But the fact is that anti-Semitism is not peculiar to any one creed or nation: it is to be found everywhere, not least in atheistic cultures. There was no escape from chastisement for Jews, wherever they were in the world, a fact which continues still, despite the formation of the state of Israel.

Grace and Mercy in the midst of Chastisement.
There were, however, in all this severe chastisement, seasons of extraordinary grace. These are hinted at in words that Jeremiah wrote to the first exiles in Babylon: *"Increase in number there. Seek the peace and the prosperity of the city to which I have carried into exile, because if it prospers you will prosper ... I have plans to prosper you"* (Jer. 29: 4-7). Jeremiah spoke of "prosperity" in exile, and the exile has in fact always been punctuated by periods of amazing prosperity, as for example in Babylon and Spain in the first millennium AD. The present U.S.A. dispersion (the "modern Babylon") could be seen as a current example, a long period of prosperity that has lasted for a century. A plethora of gifted Jewish intellectual, cultural, business, financial and political leaders has

also emerged over the whole time span of the dispersion, with Jews achieving the highest positions in nation after nation. This has been a most remarkable feature - a divine feature, a sign of mercy on the nation; and yet, even this tragically tended to bring about an anti-Semitism rooted in bitter envy and making the most brilliant achievements all the more dangerous.

2. THE PRESERVATION OF THE NATION

"... when they are in the land of their enemies, **I will not reject them or abhor them so as to destroy them completely,** *breaking my covenant with them ... I am the Lord." Lev.26:44 NIV*

*"This is what the LORD says, he who appoints the sun to shine by day, who decrees the moon and starts to shine by night ... - the Lord Almighty is his name: "**Only if these decrees vanish from my sight, "declares the Lord, "will the descendants of Israel ever cease to be a nation before me.***" Jer. 31:35-36 NIV*

In the verses quoted above God made it plain to the Israelites that no matter how severely he punished them for their sins he would not completely destroy them. The reason for this was clear: if he did so he would be breaking his covenant with them which he made through Abraham. In that covenant he said he would be their God for ever, so implying a nation that would never die out. Jeremiah, prophetically endorsing the covenant, said the nation would last as long as creation.

This is a very clear and bold statement made to a specific nation in history, and in making it God tied his credibility to the historical process. What happened to the Jewish nation would either vindicate God or expose him. Perhaps it is more appropriate to say that he gave a particular promise by which the world, if it is observant, might come to recognize through its fulfilment that he is indeed God and the Lord of history. He invites us to cast our eyes over history,

read its testimony and recognize the divine hand. He invites us to recognize the continuance of his covenant with Israel.

A Very Vulnerable Nation

A sceptic might be tempted to remark that there are numerous nations which have lasted for more than two millennia, and that there is, therefore, nothing remarkable about the Jewish experience. What about the Egyptians, for example? On the other hand there are many peoples and nations which have disappeared through being destroyed or assimilated. Survival has never been a certainty, and this has been particularly the case where the Jews are concerned for there were two factors which made the Jewish nation extremely vulnerable and a prime candidate for disappearance. **First,** unlike Egypt or Persia, it was a small nation, a despised people. It was formed from a petty tribal group, spent four centuries in bondage in Egypt, and eventually inherited a relatively small piece of land bridging two continents and over which great empires fought. Thus it was not only very small but very exposed and vulnerable. Its moments of glory and empire under David, Solomon and Uzziah were very brief indeed and happened only when the great empires were dormant. It was not destined to be a great ruling political force in the world, but was at the mercy of the world. It was a nation that in fact lost its land to the rule of successive world empires two thousand five hundred years ago and has only recently recovered part of it. **Second,** for that same span of time it has been a nation of which the large majority of its people has lived dispersed in other lands. The story of exile has been one of constant oppression, harassment, violence, dislocation and, more lately, of genocide. The exile has been a place of great vulnerability where the Jews have struggled to survive, and frequently longed to assimilate with their hosts. Thus there have been two great threats to the existence of the nation; being small it was always open to destruction, and being in exile it was always open to being swallowed up in the melting pot of assimilation. But the Jews remain. Seen against this background, the covenant promise takes on a much more convincing note, and even, at times, an awesome note.

Survival from Destruction

Some specific instances from Jewish history might help to illustrate more precisely the danger of destruction that threatened this small

nation. As far back as two and a half millennia ago the Babylonians threatened the Jews with extinction. In 586 BC they left Jerusalem in ruins, with its temple destroyed, and what remained of its people, all bar a few poor, removed to exile in Babylon for slave labour. There was absolutely no certainty of return – the exile was not a temporary expedient! Indeed Judah's sister nation, Israel, had been destroyed and exiled in 722 by the Assyrians and there had been no return of its people to their land in northern Palestine. They disappeared. It was certainly no forgone conclusion that the Persians, when they in their turn conquered Babylon, would allow the rebellious Jews to go back to a piece of land that was a strategic gateway to Egypt. But in fact that is exactly what they did allow. Cyrus, the Persian king, made an edict and the Jews from Judah were encouraged and helped home. The point is that while we might accept the historical twist here as seemingly natural, it wasn't at all quite as natural as it seems. The prophet Isaiah saw the real point clearly; Cyrus was God's anointed agent in history for the sake of the Jews to get them home (Is. 45:1-4). To spiritual eyes there was much more here than a natural process; there was an act of God.

A major threat of genocide against the whole nation scattered throughout the Persian empire came when the king's favourite, Haman, angered by the Jewish leader, Mordecai, made a careful plan for their complete annihilation (Book of Esther). The providential position of a Jewess as queen brought deliverance from a plan that might well have been carried out.

The most destructive episode for the nation took place in Roman times, six hundred years later. In AD 70 Jerusalem and its temple were once more laid waste with massive loss of life, and in AD 135 a further act of Jewish rebellion led to the complete razing of the city, the erection of pagan altars and the prohibition of Jews from living there. In addition large areas of land around Jerusalem and in Galilee were laid waste with enormous loss of life. The nation lost its major institutions of kingship, priesthood and temple, and for a time even the teaching of Torah was forbidden. The Romans were explicitly intent on destroying the national roots. These two catastrophes formed a hammer blow from which the Jewish nation in the homeland never recovered. It seemed it *"ceased to be a nation before him"*. For any other nation it might well have been the end, but in the providence of God there remained one thing that would

ensure the continuance of the people; that was the "Dispersion" (the "Diaspora") or, more accurately the exile (the "Gulat").

When the Romans destroyed Jerusalem the Jewish Dispersion had already been in existence for 500 years. It was particularly strong in Babylon, but it was found all over the Roman Empire (Acts 2:1). Most Jews in fact lived in the Dispersion. It is extraordinary that the very thing that in large measure formed the judgement of God on the nation, the "*Gulat*", now became the salvation of the nation. God turned his very judgement of exile into an ark that would preserve his people for two thousand years. Over those two thousand years there were many instances of attempted destruction of the Jews, but it is very difficult indeed to destroy a nation that is dispersed among many other nations. The exile stands as a divine master stroke, combining judgement and preservation. Thus, though Spanish Christians in the Dark Ages sought their destruction, though the Crusaders killed Jews wherever they found them across Europe, and though, later, Spain, England and France etc all expelled their Jewish populations, such destructive events never reached all Jews. In extremis, Jews sought refuge in other lands, which, at critical moments always seemed providentially to open up for them. In more recent history, the 19C and 20C Russian and Polish pogroms could not reach all Jews, and, more particularly, even the Nazi programme of total genocide, much the greatest attempt to destroy the Jewish people of all time, though appalling in its destruction (2/3rds of European Jewry were killed) could not reach the whole "nation". A new providential door in N. America let in 2 million Jews. None the less, had the German armies succeeded in their Russian and Middle Eastern campaigns the outcome for the Jewish nation in the 20C might well have been different, for all European and Middle Eastern Jewry would have been at their mercy. But that was not something of which the God of history and the God of the covenant was unaware. The German armies were destroyed.

Deliverance from Assimilation - "Torah", The Positive Factor
Whilst the "Gulat" proved to be in one sense the salvation of the nation, it none the less held great danger for the Jews as a distinct people. It could have been in fact the very place where they lost completely their identity, for the pressure to assimilate and become one with their surroundings was always present and powerful. The danger was made worse by the extraordinary reluctance of the Jews

throughout the centuries to leave their place of exile and return to their land. Restoration was certainly always in their prayers and thinking, but the personal cost of doing so and the opportunity seemed always prohibitive.

Two factors have been crucial in preventing the sort of assimilation that over two millennia ought on any reckoning to have taken place. The **first** of these was the adoption of the Torah (5 books of Moses), with its associated literature, as the basis of Jewish law and society. This produced a clear national identity throughout the dispersion. The **second** was the fact that the nations amongst whom the Jews were dispersed did not allow the Jews as a whole to assimilate, even when they sought to do so. Both of these factors bear the mark of a divine providence for keeping God's covenant nation alive and distinct.

The centrality of the Torah in the nation was paradoxically the fruit of the two devastating experiences suffered first at the hands of the Babylonians and then the Romans. The destruction of the first temple and the exile to Babylon forced the Jews to concentrate on their Torah literature and brought about the widespread local study of it in synagogue meetings. The synagogue, which was to have a vast influence throughout the dispersion for two and half millennia, was born in the first exile. Though the temple was rebuilt after the return from Babylon, the synagogue remained, along with those who taught from the Torah. It was not long before the "Law and the Prophets" were committed to writing, and the accompanying "oral law" (explanations and comments of the Torah) carefully remembered. When the Romans, after the death of Jesus, in their turn destroyed temple and kingdom an even more powerful development of the "book and synagogue" culture followed. In the five centuries that followed the Roman destructions, the oral law was committed to writing (The Mishnah), and the comments on the oral law were also written down (Talmud). Schools and colleges appeared and Rabbis became the national leaders. The behaviour, the beliefs and the identity of the Jews became very clear. This set them as a "people apart" in the exile. Whilst, therefore, it was their attitude to the Law that blinded the Jews to their Messiah in the first century AD, it was the Law, and the huge amount of study they invested in it that, in the mercy and providence of God, preserved their identity across the dispersion for centuries.

Deliverance from Assimilation - The effect of anti-Semitism
To be a minority people with a clearly different culture and behaviour is naturally to invite suspicion, misunderstanding and antagonism. That happened wherever the Jews went in the dispersion, except when they proved useful to the people or rulers around them. The Jews faced a greater danger, however, than mere ostracism. From the 4th Century AD they lived in Christian lands and from the 7thC they found themselves living in Moslem lands. Neither religion was friendly to them, and both oppressed them, particularly so the Christian states, where over the centuries they became a distinctly "pariah" people. The pain and oppression of this in itself brought pressure to the Jew to assimilate, or at least conform outwardly, but such a course never proved to be viable option. Grotesque slander and misrepresentation, refusal of status and normal employment, all fuelled by religious hatred proved an impassable barrier and they were never allowed to make the leap. Until the 18thC anti Judaism kept them separate, and in the 19thC and 20thC, when liberalism for a time held out high hopes of assimilation for Jews, a more virulent anti-Semitism burst on the scene which violently identified them racially and ultimately lead to the Holocaust, making them realise they were for ever the outcast. Both anti-Judaism and anti-Semitism were, of course, expressions of insensate evil, but in the overriding providence of God they were also instrumental in preserving the identity of the nation. Indeed the 20thC Holocaust was a major cause of the new State of Israel. It is precisely in such convoluted historical processes that we perceive the hand of God: what was intended for evil was made to work for good. The nation remained.

God was fully in the historical process of the centuries, and the Jewish nation was preserved. Has it been preserved for no purpose? Is the covenant to no purpose? That simply is not credible. Every instinct demands a purpose, and both the covenant and the prophetic word demand an outcome involving national restoration with blessing for the world.

3. THE COMING OF THE STATE OF ISRAEL: ANTI-SEMITISM AND THE HAND OF GOD

"As surely as I live, declares the Sovereign LORD, I will rule over you with a mighty hand and an outstretched arm and with outpoured wrath. I will bring you from the nations and gather you from the countries where you have been scattered—with a mighty hand and an outstretched arm and with outpoured wrath."

Ez. 20:33-34

The bible unequivocally reveals God as a God who reveals himself in history and works out his purposes through history. It is for this reason that the extraordinary re-emergence of the nation of Israel in 1948 demands our attention.

It certainly was an extraordinary emergence, indeed in the eyes of many Jews little short of miraculous. It was only toward the end of the 19thC that the idea of actively restoring the state gained any momentum, and its implementation faced huge and intractable obstacles. Yet within a mere two to three generations a bedraggled, poverty stricken group of individual Jews in Palestine has become a state numbering millions.

The fact that the state of Israel became a reality against all odds was the result of an interweaving of powerful historical forces on a large canvas, forces which inexorably removed all the obstacles and brought about the arrival of the new state. It is in the operation of these forces that the divine hand can best be discerned. The two essential obstacles were Jewish inertia and international politics. Though that hand can also be seen in some extraordinary specific moments of providence. We need to look carefully, therefore, at how these obstacles were removed. Essentially they were twofold; the first was the huge inertia within Jewry itself to any restoration in Palestine, and the second was the complexity of international politics which made a Jewish state seem virtually impossible. This pamphlet addresses the first obstacle - Jewish inertia.

Jewish Inertia
Jewish inertia in regard to possessing the promised Land has a long history. Even Moses found it very difficult to get the Israelites out

of Egypt. When, later, Cyrus allowed the Jews to return to Palestine after their 70 yrs. exile only a minority took the opportunity, the rest preferring to remain with the luxuries and opportunities of Babylon. In the great exile from the early 2thC AD right up to the 19thC, the Rabbis, though well aware of the promises of restoration to their own land of Israel, made no effort at all to encourage any large scale move back to Israel. They took the view that any such upsurge for a return to Israel would be merely human endeavour and would fly in the face of a God-inspired Messianic return. And, of course, there was certainly no attraction in returning to what was a derelict, barren and hostile land totally lacking in opportunities.

This negative outlook was universal throughout the Dispersion right up to the 19thC, and it was implacably and bitterly opposed to the new Zionism emerging later in the 19thC. Even the newly enlightened and liberal Jews of the 19thC remained very opposed to Zionism, preferring assimilation. Nor were the Jews particularly drawn to their historic home by the new spirit of nationalism that burst out in Europe in the 19thC. Orthodox or enlightened, they were not prepared to move.

This stubborn inertia would obviously require some massive force to cause it to break if any return was to happen. That force came in perhaps the only possible form it could come - virulent anti-Semitism. Jews throughout the centuries had always tended to stay wherever they were allowed to settle, and only intolerable persecution had ever moved them on. Significantly, the late 19thC and the first half of the 20thC were to see the emergence of two vast cauldrons of violent hatred toward the Jews, one in Eastern Europe and the other in Central Europe. It was these that caused the Jews to move on, and some to move on toward a Jewish state. They broke the inertia.

The Eastern Cauldron - Russia and Poland - 1881-1914
Towards the end of the 19thC there were some 4 million Jews in Russia and Poland, the large majority of whom were herded together into an area of Western Russia/Poland called the Pale. They were without citizenship or opportunities and were constantly oppressed by the Russian authorities and native populations. In typical fashion, however, they tried to survive and trusted for some liberal intervention from the Tsar.

That hope was never realised. From 1881 to 1884 violent pogroms broke out across the Pale, leaving hundreds of thousands of Jews homeless and ruined. Instead of alleviating the situation, the Tsar in 1882 instigated a severe programme of repression on the Jews (The "May Laws") by which they were not allowed to rent land, and were forcibly driven off the land into the growing cities. This meant huge loss of livelihood and great concentrations of pauperised Jews. The Tsar's programme was relentless, even when the pogroms eased, and was made worse by the forcing of 500,000 additional Jews into the Pale. In 1903 a fresh round of unusually violent pogroms started at Kishinev, a name which in its day had similar connotations as Auschwitz had later. More followed in 1904 and 1905, bringing wholesale destruction of property, killings and abuse of all kinds. This went on until the Pale became the eastern battleground of WW1, adding to the carnage. A massive exodus of Jews was inevitable. It lasted three decades, and some 2 million Jews went to North America alone, a fact of critical importance for the support of the Jewish state later.

The Early Zionists
It was in this cauldron that the state of Israel found its beginnings, for not every emigrant set out for the West or for America. There was a very small number for whom the preferred goal was *"eretz"* Israel (*the land* of Israel). These became the early "Zionists".

In 1882, one year after the pogroms started, the *"Hibbat Zion"* "Love of Zion" came into being. Its eventual mentor and leader was Leon Pinsker, a doctor and a Polish Jew, who at the age of 60 was profoundly affected by the pogroms of 1881. For years an assimilationist he suddenly realised that anti-Semitism would always prevent the Jews from finding a true home in the dispersion, no matter how enlightened they might become. They needed a national home of their own. The *Hibbat Zion* movement aimed at precisely that and began to establish agricultural colonies in Palestine and to build factories there, all manned by Jews. Its philosophy was captured in Pinsker's book, *"Self-emancipation"* and it represented an unprecedented new attitude toward Palestine, a profoundly new spirit - a vision of a new Jewish home. It was unparalleled in eighteen centuries of Jewish history. The difficulties were enormous, the barrenness of the land, Turkish and Bedouin hostility and constant financial shortages. Yet by 1903 some 25,000

"*olim*" (Hebrew for "ascenders") had settled in Palestine and there were 700 independent farms. It was small and vulnerable but very definitely a bridgehead for the future.

Hibbat Zion became a crucial part of a greater initiative when in 1897 Theodore Herzl, a Jew from Vienna, called for a World Zionist Conference. Herzl, like Pinsker, had been an enlightened Jew but in 1894 experienced the same profound change of heart as Pinsker through the vicious and blatant anti-Semitism of the French "Dreyfus affair". For him also there could never be any safe haven for the Jews in anything but their own country. He put down his thoughts in his book "*The Jewish State*" in 1895, a powerful plea and a practical proposition for the establishment of such a state. 90% of the attendees of his 1897 conference were from Russia and Poland, but though the Eastern Jews remained Zion's foot soldiers, his successive conferences put Zionism on the map in the West. Thus the "Zionist idea" was born out of sheer desperation over 19thC anti-Semitism. It was also a unique visionary idea, for though it was almost entirely secular and pragmatic in origin, it was the first real serious attempt to "restore" Zion for two millennia.

The decade 1904 to 1914 saw no diminution of anti-Semitic pressure on the Jews either from the Tsar or from the Russian and Polish communities. Inevitably this all led to a further surge of emigration to Palestine, and by 1914 some 85,000 "*olim*" had settled in Galilee and around the newly founded Tel Aviv. The crucial institutions of the Anglo- Palestine bank and the Zionist Organization Palestine office also appeared. The bridgehead had been substantially strengthened.

The Central European Cauldron 1919-1945

Unlike Russia and Poland the more enlightened countries of western and central Europe gradually gave their Jews full citizen status. Most Jews avidly embraced the educational and employment opportunities such status provided. By the beginning of the 20thC, they had become dominant in science, literature, industry, banking and the professions, and particularly so in Germany and Austria. However, their aim was assimilation and they bitterly opposed Zionism. There was widespread belief that any vestige of their former status as a pariah nation would eventually die out. The 20thC, however, was to destroy this hope completely; an anti-Semitic cauldron of unparalleled intensity, much greater than that in

Russia, was brewing that would destroy 2/3rds of European Jewry, a cauldron that ironically would be centred on Germany and Austria.

The fact was that, despite political emancipation, anti-Semitism as a social force never ceased to smoulder just below the surface of European society. In the late 19thC it surfaced in France in the Dreyfus affair and at the same time it surfaced in Germany with the pseudo-scientific myth of Aryan racial superiority and Jewish inferiority, a view championed, amongst others, by the composer Richard Wagner. Reactionary forces were re-appearing everywhere on the Continent as the 19thC came to a close, and it would only take some drastic event to bring them to the boil.

The First World War and the political and economic chaos which ensued was precisely such an event. That chaos enabled anti-Semitic forces to gain a very strong grip in central Europe and especially Germany. In the political chaos of 1919 Russian and eastern Jews were found leading attempted Bolshevik-style take-overs in Germany, Poland, Rumania and Hungary. They were thwarted but thereafter the Jews were stigmatised as the extreme left, the Bolshevik menace. This would prove fatal for Jewry when right wing Fascism was later gaining power. In the economic chaos the assimilated middle class Jews with their huge financial and industrial power were an easy scapegoat for the economic ills overwhelming Germany.

Jewry may none the less have survived had it not been for the Great Depression of the late 20s and early 30s. It was this chaos that opened the way for Hitler, the Nazi leader, to massive gains of seats in the Reichstag (the German Parliament) and thence to become Chancellor. He unashamedly used the force of his para-military supporters and the burning down of the Reichstag building in 1933 to seize rule by administrative decree. From that point it was a straight path for him to total and brutal fascist power.

Hitler was able to get to this point because he brought together so many strands that deeply appealed to German people at large. He was completely taken over by the popular myth of the Nordic German racial supremacy; he was a reactionary who expressed the military values of the old "Empire" and so connected with the aristocratic military who was still very active in German politics; he pleased the Pan-German party looking for as greater "Reich"; he formed an alliance with Thyssen and other very powerful industrialists who saw him as the only alternative to economic

chaos. But above all these things he embodied the growing widespread mood of virulent anti-Semitism. There is a consensus that Hitler's life was decisively shaped by racist ideology. In 1919 he wrote that the Jews were the reason for the wartime defeat and deserved to be eliminated from all levels of economic and cultural life. He emphasised anti-Jewish items in the Nazi programme in 1920, and *Mein Kampf* was virulently anti-Semitic. Once in power he rode a strong, European-wide wave of anti-Semitism and fascism, first expelling the Jews, and then as he conquered Europe, destroying six million in a "final solution" of Holocaust.

There were three main results of this appalling and totally unparalleled cauldron pertinent to the emergence of the State of Israel in 1948. The first was that in the period 1933 to 1939 a further 90,000 Jews went to Palestine. The second was that the appalling event of the Holocaust profoundly strengthened an already growing radical determination among Zionists that the Palestinian home must be secured at any cost, even though it meant war with the British mandate in Palestine. For the Jews there could be no going back after the Holocaust It was the defining moment; the inertia of centuries gave way to a readiness to fight to the death for a homeland. It was this spirit that really motivated Ben Gurion to grasp the half chance that the U.N. Partition plan offered in 1948 and declare unilaterally the state of Israel. The third result was that the Holocaust provided a moral impetus in the Western world to do something for the Jewish tragedy. This was particularly important in shaping post war American attitudes and helping to bring American recognition of Israel. As so many have observed there was a direct connection between the Holocaust and the founding of the Israeli State. It was a resurrection moment.

Conclusion
Clearly the Jews were not in control of the events in East and West Europe that led to their new state; rather such events were driven by huge waves of violent anti-Semitic hatred which propelled the Jews over all obstacles into a return to Palestine. Even the "Zionist idea" itself was the result of that hatred. All the agony and pain of the exile has always been under God's control - he sent the Jews into exile, and he chastised them there. He cannot have been uninvolved in the horrific chastisements of the 19thC and 20thC by which they were led to the shores of their promised land. In the previous history of

exile in Europe God had always providentially opened up new refuges for the Jews at a time of persecution. In the 20thC he seems to have uniquely opened up Palestine.

The story is very sobering and raises many questions, but it is hard not to conclude that God was at work among the Jews in their return, and that events were working toward an outcome that, though horrific in so many ways, was yet foreordained.

4. THE COMING OF THE STATE OF ISRAEL: POLITICS AND THE PROVIDENCE OF GOD

"Nations will take them and bring them to their own place."
Isaiah. 14:2 NIV

Those 19thC visionaries who took the pathway to a new Jewish state in Palestine had to face a crippling inertia from within the Jewish world itself. At the same time they also faced a daunting international political problem, namely securing recognition for their state in a Palestine that was already occupied land. This pamphlet deals with the way in which that second obstacle was overcome. There are two main phases in the story, and both phases show extraordinary providences.

Phase 1. 1895-1919: from Herzl to the Balfour Declaration

When Theodore Herzl penned his book *"The Jewish State"* in 1895 his plan to implement such a state was naively optimistic. He believed that because the gentile nations did not want the Jews they would be only too glad to help them find somewhere of their own to live and help them get there. In this way the Jewish state would secure political endorsement, and would happen peacefully. Herzl's optimism was helped by the fact that in his original plan he did not specify Palestine - any suitable area in the world would do. However, the *"Hibbat Zion"* settlers in Herzl's World Zionist Congresses wanted only Palestine, and though Uganda was canvassed by Herzl in 1904, he eventually had to agree to Palestine.

But Palestine was neither suitable nor free; it bristled with difficulties.

Correctly identifying the crucial need for political recognition of the new state, Herzl worked ferociously at getting the leaders of the European states to forward that goal. Before putting pen to paper he had already approached the two great Jewish bankers, Rothschild and Hirsch, who had the ear of national statesmen and were already supporting Jews in need, but they had rebuffed him. Unperturbed, Herzl gained access to the German Kaiser and the Sultan of Turkey in whose domain Palestine lay. The Sultan, of course, had no desire for a Jewish state in his Moslem land, even though Herzl tempted him with the idea of the Jews servicing the huge Ottoman national debt. The Sultan was in fact already making life difficult for the *Hibbat Zion* settlers. Herzl's optimism received a sobering reality check.

However, with these activities Herzl none the less put Zionism on the European political map, and before he died, worn out with his efforts, he sowed a seed in the minds of the up and coming political leaders of Great Britain, seed that was to bear critically important fruit in the future. Britain in the late 19thC and early 20thC was good soil for Zionism. It provided a contrast with Germany and France in its attitude to the Jews. Whilst Germany was echoing with many virulent racial and anti-Semitic publications and France was raging with the huge Dreyfus debate and with Drummont's anti-Semitic writings, Britain was reading George Eliot's novel *Daniel Deronda* and Disraeli's *Tancred,* both of which were pro-Jewish. Both books were particularly widely read in political circles and pre-disposed many politicians towards Jewish Zionism. When Russian pogroms brought an influx of refugee Jews to Britain in 1902 a Commission was convened to examine the Jewish problem, and it called on Herzl as the leader of Zionism to give evidence. Herzl was able to declare that the ultimate solution to the Jewish refugee problem was "a legally recognised home". It was this that gave rise to discussions with Britain about Uganda, and though they came to nothing, the active idea of a Jewish home was effectively lodged in the minds of men like Lloyd George, the future wartime Prime Minister.

Herzl died in 1904, and for a decade the high level political activity hung in abeyance. The profile of the World Zionist organization slowly grew, however. In 1910 a certain Chaim

Weizmann, a Russian refugee educated in Germany and Switzerland, came to teach chemistry at Manchester and became a British subject. He also became Herzl's successor as the Zionist leader. By 1914 Weizmann had met Balfour, Churchill and Lloyd George, all of whom he impacted, all of whom were to become cabinet members and all of whom were disposed toward a Jewish homeland in Palestine. It was quite astonishingly providential that this very able and diplomatic Weizmann was able to pick up the reins with the British leadership where Herzl had dropped them and, moreover, at a momentous time when the ruling power over Palestine was about to change.

That momentous time was World War 1. Its significance for the future of the Jewish state lay in the fact that the Ottoman Sultan had joined Germany in the conflict. That meant with the Allied victory his empire would be dismembered. What would happen to Palestine? Two factors decided the issue. The first was that the British cabinet agreed that British post-war interests in the Middle East would be best served by British control of Palestine under the form of a "protectorate", and the second was that the cabinet, already ideologically disposed toward a Jewish homeland in Palestine, thought a petition from Jewish leaders for such a homeland would help secure such a protectorate. The Jewish leaders duly responded and actually worded a declaration that the British might make concerning such a homeland. The result was the Balfour Declaration of 1916 in which Britain undertook to facilitate a Jewish home in Palestine. After the allied victory the League of Nations confirmed the Protectorate and its obligation to the Jews. The Balfour Declaration was powerful in that it *required* Britain to secure a Jewish national home, and affirmed that the National Home existed as of right, not by Arab sufferance.

Thus in a mere twenty years after Herzl's *Jewish State* was written the impossible had taken place. It was a staggering outcome, the fruit of an extraordinary collusion of Jewish vision, British ideology, British strategic need, and the outbreak of a brutal war which redrew the Middle Eastern map. If God is in the wide sweep of history, he was certainly here. If he is in "miracle moments" he was certainly in Weizmann's appearance.

Phase 2 1918 - 1948: from British Mandate to the State of Israel
Understandably in 1918 optimism was very high among Jews at the prospects for the Jewish Home. No Arab objection was registered to the Declaration, and Weizmann and Feisal Hussein of Transjordan appeared set on a course of open co-operation. Many Arabs could see benefits from a Jewish homeland. Only a farsighted few were nervous about Arab reaction, and with good reason. The truth was that the war had in fact encouraged the development of Arab nationalism, and this made itself felt as early as 1920 when violent disturbances broke out against the Jews as they returned to Palestine from wartime exile and from the post war killing fields of Russia. From that moment violent Arab nationalism would increase in direct proportion to Jewish immigration. Though officially a door was open to the Jews, there would now be increasing Arab pressure to close it. This fact provides the clue to the tortuous 30 year run up to the Jewish state (and beyond); Arab nationalistic pressure was strong enough eventually to virtually close down Britain's attempt to implement the Balfour Declaration.

The problem for Britain was not simply one of Arab violence. That alone could be put down, but the goodwill of the Arabs was a crucial plank in Britain's Middle Eastern strategic policy. The link to the Far Eastern part of the Empire, and especially India, lay through Suez, and the Arab nations could be a great threat to that if antagonised. This need for unimpeded British communication with the Far East became critically important in the 1930s as the German war machine began to re-assemble and threaten all Europe. An Arab revolt must, therefore, be avoided at all costs. The Jews posed no such threat. It was policy, therefore, to court the Arabs at Jewish expense.

The real problem with Arab nationalism was that it was not just sporadic and aimless, but from the early 1920s became violently radicalised and clearly targeted against Britain's obligations to facilitate a Jewish homeland. Herbert Samuel, a Jew and a Zionist became High Commissioner of the new protectorate but misguidedly appointed a radical and violent anti-Zionist and anti-British Arab as both the *mufti* of Jerusalem (Palestinian Arab leader) and the leader of a new Supreme Muslim Council. This *mufti* worked tirelessly to radicalise the Arabs against Jewish settlement right up to 1939 both on racial and religious grounds, and he was not afraid to use violence either against Jews, the British or even

Arab opponents. From the moment of his appointment any hope of Arab moderate opinion accepting the developing Jewish home was completely lost. The *mufti*'s avowed aim was the annulling of the Balfour Declaration and the British protectorate and the achievement of Arab sovereignty over Palestine. He knew how to use Jewish immigration to work up violence to achieve that end.

It is not surprising, therefore, that in 1929 after an Arab massacre of 100 Jews at Hebron and an uprising at Jerusalem that left thousands of Jews homeless, the British government temporarily stopped Jewish immigration to appease Arab unrest. The real pressure on the British came, however, later, in the 1930s, as large numbers of Jewish refugees began to pour in from Europe. By 1937 the Jewish population had shot up to 400,000. The Arab response was acts of violence, a general strike and refusal to pay taxes. Not surprisingly the British once more appointed a Commission to consider Arab demands, and a partition of Palestine between Arabs and Jews was proposed. The Jews accepted, but 400 Arab leaders conferring in Syria demanded the whole of Palestine. Britain's attempt to implement the partition plan was a signal for further widespread acts of Arab violence on Jews, oil pipelines, transport, police etc. The British response was initially strong; the *Mufti* was dismissed and harsh measures were taken against rebels. But it was the British who eventually capitulated as war with Germany became imminent. In 1939 Britain abandoned partition, allowed a final 75,000 more Jewish immigrants, promised an Arab dominated Palestinian state and refused entry to desperate refugees from Europe in 1940-41. This kept the Arabs quiet, but it was a death sentence to Jewish hopes and to the Balfour Declaration. The success of Arab violence against Britain pointed the way for the Jews; they too would need to "declare war" on Britain if its policy did not change. Such a strategy was postponed by the 1939-45 conflict, but the Jews took advantage of the war both to train men and secure arms. After the British victory at El Alamein the German threat to the Middle East faded, and Jewish extremists began attacking British targets. This rapidly escalated after the war when Ernest Bevin as Foreign Secretary took over the Palestine issue and pursued the pre-war policy of seeking Arab goodwill and totally refused entrance for any Jews. This was immediately after the Holocaust when there were 500,000 desperate Jewish survivors in refugee camps across Europe. Bevin refused U.S. pressure to take

even 100,000, and systematically, and in the eyes of the world, cruelly blockaded any illegal entry. Inevitably the Jews as a whole "declared war" on the British in Palestine. They fought with the ruthless determination of those whose very existence was at stake. With the Holocaust as the background Jewish psychology underwent a radical change and a new militancy was born.

Bevin survived the Jewish onslaught for just two years, until in 1947 he decided that the British Palestinian mandate was no longer strategically valuable enough to warrant the cost of such a conflict. Accordingly he handed the mandate back to the United Nations, and planned a British withdrawal from Palestine for 1948. The U.N., acting on a totally uncharacteristic Russian initiative, decided on partition for Palestine. There was Jewish approval, but not Arab. At this point, however, the militant Jewish leadership (and an equally militant Arab leadership) had their sights on the British departure. Both knew it would come to a fight. Indeed the struggle began before the British left. The moment the British withdrew Ben Gurion unilaterally declared the existence of the state of Israel on the basis of the partition plan. It a was daring and historic move, knowing that Israeli borders (and indeed Israel's existence) would be determined less by the partition plan than by the fighting that was bound to break out. However, the U.S. Immediately recognised the state *de facto*, and the Russians *de jure*. It was an unbelievable and astonishing outcome, capped only by Czechoslovakia's arming of the Jews, and the defeat of Arab armies by a fledgling Israeli army. The defeat of the British had paid huge, if risky, dividends for the Jews. If the British had not departed at that moment of history there would have been no state of Israel; it was a unique historical moment for its birth, a very narrow window of opportunity.

Conclusion
It is important to acknowledge that all these extraordinary providential happenings are not on account of any special moral virtue of the Jewish race. If the Jews do have one outstanding feature it has to be that they have clung to the "Jahweh" God of their Fathers, whose laws are profoundly moral and upright. That attachment, however, was, and still is, held very loosely by a great many Jews. They are, like any other nation, imperfect and pay the price of their imperfections. "In particular their genocidal acts during the dispossession of the Palestinians from their lands in the "Nakbah", which have been carefully catalogued by two outstanding

historians, one a Jew (Pappe) and the other a Palestinian (Khalidi), will not have gone unnoticed by the "Judge of all the Earth".The fact is that the providences of God which are among them are, and continue to be, the result of His intention to fulfil his ancient promises to them as a nation irrespective of their disobediences. And, as was made clear to Abraham, he will fulfil his promises to the Jews ultimately not simply for the Jews but for the blessing of all the nations on the earth.

5. THE STATE OF ISRAEL, THE RETURN OF THE JEWS & THE HAND OF GOD

*"I will even gather you from the people, and assemble you **out of all the countries** where you have been scattered, and **I will give you the land of Israel"** Ez. 11:17 NIV*

*"I will bring your children from the east and gather you from the west. I will say to the north, 'Give them up!' and to the south, 'Do not hold them back. Bring my sons from afar and my daughters **from the ends of the earth.** " Isaiah 43:5-6 NIV*

Two features particularly stand out in the return of the Jews to the State of Israel and indicate a divine providence. First, they are back to their land in large numbers and from all nations. Second, their physical absorption was nothing short of miraculous.

1. The large scale return of the Jews from all nations to the state of Israel after 1948 is the single biggest factor arguing the case that the 20thC witnessed God at work in history through a genuine fulfilment of biblical prophecy. Such prophecy (see texts above) made two essential claims: the Jews would be restored to their own land, and they would be gathered from all the nations where they had been exiled. Facts and figures are critical to demonstrate fulfilment, and they are readily available. The table below shows the astonishing phenomenon of the 20thC return, and is so compelling that those who doubt a prophetic fulfilment bear the onus of providing an alternative explanation.

Return of the Jews to Israel 1948-64 (the period of foundation and consolidation)

Iraq	123,000
Morocco	120,000
Rumania	119,000
Poland	104,000
Egypt	75,000
Czechs	40,000
Yemen	40,000
Iran	39,000
Turkey	37,000
Bulgaria	37,000
Libya	35,000
Tunisia	30,000
Syria	26,000
Hungary	14,000
Germany	9,000
Yugoslavia	8,000
Aden	6,500
France	4,000
Afghanistan	4,000

7 other European countries show lower numbers

This table of the first 16 yrs. of the State of Israel shows us just how many countries in the Middle East and Europe were involved in immigration, and it also shows how significant were the numbers. From 1948-62 the population of Israel rose from 650,000 to **2,050,000.**

If we were to make a similar analysis but over a longer period, namely from 1948-2003 we would find the facts still more compelling. After 1964 the return to Israel of Jews **from Europe and the Middle East** continued unabated. For example the number of Jews from Morocco increased to 270,000 in total, from Poland to 172,000, from Rumania to 275,000, from UK from 2,000 to 33,000, from France from 4,000 to 42,000. The major increase by far was from the former USSR as 1,100,000 Jews returned.

Moreover, if we look beyond the Middle East and Europe and at the global scene there were an additional 295,000 Jews who returned to Israel from other parts of the world. The main bulk came

from USA (86,000), Argentina (59,000) and S. Africa (72,000). But Jews also returned to Israel in very significant numbers from virtually every country to which they had been exiled, that is from over 80 different countries. Of particular note is the fact that this restoration brought about the rejoining of the two major Jewish groupings, the Ashkenazi (Western Jewry) and the Sephardim (Eastern Jewry) after centuries of separation. This in itself was a very distinct and unique mark of something quite extraordinary. So also was the complete evacuation of Iraqi Jews which finally brought about the end of the 2½ millennia long Babylonian exile.

In total from 1948-2003 the Jewish population of Israel grew to **over 5,000,00**, which means that **over one third of world Jewry had returned,** and the State of Israel became the predominant focus of Jewry in the modern world.

There is, therefore, a very remarkable precision between the prophetic words and the historical facts of Jewish 20thC. history.

Three essential features emerge:
First, the return is universal. Jews have come literally from all the four corners of the earth. Jews have, of course, been constantly on the move throughout the last 2½ millennia of their dispersion but there has never been anything remotely like a movement which has involved Jews from all parts of the dispersion and directed them to the Holy Land.
Second, the return is one of very significant numbers. The 4 million Jews who have come to Israel in the last 50 yrs or so overtakes even the huge migration of Jews to the USA, when in the 50 years up to 1914 some 2 ¼ million Jews went from Russia and Eastern Europe. The return to Israel is in fact the most significant movement in terms of numbers that the world of Jewry has seen in its entire history. Not only have significant numbers come from most countries of the dispersion, but from some of the Middle Eastern countries virtually the whole of the Jewish population has come.
Third, since 1948 the return has been marked by a **breathtaking suddenness.** There was a fairly lengthy preparatory stage from the latter part of the 19thC until 1948 during which it took some 70 years for the Jews in Palestine to reach 650,00 in number, Eastern European and Russians predominating. But in the fourteen years from 1948 and to 1962 the population virtually tripled to over

2,000,000 from all across the globe. Anyone looking back from the year 1962 and recalling the situation in 1948 could be forgiven for thinking they had indeed watched a miracle rather than a normal historical process.

Some Extraordinary Moments in the Return.
The overall picture of such historical trends is bound to cause any person versed in the prophetic promises to pause and carefully weigh the extraordinary fact of fulfilment. At the same time, however, the details also have something of a divine mark on them.

The Jews of Yemen are an example. They trace their origin back nearly two millennia, during which their piety tenaciously held on to the promise of a return to Zion despite bitter persecution. In the years 1949-51 under violent persecution some 48,000 were airlifted by the Jewish Agency to Israel. This "Operation Magic Carpet" meant the Yemenites were a Jewish community virtually totally transported to Zion.

In 1948 some 30,000 dark skinned African Jews lived in Ethiopia, (the Falashas), the descendants of Africans who had been converted to Judaism in the Middle Ages and of whom there had once been some 250,000. From 1981-83 some 9,000 were taken out by the Jewish Agency, over 5,000 of them by airlift ("Operation Moses"). A further 14,000 Falashas were airlifted from Addis Ababa in 1984 from under the noses of a besieging rebels ("Operation Solomon").

"Operation Ali Baba" from Iran was a further airlift of Jews who were totally blocked in by an Arab blockade from any other form of travel.

In all these cases the commitment and tenacity of the Israeli authorities along with the brilliance and competence of their actions, not to mention the cost, points to a most extraordinary and unusual dynamic behind the restoration process of "Aliyah".

2. The Miracle of Integration
If we might legitimately describe the extent of the Jewish return as miraculous, we might also describe as miraculous the successful absorption and integration of such a vast influx by a very small state with minimal resources and under grave economic and military threat.

Mass immigration was crucial both for the defence and the populating of the new Israel, and one of the first acts of the new State of Israel was the granting of the right of return to any Jew from whatever country. Such a declaration, however, involved huge social, economic, financial and logistical problems and entailed vast risks. Israel in 1948 was only just finding its feet with its independence and its new national institutions. No one knew how big the response might be; it could be overwhelming.

A serious complicating factor was that the hundreds of thousands of Jews who began to make their way to Israel were derelict and poverty stricken, being initially survivors of the European war and later refugees forced out of Middle Eastern Arab countries. They had little or no resources of their own, and the very process of getting them to Israel was enormously costly. Not only did much of the transport have to be provided, but in a great many cases they had to be "bought". The Falasha immigration involving just 30,000 Jews cost millions of dollars in airlifts and also millions of dollars paid to government figures in Ethiopia to persuade them to let Jews go freely. Similarly. there was no free emigration from the European Communist states; the Hungarians wanted $80 a Jew, the Rumanians $100 and Bulgarians $300. In the end, mainly through USA Jewry, $5 million was paid to Rumania and Bulgaria for 160,000 to emigrate.

Once in Israel the task was to house them, find them productive work in a small country with sparse resources, provide medical care and education, build essential infrastructure and integrate many very different nationalities and languages. The first 100,000 were Displaced Persons from refugee camps in war-torn Europe, presenting a huge rehabilitation task, many being chronically sick, broken, traumatised and beyond long term self-support.

The idea of finding the resources for doubling or tripling the population in 10 years in a constructive manner would have seemed utterly beyond reason in 1948. Israel lacked vital raw materials for industrial development, especially oil and iron. Industry required expensive imports, technical expertise was lacking, the development of the Dead Sea area minerals and the infrastructure of roads, ports and shipping was rudimentary. Agriculture faced massive problems. The land had still largely to be reclaimed from disuse, the challenge of the desert in the Negev was huge, and the major problem of water

for irrigation, had still to be solved. All this required huge investment.

However, all this had to be achieved at a time when Israel faced the very heavy demands for national defence against a real and immediate possibility of a second Holocaust at the hands of the surrounding Arab nations. Arab intent to destroy Israel did not end with the armistice of the 1948 War of Independence; it only hardened. Israel would not be really safe until the mid-60s. This meant there was not only a huge drain on Israeli resources to purchase arms, but the Arab world and its supporters were fully intent of effecting an economic blockade against the new state in an attempt to strangle its agriculture and new industries by removing their markets. Controlling oil supplies the Arab nations could even put economic pressure on Western states to join them. The Arabs sealed all borders with Israel at a time when Israel was utterly dependent on exports to pay for life-giving imports.

The resettlement process, inevitably, was never without its flaws; many spent many months in what was virtually refugee accommodation, cheap temporary huts, with long waits for work and permanent housing. As a consequence considerable numbers moved back out of Israel altogether. With so many previous different nationalities among the Jews there was inevitably jealousies and friction, especially between East and West Jewry. There was friction between secular and religious factions. None the less the ultimate result was eventually a largely cared for, productive and united nation with great desire to succeed. Roads were built, large tracts of land were reclaimed and hundreds of miles of new pipeline distributed the waters of the upper Jordan area to the population and to the new agricultural areas. New towns went up and the ports of Ashkelon and Eilat were built. Massive advances were made in scientific and technological expertise. On any criterion the first ten years of resettlement constituted an astounding achievement against extreme odds, and for many it pointed all too clearly to the hand of divine providence.

How did this happen? Where did the massive financial provision come from? Personal Christian testimony is never short of instances of divine provision at difficult times, and discovering national provision is essentially no different. Certainly evidence abounds in the story of the settlement of Israel's immigrants of extraordinary provision. A large flow of monetary gifts came especially from

USA, some $35 million annually. Created by the 19thC persecution in Eastern Europe and Russia, Jewry in the USA became an essential buttress of the State of Israel in the latter part of the "20thC. It also enabled the Jews to float bonds and raise funds for investment. USA Jewry was a major item in divine planning. A very unusual provision came from West Germany, whose Chancellor, Konrad Adenauer, offered to make reparations to the Jews in Israel, a sovereign and unexpected gesture which brought in massive sums of $120 million per annum in a very critical decade.

Two other features are worth noting which seem very much to have a divine stamp. First, though the influx was massive it was in a sense controlled, for the huge inflow of one million Jews from the USSR was held back until the 1970s by Russian policy decisions. Had it come in the first two decades of Israel's history it undoubtedly would have swamped the country. Second, though the 1920s and 30s had been very difficult times for the Jews in Palestine, they were the times when the embryo national institutions had been providentially born to form the skeleton of the new state. Flimsy though it was, it was just sufficient to take the weight of a rapidly growing independent state.

JESUS IN ISAIAH

CONTENTS

Introduction.

JESUS' ENDORSEMENT OF ISAIAH'S PROPHECIES
CONCERNING HIMSELF
(Isaiah 61:1ff and Luke 4:16-19)

Not long after he had received the Holy Spirit at the river Jordan, Jesus went into the synagogue in Nazareth, opened the scroll of Isaiah at what is now chapter 61 and read the words, *"The Spirit of the Lord is upon me because he has anointed me to preach ......"*. He read a few further verses, then sat down and said, *"Today this scripture has been fulfilled in your hearing"*. Jesus was claiming that Isaiah's words about the coming "anointed one" had been fulfilled in him. Using Isaiah he was explaining to the people the nature of the power that rested on him and the ministry he was

136

undertaking. It conveyed precisely the love, grace, compassion and mercy that would flow through his anointing to meet the needs of the poor, the oppressed, the broken hearted, the grief stricken.

Isaiah 61 is one of a series of major prophetic passages in Isaiah pointing to the Messiah (they can be found in chapters 9, 11, 42, 49, 53, 61). Being deeply versed in the Old Testament, Jesus must have known these passages in Isaiah from boyhood, and there is every reason to believe that they were used of the Holy Spirit to enlighten him as he grew up as to the true nature of his own person and the nature of the work and ministry that he was to perform. It is equally reasonable to presume that he schooled his own disciples in the same Messianic passages, especially, as is clear from Luke, in the period after he rose from the dead and before he ascended. Certainly the substance of these passages of Isaiah lie very much at the heart of the New Testament witness to Jesus.

The striking feature of these Isaiah passages is the extraordinary comprehensiveness of the teaching they provide about Jesus. They reveal a remarkably detailed commentary on the life of Jesus, and on his death and the reason for it (Is 53). They add enormously to the depth of our appreciation of the meaning of the gospel story. The passages are not, however, only confined to his earthly ministry; they also range over his ascended ministry to the Gentiles and the gathering in of all his chosen people.

These striking prophecies concerning Jesus constitute the major offer of hope which God gave through his prophet to his own contemporary generation, battered as it was by appalling judgements. They remain the source of hope whenever God's judgements threaten, and are certainly extremely pertinent to our modern world and generation, which is suffering severe reminders of judgement. Jesus always remains the rock in the storm.

1. "A GREAT LIGHT" and "MIGHTY GOD"

Isaiah 9:1-7 NIV

Isa 9:1 Nevertheless, there will be no more gloom for those who were in distress. In the past he humbled the land of Zebulun and the land of Naphtali, but in the future he will honour Galilee of the Gentiles, by the way of the sea, along the Jordan—2 The people walking in darkness have seen a great light; on those living in the land of the shadow of death a light has dawned. 3 You have enlarged the nation and increased their joy; they rejoice before you as people rejoice at the harvest

Isa 9:6-7 For to us a child is born, to us a son is given,
and the government will be on his shoulders.
And he will be called Wonderful Counsellor, Mighty God,
Everlasting Father, Prince of Peace.
Of the increase of his government and peace there will be no end.

1. Galilee in the Spotlight

The opening verses of Isaiah 9 are prophetic words directed at the geographical area of Galilee of the Gentiles. There is an obvious New Testament feel about that expression, "Galilee of the Gentiles", and though the area is also described by Isaiah as "*the land of Naphtali and the land of Zebulun*" (because that is where those two tribes settled when the land was first taken by Joshua) the title "Galilee of the Gentiles" is the title that stands out. It is a uniquely appropriate description for a unique prophecy.

The gist of the prophecy was that Galilee of the Gentiles was to "*see a great light*" (9:2), and to be a "*place that God would honour*" (9:1). As the light shone there would be a tremendous release of joy in that land, joy that could only be compared to the joy of harvest and the joy of victory over enemies (9:3). It would be like the day Israel was delivered from the oppression of Midian (9:4), when war became a thing of the past (9:5). Joy would be the key outcome of the "great light" that was to shine.

This prophecy of exuberant joy for these northern parts of Israel stands in sharp contrast to the prophecies in the surrounding chapters of Isaiah, for those other prophecies speak of severe judgement.

Their foremost theme was of the imminent disaster that was to come to the Kingdom of Israel, of which the Galilean lands formed a part. In fact Galilee was destined to be the first area of the Promised Land that would experience the deportation of its people into exile. Yet in the midst of this flow of prophecies of judgement, Isaiah burst out with this incredibly striking prophecy of the glory that would be be seen in Galilee. The land that was to know the *"gloom and distress"* of judgement, and would be characterized as the *"land of the shadow of death"*, was destined one day to be honoured and filled with light.

It was a totally unexpected prophecy, relating to a totally unexpected region and speaking of a totally unexpected blessing. It was also a prophecy of great hope.

2. Jesus and Galilee

In Isaiah's prophecy this great deliverance and this great light for Galilee were intimately connected with the birth of a child. This is made clear in verse 6 which begins with the words, *"**For** unto us a child is born, a son is given"*. The light and the joy were to be the result of the emergence of an extraordinary person. It is when we put this prophecy alongside the astonishing ministry that Jesus actually exercised in Galilee some six hundred years later, and the enormous light he brought to the area, that we begin to appreciate something of the meaning and accuracy of this prophetic word. For the fact is that Galilee was the epicentre of the earthly ministry of Jesus; it **was overwhelmingly in Galilee that his glory was displayed, and his light shone**. No man could have dreamed up such a ministry in such a place just to "prove" a prophecy! No man could have dreamed up such an unlikely prophecy about Galilee in the vague hope that it might happen! The fact is that God spoke through his prophet and what he said, though very unlikely indeed to happen, humanly speaking, actually came to pass.

Jesus grew up in Galilee, at Nazareth, and was known as a Galilean. His ministry proper, after a short period in the Jordan valley alongside John the Baptist, began in "Galilee of the Gentiles", with Capernaum on the shores of Lake Galilee as his base. This ministry to Galilee went on for some two to three years, and it was punctuated only by periodic visits to Jerusalem for certain feasts, and by very rare forays into a few places such as Samaria and Phoenicia. It was a thorough, intensive, itinerant ministry and covered all the villages of the Galilean area. It grew in impact as the

twelve apostles were also sent out to itinerate, followed later by seventy other disciples. There was clearly an impulsion on Jesus to cover the whole area, for we know that on one occasion he refused to re-enter Capernaum saying, "*I **must** preach the good news of the kingdom of God to the other towns for this is why I was sent*" (Lk. 4:43). This indicates that Jesus himself had thoroughly digested the implications of Isaiah 9 as far as Galilee was concerned, and so gave himself totally to fulfilling what he recognized to be the prophetic purpose of God in that land. He knew he was the "child to be born", and he knew that he was the light promised to Galilee. It would have made very great sense to him that he had been brought up in Galilee, knew the people intimately, and was well able to speak their language. He would have been very aware that everything was providentially prepared for his destined ministry.

3. The Great Light
The extent and depth of his work of preaching and healing was totally without precedent. To describe Jesus as *"a great light"* was no exaggeration. The Old Testament prophets had healed individuals, but there had been nothing remotely on the scale of Jesus' ministry. The dead were raised, the sick were healed from every kind of disease and deformity and, very significantly, a great many were delivered from demons. To add to it all, the poor were taught of the kingdom of God and its mysteries. A report in Luke's gospel (Lk 6:17-19) gives the flavour of those times: *"A large crowd of his disciples were there, and a great number of people from all over Judea, from Jerusalem, and from the coast of Tyre and Sidon, who had come to hear him and be healed of their diseases. Those troubled by evil spirits were cured, and the people tried to touch him, because power was coming from him and healing them all.* (Lk. 6:17-19 NIV). When Luke here reminds us that people even came up from Jerusalem and from neighbouring cities like Tyre and Sidon we become aware that the *"great light"* in Galilee was one that could also be seen well beyond its own borders. It was something that had never been witnessed before in the history of Israel, not even in Jerusalem, let alone in such a despised area as Galilee.

It is easy to see how Galilee became a place of immense joy, as Isaiah 9:3 so strongly stresses. We have only to think of Jairus seeing his daughter given back to him alive, the widow of Nain

seeing her only son likewise given back to her, the centurion rejoicing over his servant, the woman healed from her issues of blood after years of suffering and ostracism, and even Zacchaeus freed from a bondage of greed and corruption; all of these people would have known one thing in common, a huge release of joy in their lives. Yet these are but a few examples of what must have been happening to literally thousands who were released and delivered by the power of Jesus. It was a time that was indeed like the joy of harvest.

Why did God choose to shine the light on Galilee? One reason has to be simply that it was a prophetic statement of what was to come in the world-wide "Gentile" missions that followed his resurrection and ascension. Jew and Gentile mixed in close proximity in Galilee, and he could not but touch the Gentile world in Galilee, and so provide a foretaste of what was to come. It is true that Jesus declared that he was sent *"only to the lost sheep of the house of Israel"*, but, even in the very act of making that statement, he was happy to respond to the faith of a Syro-Phoenician woman and heal her daughter (Matt 15:21ff).

A further reason for the choice of Galilee may well be that it was a region that symbolized the despised and the rejected, the needy and the blind, the very people for whom the child was born.

4. "Mighty God and Everlasting Father"

The child to be born was, then, to impact Galilee, but Isaiah has more to say about the child than what he would do. He speaks prophetically and directly about the nature and person of this child. In fact he makes an astonishingly comprehensive statement of the child's essential divinity.

Before examining this, however, we should not lose sight of the fact that the prophecy first speaks of this immense figure as having a human birth. This is a person who has true human origins and so is born like all humanity. He is no ethereal manifestation of the Godhead, no phantom. He is a real human person, not some being who just appears suddenly on earth as a God-human person and then disappears.

In the same verse, however, that his birth is foretold, this child is also called "Mighty God" and "Everlasting Father" (v.6). The exact expression "Mighty God" is used by Isaiah again in 10:21, and there it refers plainly to the God of Israel, having the full meaning of

divinity. There is no reason to think that it is used in any lesser sense in 9:6. The actual Hebrew word used here for God is "El", and, as one commentator asserts, "it is significant that the word for "God" in this expression is not "Elohim", which may be used in a lower sense for those who are representatives of God (e.g. Ex. 7:1). "El", on the other hand, is never used by Isaiah, or any other Old Testament writer, in any lower sense than that of absolute Deity".

It is sometimes suggested that we have here in this term "Mighty God" a rather exaggerated description of kingship appropriate for an earthly coronation, and reminiscent of some pagan rites. However, though debased at this time, the Israelite tradition was unlikely to have confused their king with God himself, and ascribed the name of God to their king. In any case we are looking less at Israelite tradition and much more at a prophet speaking in the name of God. Isaiah would have been the last person to have been guilty of such an exaggerated, pagan confusion. The expression *"Mighty God"* remains, therefore, breathtakingly direct in its implications of the child's divinity.

The expression *"Everlasting Father"* lends further support to this prophetic revelation of the divine nature of the child. The word "Father" is not current in the Old Testament as a title of the kings. Neither is the word "everlasting". Both descriptions lend themselves much more easily to descriptions of God himself, and, certainly in the light of the use of the expression *"Mighty God"*, fit much more comfortably with a continuing description of the divinity of the child to be born.

5. Jesus, Prince of Peace.

The rest of the language in Isaiah 9 that is used to describe the new child relates to the fact that he will be born to kingship and to government. Thus the first expression Isaiah uses in describing the child's role is that *"the government will be on his shoulders"* (9:6). In other words he will rule. This government will keep increasing (9:7). He will rule as king, and he will reign on David's throne (come from David's line, 9:7). Kingship is fundamental to this messianic figure, a kingship which has links both to the line of David and to the one who truly is King, God himself. It is not at all surprising, therefore, that when Jesus came to Galilee he came with a proclamation essentially about a kingdom *"The Kingdom of God is at hand!"*. Neither is it surprising that he declared himself king

(e.g. on Palm Sunday). The coming of the kingdom, the nature of the kingdom and his own role as king were his great themes in precisely the way that they were foreshadowed in this great messianic passage of Isaiah 9.

Isaiah 9 certainly foreshadowed the nature of the kingdom: it was to be a kingdom of peace – the child was to be the *"Prince of Peace"* (9:6). In his kingdom there would be be no hatred, no war, no aggression, no pain, no hurt, no anger, no bitterness, no grief, no mourning, only peace. It was a tremendous prophetic vision. This was kingship for the true benefit of those ruled. In the exercise of this kingship, the king would be a *"Wonderful Counsellor"* (9:6), "wonderful" implying that which is beyond the purely human. In other words this king would have the wisdom of God, and that wisdom involved *"justice and righteousness"* (9:7).

On any reckoning his prophetic Messianic word in Isaiah 9 is quite astounding in the accuracy of its fulfilment in Jesus. Not only does it describe the nature of his ministry an where it would take place, but in every detail prophesied precisely the claims that Jesus was to make about himself as Lord and King.

2. THE SHOOT OF JESSE

ANOINTED KING and BANNER FOR THE PEOPLES

Isaiah 11:1-10 NIV

Is. 11:1 NIV A shoot will come up from the stump of Jesse; from his roots a Branch will bear fruit. 2 The Spirit of the LORD will rest on him— the Spirit of wisdom and of understanding, the Spirit of counsel and of power, the Spirit of knowledge and of the fear of the LORD— 3 and he will delight in the fear of the LORD.

11:10 NIV In that day the Root of Jesse will stand as a banner for the peoples; the nations will rally to him, and the place of his rest will be glorious.

1. The End of the Kings of Judah

Isaiah received his call as a prophet in the same year that saw the death of one of the most powerful and prosperous Jewish kings, Uzziah king of Judah (Is.6:1ff). No king had been more prosperous since Solomon. However, on his call, God immediately commanded Isaiah to prophesy an end both to the national prosperity and the kingship of Judah. He was told to prophesy judgement *"until the cities lie ruined and without inhabitant, until the houses are left deserted and the fields ruined and ravaged, until the LORD has sent everyone far away and the land is utterly forsaken"* (Is. 6:11 NIV). Destruction and exile was to be his word. The outlook, therefore, was bleak for Judah and its kings. The nation would no longer spread out like a great luxuriant tree but would be cut down and left like a mere stump in the ground (Is. 6:13), and the same would happen to the kingship (Is. 11:1). Where all had been so fruitful and prosperous, only roots would remain.

2. Hope for the Future - The "Root of Jesse"

However, the word of God is never without hope, and this is true of the prophecies of Isaiah. Whilst the word of doom was that Judah and its kingship were to be reduced to a mere gnarled stump, the word of hope was that that very same stump would, at some future point, spring into life, and in a way never seen before. It was toward that stump that God directed Isaiah's attention, and from the imagery of the stump came the extraordinary prophetic pronouncements of Isaiah 11 concerning the future.

In Isaiah 11 God says explicitly that the *"stump of Jesse"*, that is to say the kingly line of David (for Jesse was David's father), though seemingly dead in the ground, would burst into life and would produce a new *"shoot"* or *"branch"* (Is.11:1). In other words a new king would emerge. A century or so later Jeremiah took up the same imagery as he personally witnessed the final death throes of the Davidic kingship of Judah. Even as he watched it dying Jeremiah's said: *"The days are coming"*, declares the LORD, *"when I will raise up to David a righteous Branch, a king who will reign wisely"* (Jer. 23:5 see also Jer. 33:15). Thus the new king, the new David, the shoot of Jesse, the Branch, became embedded in Jewish prophetic thought. It was the great hope of the nation. It was a Messianic hope.

3. "The Spirit of the Lord will rest on Him" - the Kingly Anointing.

The expression *"shoot from Jesse"* makes it abundantly clear that God is speaking through his prophet about a real human person, someone from David's line. However unique his character might be in other ways and even if he would be called *"Mighty God"* or *"Everlasting Father"*, the king who was to come would have a human birth.

The fact that he would be human would have, however, an important implication. Because of his humanity this king would need to be equipped with the Spirit of the LORD, for a human person can only fulfil a God-given kingly role through the Spirit. Accordingly, the prophecy in Isaiah 11 announces that *"The Spirit of the LORD will rest upon him"* (11:2), and then goes on to describe in detail the nature of the Spirit's presence on him (vv. 2-5). This would be essentially a kingly anointing to enable him to perform his kingly role.

What God is saying here through his prophet unmistakably points to Jesus. Jesus was in fact born of David's line and in his humanity received such a kingly anointing. He came speaking of a kingdom and acting like a king, though not an earthly kingdom of an earthly king. Jesus was an astonishing fulfilment of an astonishing prophecy. The prophecy, however, is immensely valuable not only for its startling accuracy concerning Jesus, but also because of the clarity with which it describes the nature of the kingly anointing that would rest on him.

First, the Spirit resting on him is said to be the *"**Spirit of wisdom and of understanding**"*. The two terms, "wisdom" and "understanding" are reflected in God's words to King Solomon, *"I will give you a wise and a discerning heart"* (1 Kings 3:12 NIV) after Solomon had asked God for *"a discerning heart to govern your people and to distinguish between right and wrong"* (1 Kings 3:9). *"Wisdom"* here is that which distinguishes what is right from what is wrong, and *"understanding"* is that which sees right to the heart of issues. These two characteristics of the Spirit enable a ruler to do the right thing in the right way for all those he rules, especially for those who are underprivileged and oppressed.

Second, the Spirit is said to be the *"**Spirit of counsel and power**"*. These two words appear again in Isaiah 36:5 where they are translated *"strategy and military strength"*. *"Counsel"* (strategy),

therefore, refers to an ability to devise a right and successful course of action, to put forward a plan that looks to the future and brings things to a proper conclusion. *"Power"* (military strength) refers to the ability to see the strategy through to a successful conclusion: it is the equivalent of the New Testament *"dunamis"* or *"enabling"* of the Spirit. Thus the new king would have all that was required both in terms of strategy and of power to bring about the Kingdom of God in the world.

Third, there would rest upon him the ***"Spirit of knowledge and the fear of the LORD"***. *"Knowledge"* here is essentially the knowledge of God and his ways. The Spirit of God knows God just as the spirit of a man knows a man (1 Cor.2:11). Thus through the Spirit the king would actually know God, not just know about him. The *"fear of the LORD"* is a true reverence for God, giving due respect to God's moral nature, his love of righteousness and his hatred of evil. The *"fear of the LORD"* is, therefore, the true motivator for obedience, godly behaviour and worship. Moreover, this *"fear of the LORD"* would not be a hard thing for the king, but will be a matter of delight. When such a Spirit rests upon a man, righteous living and godly behaviour is a matter of intense joy and delight, not a matter for grim determination. *"I delight to do your will, O Lord!"* (Heb. 10:7) was its vocal expression on the lips of Jesus.

Having described the nature of the anointing in vv.1-3a, Isaiah goes on to give us a short picture of how it would be recognised in the way the king acts (vv.3b-5). He tells us that the king would not judge by mere outward appearance, whether by hearing or seeing, but would act only with justice. His eyes would be on the needy and the poor and he would seek out their cause to give them justice. This is brought out very forcibly in another passage of Isaiah, Is. 61:1ff. There we have the King himself speaking through Isaiah and saying that *"The Spirit is upon me to bring good news"*, *"to heal"*, *"to release"* and to *"comfort"*, and they are words that Jesus used specifically to describe the heart of his anointing. These words bring into focus that fact that the royal anointing is not an expression of some impersonal justice and right-doing on God's part, but that it is also an expression of his heartfelt mercy and compassion. Justice and right-doing from God are really love in action, and are based on mercy and compassion. Love is the rule of the Kingdom. Thus the "rule", the "kingdom" is hugely concerned

to deal with broken humanity. The righteousness of the king is a righteousness that restores and heals, especially where people have suffered through oppression and injustice. The anointing on the king puts the focus of the king's attention unmistakably in the direction of the oppressed and the needy.

Here, then, in this anointing we see the essence of true kingship or rule. It is totally orientated toward bringing righteousness and justice for those who are under the king's rule. The king acts with justice always, motivated by a love of what is morally upright and by a hatred of evil. Such a king exercises all his power and authority to make sure that righteousness is promoted and injustice removed. Such a king was Jesus, and his essential work was to build his kingdom. This is what he proclaimed throughout Galilee – "*the kingdom of God is near*", for the king had arrived. As Jesus walked through Galilee, he walked not simply as "rabbi" but as "*king*". His actions, his authority, his righteous wisdom, his love and respect for his "*Father*", his concern for the poor were all manifestations of the kingly anointing.

A "Banner for the Peoples"

It is not difficult, therefore, to see the prophecy of an "anointed" Shoot of Jesse as pointing to the earthly ministry of Jesus and being fulfilled in that ministry. There is, however, an aspect of the prophecy about the Shoot of Jesse in Isaiah 11 that seems to take us beyond the earthly ministry of Jesus. This aspect is expressed in verse 10, "*In that day the Root of Jesse will stand as a banner for the peoples; the nations will rally to him, and the place of his rest will be glorious*". One thing in particular indicates that this was not fulfilled by the Galilean ministry; it has in focus a ministry not to Galilee and the Jews but to the "*peoples*" (the Gentiles), and the ministry to the Gentiles did not properly begin until after the ascension of Jesus, Jesus himself being sent in his earthly life only to "*the lost sheep of the House of Israel*". It must have meaning, therefore, beyond the earthly ministry of Jesus in Galilee.

The description of the Root of Jesse as a "*banner for the peoples*" is both powerful and suggestive. There are three important features of a banner. First, a banner proclaims something or someone. Second, it is something that people rally to. Therefore, third, a banner is always made to fly where all can see it. Thus in saying that the root of Jesse would be a banner to the nations,

Isaiah implies that the Root of Jesse and what he stood for (salvation and justice), would be exhibited in such a way that the nations could see it and rally to him. The image of the banner amounts to a direct prophecy that the new king and his kingdom would have a high profile and he would be proclaimed throughout the nations.

The same "banner" theme appears in other parts of Isaiah. Take for example the following; *"This is what the Sovereign LORD says, 'See, I will beckon to the Gentiles, I will lift up my banner to the peoples'"* (49:22 NIV); *"Prepare the way for the people, build up, build up the highway! Remove the stones. Raise a banner for the nations"* (62:10). The same concept underlies Is.52;10, *"The LORD will lay bare his holy arm in the sight of all nations and all the ends of the earth will see the salvation of our God.".* The banner is always associated with the Gentiles or the nations. This king had a work to do among the nations; indeed his destiny was to become king of all the nations. The theme is written large in the prophets, and in none more so than Isaiah.

Such verses could, of course, point to the reappearance of the Shoot of Jesse at an end time in history. But the simple fact is that from the very earliest days of the church the name of Jesus, the one who laid claim to title the Son of Jesse, has been raised in a very obvious way as a banner for the Gentiles. One of the most important themes of the New Testament is the manner in which the gospel, under the direction and power of the Spirit, became quickly available to the Gentiles and, also, was widely responded to by the Gentiles. It would seem fairly obvious that Jesus himself must have recognised immediately in these prophecies of a banner that, after his death, resurrection and ascension, the good news of the salvation that he had won would be preached throughout the entire world. Indeed he anticipated it would be so, and commanded his disciples to embark on the task. He was determined his name would be proclaimed to the nations, to the *"ends of the earth"*. The proclamation of what he had done through his death and his resurrection would be the unfurling of the banner. In his ascended glory he, the Root of Jesse, would stand as a banner to bring to all who will rally to it a peace that is glorious.

So, Isaiah prophesied that out of the gnarled stump of the devastated kingship of Judah would come a new king with a pure

and righteous kingly anointing. His destiny would be one, however, not simply of being king of the Jews but king of the nations. The restoration that Isaiah is speaking about is nothing less than a world-wide restoration. What a massive and glorious hope this is, coming as it did out of the most devastating word of judgement!

3. THE SERVANT OF THE LORD

"A LIGHT TO THE GENTILES"

Isaiah 42:1-7 NIV ; Isaiah 49:1-7 NIV

Is. 42:1 "Here is my servant, whom I uphold, my chosen one in whom I delight; I will put my Spirit on him and he will bring justice to the nations.
2 He will not shout or cry out, or raise his voice in the streets.
3 A bruised reed he will not break, and a smouldering wick he will not snuff out. In faithfulness he will bring forth justice;
4 he will not falter or be discouraged till he establishes justice on earth. In his law the islands will put their hope."
Is. 49:6 "I will also make you a light for the Gentiles, that you may bring my salvation to the ends of the earth."

1. The Failure of Israel as God's Servant
It fell to Isaiah, amongst others, to speak out the indictment Judah was to receive for its disobedience. Isaiah announced the failure of Israel's servant role. Israel had become a *"blind servant, a deaf messenger"* (42:18-19 NIV). As a consequence the nation would taste judgement through the flames of war and exile. As for the nations, they would lose a light that had been intended for them.

However, this same Isaiah, at the very time that he was called upon to proclaim Israel's judgement, also received a series of prophetic messages about another servant figure that was to be raised up for the blessing of the nations. Israel may have failed as

the servant of God, but God already has someone else in place who would not fail. We can see this figure emerging in Isaiah 9 where he is seen as a "great light and mighty God", and he appears again in Isaiah 11 where he is seen as the kingly Shoot of Jesse. He then appears a further four times in Isaiah (42; 49; 52-53; 61) as the servant of the LORD and the anointed one. These passages are the great peaks of Messianic prophecy. It is very obvious that the passages are pointing to one and the same person. He is consistently displayed in his divinity, his humanity, his anointing, his kingship and his concern for Israel. But for the purposes of this study we need to note that he is markedly portrayed as one who has a profound ministry to the Gentiles and to the nations. He is a figure with nothing less than the restoration of the world in his view. He is the great Messianic hope for the world.

3 The Identity of the Servant.
Before addressing that world theme, however, it is worth clarifying who this new servant is. It has been argued that the servant references could be applied still to the nation, Israel. It is pointed out that Israel is referred to explicitly by God in Is. 41:8ff as *"you, O Israel, my servant, Jacob, whom I have chosen ... I said 'you are my servant and I have not rejected you")*, and the expression, *"my servant Israel"* is actually used in the second Servant Song (Isaiah 49:3). There is, however, an insurmountable obstacle to the servant being identified with the historic nation of Israel: this servant that Isaiah announces is told that he was *"formed in the womb to be his servant to bring Jacob back to him and gather Israel to himself."* (49:5). Quite obviously, therefore, Isaiah's servant is someone who stands outside the nation and is himself charged with the responsibility at some point of bringing back the Jewish nation to God. Moreover in the depiction of the servant in Isaiah 53 he is described as being a *"guilt offering"* (Is. 53:10), one who *"for the transgression of my people (i.e. the Jews) was stricken"* (Is 53:8 NIV). Here again, he stands outside the nation and as one who suffered for a nation that had transgressed. Moreover, Isaiah 53:10 shows a servant without sin, for such is the implication him being a guilt offering. What is very clear from the prophecies of Isaiah is that Israel cannot in the least be said to be without sin: it is the gross nature of its sin that is Isaiah's burden along with the judgement about to fall on it. If, then, Is. 41:18 addresses the new servant as

"You are my servant, Israel, in whom I will display my splendour" it can only mean that the new servant has now taken over Israel's role and embodies all that Israel as a servant was intended to be.

Others have tried to identify the new servant, not with the nation, but with Isaiah himself or some other prophet. However, Isaiah, if anything was called to preside over the destruction of the nation, not its restoration; he might prophesy of the latter but he would in no way effect it. Neither is there any way in which the prophet could measure up to the glory and majesty of the figure that the prophecies portray. Neither could any other figure of that time claim to be "a light to the Gentiles" or "a covenant to the peoples" or a "guilt offering" or "mighty God".

History has revealed no one remotely like the figure described in these great Messianic passages, except for the figure of Jesus of Nazareth, and he presents unmistakably in his person, his ministry and his death and resurrection an astonishing fulfilment of the huge call involved in Isaiah's predictions.

4. The Mandate of the Servant
As we have stated previously, the main mandate that God gives to his new servant is to be a *"light to the nations"*. This particular phrase, *"light to the nations"*, is used in the two servant songs of Isaiah 42 and 49. In Isaiah 42:6 NIV God said to him: *"I will keep you and will make you a light for the Gentiles that you may bring my salvation to the ends of the earth'"*. In Isaiah 49:5 he said: *"It is too small a thing for you to be my servant to restore the tribes of Jacob .... I will also make you a light for the Gentiles that you may bring my salvation to the ends of the earth"*. The mandate was nothing less than a worldwide task. The servant was to be light to bring salvation to the very ends of the earth. This is a magnificent declaration of hope to a scarred and sinful world: God has made plans to redeem it. It is a mandate far beyond restoring the Jews, important though that is to God, for the servant is specifically told, *"It is too small a thing for you to be my servant to restore the tribes of Jacob .... I will also make you a light for the Gentiles"*.

This worldwide salvation is the essential theme, therefore, of these two servant songs of Isaiah 42 and 49, but it is a theme by no means confined to those two songs. There is a very significant reference to the same theme in the song of the suffering servant (Isaiah 52 -53) where we are told (Isaiah 52:15) that the servant "

will sprinkle many nations, and kings will shut their mouths because of him". The word *"sprinkle"* is used elsewhere in the Old Testament for hallowing people, for cleansing and for atonement. Thus the servant was intended to be a guilt offering for sin and to bring cleansing and atonement for the nations. This, we are told, would one day be a great shock to the rulers of the nations and render them speechless.

Moreover, we find the same theme of worldwide ministry when we look back to the Messianic passages of Isaiah 9 and 11. In 9:1 Galilee of the Gentiles is to be honoured by a great light and much joy, something that came to be fulfilled in Jesus' earthly ministry and pointed to the greater Gentile ministry that was to follow. The light that is depicted in Isaiah 9 as bringing unparalleled joy to people is the same light that the servant of Isaiah 42 and 49 is to convey to the nations. In Is. 11:10 NIV the worldwide theme is powerfully voiced in the words, *"In that day the Root of Jesse will stand as a banner for the peoples; the nations will rally to him"*, words which are repeated in 11:12. In a gloriously poetic statement Isaiah declares in 11:9, *"the earth will be full of the knowledge of the Lord as the waters cover the sea"*.

This great prophetic hope is not even confined to these acknowledged Messianic passages. It is a theme that readily surfaces in many other parts of Isaiah. To mention just a selection of examples, Is. 51:4-5 NIV says, *"The law will go out from me; my justice will become a light to the nations .... My salvation is on the way, and my arm will bring justice to the nations"*. Isaiah 52:10 NIV says, *"The Lord will lay bare his holy arm in the sight of all the nations, and all the ends of the earth will see the salvation of our God"*. Isaiah 56:7 declares, *"My house will be a house of prayer for all nations"*.

Some Key Words

There are three key words which are used in these passages to describe the blessing that God intends to bring on the nations: **"light"**, **"salvation"** and **"justice"**. As we have seen, the light which was to shine on Galilee of the Gentiles in Is 11 was a light that brought unspeakable joy; it was like the joy of harvest or full provision, the joy of freedom from oppression, war and hatred, the joy that came from genuine peace. That joy represents an essential part of the all-embracing term "salvation", which means fullness of

health in every dimension. Salvation embraces peace and contentment, wellbeing and satisfaction in the fullest possible manner.

Justice is a word emphasised particularly (though by no means exclusively) in Is 42, where we are told, the servant was to *"bring justice to the nations"* (v.1); *"he will not falter ....until he establishes justice on the earth"* (v.4); *"in faithfulness he will bring forth justice"* (v.3). The immediate idea we associate with the word justice is doing "that which is right", or securing "righteousness" and "truth". Justice speaks of a moral law. The law that God gave to Moses on Sinai epitomised such justice. So the idea of bringing justice to the earth means enabling nations to do things the right way, to act out of genuine concern for others and in the best interests of others. However, the Hebrew word used here for justice has the wider meaning of describing the way God determined everything in his universe should be ordered. To bring justice to the nations was to bring in to being God's predetermined order and pattern for the life of the nations, to shape the nations, and their behaviour and relationships in exactly the way he wants them to be. God's justice is his decreed righteous order of things and this is what the servant will re-establish. This would indeed be "light to the Gentiles".

The world-wide scope of this mandate of blessing is very striking on any account, but it is particularly so in the context in which it was announced by Isaiah, for Isaiah spoke at a time when the nations of that day were in confusion, when the ravages of Assyria (and later Babylon) were creating unprecedented fear and destruction and when there was little or no justice to be seen anywhere. Isaiah's message was one, therefore, of hope in a very dark hour. It was a re-affirmation in a most extraordinary way of the fact that God had always had in his heart a blessing for the whole world, and that, despite everything, he would in fact achieve it. *"The islands"* (v.4), and the *"ends of the earth"* would see his salvation.

5. The Ministry that brings Justice

The characteristics of the new servant's ministry would be totally in keeping with his mandate. His mandate was justice and love: his ministry, therefore, was to be "quiet, non-aggressive and non-threatening". He would not *"shout or cry out or raise his voice"* (Is.42:2 NIV). This triple description contains all the ideas of not shrieking at people, of not raising one's voice to dominate or shout

others down, of not making some sort of self-advertisement. This was not a ministry of coercion or of manipulation. It was a ministry of deep sensitivity and gentle sympathy, eliciting a willing response.

His ministry would be noted by the manner in which it reached the "bruised reed" and the "smouldering wick" (Is. 42:3). Both of these expressions are very suggestive. A "bruised reed" is something that can scarcely support itself, and certainly cannot be much of a support to others. The phrase speaks of those for whom a very gentle touch is needed lest further weight be placed on them and they break completely. Likewise the "smouldering wick" brings to mind the person in whom any hope or strength or inner dynamic has virtually died out. The servant would not count such people as worthless, nor despise them as weak, but rather seek to fan the ember into flame again.

Isaiah 61:1-3 NIV explains further where the focus of such ministry would be found. The servant's ministry would be *"to preach good news to the poor"*, *"to bind up the broken hearted"*, *"to proclaim freedom to the captives"*, *"to proclaim freedom for the captives"*, *"to comfort those who mourn"*. In other words it was to be a ministry that would bring comfort, beauty, gladness and praise where it was most needed, a ministry that would banish grief, despair and devastation. It would be truly a ministry of salvation.

6. His Success
This was to be a ministry that would have total and full success. It would ultimately change the whole world: *"He will not falter or be discouraged till he establishes justice on earth"* (Is.42:4 NIV). Where Israel failed he would not.

The reason for the servant's ultimate success is to be found in a promise given by no one less than the great Creator God himself: *"This is what the Lord says – he who created the heavens and stretched them out, who spread out the earth and all that comes out of it, who gives breath to its people, and life to those who walk on it, 'I, the LORD have called you in righteousness; I will take hold of your hand, I will keep you and will make you to be a covenant for the people and a light for the Gentiles ..."* (Is.42:5-6). Three powerful verbs are used in this promise for the servant: *"I will take hold of you"*; *"I will keep you"*; *"I will make you"*. The power of God would be present at every stage to provide all that was needed for this servant, who was to be born of a woman and work through

his humanity. God was determined to bring about his purpose of bringing blessing to all the nations. He had chosen his servant to fulfil it and he would resource his servant to the uttermost.

4. THE SERVANT OF THE LORD

"TO RESTORE THE TRIBES OF JACOB"

Isaiah 49:1-9 NIV

Isa 49:1 Listen to me, you islands; hear this, you distant nations: Before I was born the LORD called me; from my birth he has made mention of my name
Isa 49:5 And now the LORD says— he who formed me in the womb to be his servant to bring Jacob
back to him and gather Israel to himself, for I am honoured in the eyes of the LORD
and my God has been my strength ... 8 This is what the LORD says: "I will keep you and will make you
to be a covenant for the people, to restore the land and to reassign its desolate inheritances..."

1. The "Servant" speaks for Himself.
In the Servant Song of Isaiah 49 the servant speaks for himself: *"Listen to me you islands; hear this, you distant nations; before I was born, the LORD called me. He said to me, 'You are my servant ......'"* (49:1,3 NIV). It is very striking fact that the servant should speak for himself, and speak about his birth and life some seven centuries before it was fulfilled in the birth and life of Jesus. It certainly could not have been Isaiah speaking of himself, for Isaiah could scarcely have claimed for himself that "Kings will see you and rise up, princes will see and bow down" (v.7), nor could he have claimed he would "restore the tribes of Jacob" or be a "Light to the Gentiles" (v.6).

If this, then, is the servant speaking through the prophet, what are we to think about the nature of this servant? Whilst he may

make full reference to his humanity by saying that he was "born" and "formed in the womb", and that he was "made into a polished arrow", who was he that he should speak through Isaiah? The prophets were the mouthpiece of God and God alone. The explanation must be that we are being allowed a glimpse of the servant's divinity, hearing his living voice long before his human birth.

2. The Servant speaks of his Mandate to restore Israel

The servant first addresses the "islands" and the "distant nations" (49.1), and tells them that God has given him a mandate to *"bring my salvation to the ends of the earth"* (49.6). There is, however, another part of his mandate that is spelled out in this song and spelled out with great clarity. This has to do, not with the Gentiles, but with the nation of Israel. In v5 the servant says he was *"formed in the womb to be God's servant to bring Jacob back to him and gather Israel to himself."* In v.6 he repeats the mandate: he is *"my servant to restore the tribes of Jacob and bring back those of Israel I have kept"*. In v. 9 God speaks and says, *"I will keep you and make you to be a covenant for the people, to restore the land and to reassign its desolate inheritances"*. Though in context the servant is making the point that the restoration of the tribes of Israel is too small a mandate, and that he has the much larger mandate of bringing salvation to the nations, nonetheless the restoration of Israel is very much a part of his mandate.

The first thing to note in this mandate to Israel is that it means precisely what it says – a restoration of the nation. Israel as a nation is distinguished quite clearly from the Gentiles as nations. This is obvious from the statement (v.6), *"it is too small a thing for the servant to restore the tribes of Israel, he will also be a light to the gentile nations"*. The servant has a work to do for the Jewish nation, and that is a work of restoration. The prophet is clearly thinking nationally. **The second thing to note** is that this restoration involves two separate things for the nation: first a restoration to its land, and second a restoration to its God. Thus the servant is called *"to **restore the land** and to reassign its desolate inheritances"* (v.8), and also *"to **restore Israel to himself** (i.e. God)"*. Both themes are constantly repeated throughout Isaiah's prophecies. The restoration of Israel back to its own land, whilst clearly important, is not the final act of restoration. A much greater day is to come

when the nation is restored to God. **The third factor to note** is that these two aspects of restoration clearly presuppose a period when Israel is scattered across the world and when it is away from God. Though Isaiah could see the beginning of this in his own generation, it is evident that he is in fact prophesying about a scenario of physical and spiritual exile much greater than his contemporary world could suggest.

3. Restoring the Land

The prophetic commission of the servant to restore the land fits in with repeated prophetic statements (not just from Isaiah but from most of the other prophets) that there would come a day when the nation would ultimately return to its own land. This was the great hope offered by God to Israel and Judah even whilst a prophecy of destruction and exile was being pronounced over them on account of their sin. The restoration of the nation to its land is one of the plainest and most frequent of the promises that we can find in the prophets. So for example Isaiah elsewhere says *"In that day the Lord will reach out his hand a second time to reclaim the remnant that is left of his people from Assyria, from Lower Egypt, from Upper Egypt, from Cush (Ethiopia) from Elam (Persia), from Babylonia, from Hamath (Syria) and from the islands of the sea ... he will assemble the scattered people of Judah from the four quarters of the earth".* (11:11-12).

Clearly this scenario is not one which fits happily with the return from the exile in Babylon in the sixth century B.C. It is of much greater scope than that; these exiles are not simply to come from one place, Babylon, but from "the four quarters of the earth" (11:12). Moreover, the Babylonian return featured Judah only, whereas Isaiah distinctly mentions that the return he had in mind would be one in which both Judah and Israel (Ephraim) would be involved, and that their enmity would not appear (11:12-13). They represent a people who have been *"scattered"*, who constitute a *"remnant"* among many lands, and who come *"from the islands of the sea"* (11:11). The expression *"the islands of the sea"* denotes the outlying lands to the west and in the latter chapters of Isaiah and has been described as "virtually a technical term for the Gentile World". It is, therefore, very much more of a "world-wide" scattering or dispersion that Isaiah perceives. This wide scope of a return is something that recurs elsewhere in his prophecies, as for example in

43:5-6 NIV: "*I will bring your children from the east and gather you from the west. I will say to the north, 'Give them up!' and to the south, 'Do not hold them back. Bring my sons from afar and my daughters from the ends of the earth.*" The same basic idea of a gathering from a far flung dispersion is echoed throughout the other prophets of Isaiah's times.

The reality is that Isaiah is pointing to a much bigger scenario, a scenario that involves a truly world-wide dispersion; and it is an extraordinary fact that history has actually unfolded such a bigger scenario of dispersion. From the time of the sixth century exile to Babylon the Jewish dispersion simply grew bigger and bigger. Between 734 and 581 B.C. there were six distinct deportations of the Israelites, and more fled voluntarily to Egypt and other parts of the Near East. From this time onwards, a majority of Jews would always live outside the Promised Land. The freedom to return to Jerusalem accorded by the Persian king, Cyrus, when he conquered Babylon later in the sixth century brought some Jews back home, but it did not materially affect the momentum of dispersion. A great many Jews stayed in the homes that they had built in Babylon, and they stayed there in great numbers for a further thousand years, before dispersing to Spain and other areas of the Mediterranean. Moreover, the Jews who did return from Babylon were only to reside in Israel until the beginning of the second century A.D. At that point a greater phase of exile began with the expulsion of the Jews from Jerusalem by the Romans, resulting in the land being lost for two thousand years, and the Jews roaming the earth with no fixed abode, and being pushed and persecuted from country to country.

Living some two and a half thousand years after Isaiah's prophecy we may well feel inclined to relate his prophecy more to our own times. Certainly, as far as a world-wide Jewish dispersion is concerned, our present situation provides a much more fitting context for the fulfilment of Isaiah's prophecy of the return of Israel. The contemporary return of Jews to the State of Israel cannot but demand our careful consideration. We live in times in which the work of the "servant" and the "Shoot of Jesse" seems to be gathering pace. They are times for us to keep watch.

4. Restoring the Jewish Nation to God

The second part of the servant's mandate is the restoration of Israel to its God: he is *"to bring Jacob back to him and gather Israel to himself" (49:5* NIV). This will come because the servant is going to be made a *"covenant for the people"* (49:8 NIV). What did Isaiah mean by that? He meant simply that the servant, the Messiah, would embody a new covenant which they would accept and which would make them once again his people. What would be the nature of that new covenant?

The best starting point for examining this question is Isaiah 49:7 (part of the same servant song we are considering), where we are told that the servant (Jesus), as well as restoring the nation, would at some point be *"abhorred and despised by the nation"*. This means that there would be some historical episode or event which reflected this rejection of the servant by Israel. The crucifixion of Jesus by the nation is the only possible fulfilment (and a most astonishing fulfilment) of this event. That episode of rejection was certainly not the moment in which he restored the land or the people. In fact the crucifixion was followed in due course by the greatest scattering that Israel was ever to know, and to the total loss of the land. Thus the restoration of which Isaiah spoke must relate to a later stage of history than Jesus' first coming. Indeed it can only relate to the dispersion of the nation consequent on Jesus' death, a dispersion which became world-wide, and in which it still remains estranged from God and in need of reconciliation.

However, the fact is that it was the first coming of Jesus and the crucifixion and rejection that he experienced at the hands of the nation that laid the essential foundation for the later restoration of Israel to God and made it possible. By rejecting him and crucifying him the Jews had, albeit unwittingly, shared in the process by which God made the servant an offering for the sin of the world. His death made forgiveness possible not only for the nations but also for Israel. If Israel was to be restored to God it would have to come back to God and find restoration in the same way as the Gentiles had, namely by believing in Jesus and appropriating the benefits of his death.

Its restoration, in other words, would rest on a new basis of forgiveness. God would enter into a "new covenant" of which Jesus would be the central guarantee (Heb.9:15). That covenant would give the people forgiveness. This is exactly what God was

pointing to in Isaiah 49:8 when he said of the servant, *"I will keep you and make you a covenant for the people"*. The servant who was so badly marred and punished as a guilt offering (Is.53 NIV) would, by his death, usher in a new covenant with Israel. This is what Jeremiah meant when, a century later than Isaiah, he prophesied, *"The time is coming, says the LORD, when I will make a new covenant with the house of Israel and with the house of Judah"* (Jer.31:31 NIV). It was also what Jesus meant when, at the Last Supper he said, *"This is my blood of the new covenant, shed for you and many for the forgiveness of sins"* NIV.

The new covenant inaugurated by and through Jesus would also involve a gift of the Spirit, and through the Spirit the nation would be enlightened. The people would *"mourn bitterly"* over the *"one they had pierced"*, and would come in deep confession and repentance (Zech.12:10 NIV). Zion would then know its ultimate blessing, and finally itself bring blessing to the nations of the world.

5. Living in Significant Times

Frequently Isaiah puts together the servant's full mandate of being both a light to the Gentiles and a restorer of Israel, strongly implying a connection between them in terms of timing. In our modern world with the gospel banner now being flown world-wide and large numbers of Jews finding their way back to the land of Israel we are seeing the same juxtaposition of these two sides of the servant's mandate. This again makes our own times of the utmost significance, and times for careful watching and praying.

5. THE SERVANT OF THE LORD

"A GUILT OFFERING"

Isaiah 50:4-9 NIV; Isaiah 52:13 - 53:12 NIV

Is. 53:3 He was despised and rejected by men, a man of sorrows, and familiar with suffering. Like one from whom men hide their faces he was despised, and we esteemed him not.

*4 Surely he took up our infirmities and carried our sorrows, yet
we considered him stricken by God, smitten by him, and afflicted.
5 But he was pierced for our transgressions, he was crushed for
our iniquities; the punishment that brought us peace was upon
him, and by his wounds we are healed.
6 We all, like sheep, have gone astray, each of us has turned to
his own way; and the LORD has laid on him
the iniquity of us all.
Isa 53:10 Yet it was the LORD'S will to crush him and cause him
to suffer, and though the LORD makes his life a guilt offering,
he will see his offspring and prolong his days.*

1. Great Achievement through Great Suffering

Amid the human suffering, carnage and judgement that marked the
history of the nations of his own generation, Isaiah pointed forward
in his prophecies to the great purposes which God yet had for
blessing and restoring humanity. These were nothing less than
bringing justice and salvation to the very ends of the earth and
embracing both Jew and Gentile alike. The one who was to bring
about this worldwide restoration was referred to by Isaiah as the
"*servant of the Lord*".

However, the ultimate triumph of this servant in fulfilling these
purposes would come only through a very bitter pathway of
suffering. The first intimation of this theme of suffering in the
Servant Songs is found in Isaiah 49:7 where the prophet, referring
to the great things the servant would achieve, speaks nonetheless of
"*him who was despised and abhorred by the nation*". This short
reference to suffering is taken up at greater length in 50:5ff with the
servant himself making a statement that "*I offered my back to those
who beat me, my cheeks to those who pulled out my beard; I did not
hide my face from mocking and spitting*". Finally in Isaiah 52:13 –
53:12 we are given a detailed and graphic picture of the servant's
sufferings that makes clear for us not only their extent but also their
purpose.

These passages on suffering are, therefore, quite extensive. They
serve both as an astonishing prophetic validation of the sufferings
of Jesus and as an insight of great clarity concerning the reason for
those sufferings.

2. The Appalling nature of the Suffering

The servant depicted by Isaiah was to have a lifetime of rejection and despite. He was a *"root out of dry ground"*, having *"nothing of majesty or personal appearance that was attractive"* (53:2 NIV). The servant was a person from whom others would turn away, and they had the lowest possible estimation of him. The leaders of his day dismissed Jesus as a "rabbi" from Galilee! He was far too ordinary to be considered of note. He spoke with the wrong accent, and lacked the schooling of Jerusalem, being merely self-taught.

However the servant was to see even this rejection take a turn for the worse and become bitter and implacable hatred. Eventually it would lead to an appalling and vicious death. Isaiah spares no words in describing the agony of his death. He states starkly that *"his appearance was so disfigured beyond that of any man and his form marred beyond that of any man"* (52:14 NIV). Such a statement of comparison – marred and disfigured *beyond any man* – is not loose exaggeration but sober matter of fact. This was to be the end of the servant who was *"led like a lamb to the slaughter"* (53:7), was *"smitten"*, *"afflicted"* and *"crushed"* (53:4-5), and was *"cut off from the land of the living"* (53:8) (implying sudden, unnatural death). It was the hideous end to *"mocking and spitting"*, beatings and torture (50:6). It was a death as horrific as could be conceived, and it was the result of *"oppression and judgement"*, in other words gross miscarriage of justice. In this manner the servant who would bring so much blessing to the nations would meet his death.

Whilst crucifixion is not specifically mentioned by Isaiah, there is so much here that is foundational to the crucifixion narrative as we know it. Certainly all the horrors depicted here belonged to Roman crucifixion. One of the most suggestive words used in the descriptions of his suffering and death is the word *"pierced"*. (53:5). This takes us immediately to the crucifixion story where the piercing of his side is a matter of great significance to the gospel writers. There are, however, some other very clear pointers to the story: his *"wounds"*, *"the mockery and spitting"*, the *"assignment of a grave with the wicked, and with the rich in his death"* (53:9 NIV).

It is in this suffering that we see perhaps more than anywhere else the essential humanity of the servant. The bleeding, broken body succumbing to intense pain and death links the servant unmistakably with humanity. The servant actually was to die just as

surely as he was actually to be born, and thus as a human being was to fulfil God's purposes.

3. Suffering for a Purpose

Isaiah, therefore, clearly portrays the servant's suffering, but just as clearly he gives the reason for it. This is summed up in the expression, *"The LORD has laid on him the iniquity of us all"* (53:6 NIV). Six further statements expand and clarify this expression.

(i) Is. 53:10 says, *"It was the LORD's will to crush him and cause him to suffer NIV"*. This emphasises the idea that the suffering and death were initiated by God himself: it was The LORD who *"laid on him the iniquity of us all"*. God was personally making the death of his servant consequential by laying sin on him. When *"we considered him stricken by God, smitten by him and afflicted"* (53:4 NIV), thinking that God was punishing him for his own sin, we failed to see that there was a much deeper purpose of God in the suffering the servant was bearing.

(ii) The idea that God was laying sin on the servant is further clarified by the expression, *"The LORD makes his life a guilt offering"* (53:10 NIV). God was fashioning the earthly life of his servant so that it became nothing less than an offering for sin. The "guilt offering" was a form of sin offering and we need to understand what happened to such an offering in the temple rituals of Isaiah's time. The sacrificial animal chosen for the guilt offering was brought to the altar, hands were laid on it as sins were confessed, and the sins were transferred symbolically to the animal. It was then killed, its blood poured out around the altar, and its carcase burned, not on the altar for it was a carcase polluted by sin, but outside the camp. The imagery is only too plain. The person's sin is confessed and transferred to the animal through the laying on of hands. The animal is killed, its life (the blood) is poured out making clear that death has taken place, and the carcase is destroyed by burning, indicating the wrath of God on the sin. The animal took the sin of the offeror and died in his place. We are clearly meant to understand that this is precisely what was to happen to Jesus as the servant of the LORD: our sin was transferred to him and he died for it.

(iii) Is 53:5 spells this truth out more clearly still: *"He was pierced for our transgressions; he was crushed for our iniquities; the punishment that brought us peace was upon him and by his*

wounds we are healed". Here the transference of sin is clearly written. He was not dying for his own sin but for our transgressions and our iniquities. They were to be transferred to him, and because they were transferred he would be pierced and crushed, but we would be spared. Clearly he became a substitute for us, and suffered what we ought to have suffered for our own sin.

(iv) Isaiah 53:5 NIV also makes it plain that the servant *"was punished"*. Sin is seen to bring a punishment of suffering. The punishment was that he was *"crushed"*, *"stricken"*, *"cut off from the land of the living"* and tasted death. The word *"crushed"* is pregnant with meaning. There may have been inner crushing of the body in the process of crucifixion, but the main import would seem to be of the crushing of the inner person, the spirit and heart of the man. Such crushing would be reflected in the imagery of the sacrifice being burnt outside the camp, being banished from a holy place and from the presence of God. It was the image of the final effect of sin for humanity. It was epitomised in Jesus' great cry of dereliction.

(v) Is. 53:9 NIV makes it clear that though he was *"assigned a grave with the wicked"* the servant had *"done no violence, nor was any deceit in his mouth"*. This reminds us that a further important feature of the guilt offering imagery was that the guilt offering had to be without blemish. It tells us that the servant himself was without sin so that he might properly bear the sin of others. The implications of this fact of the servant's perfect innocence are enormous for our understanding of the nature of the servant. For what human being born in the normal human process could properly become sin for another human being? For all who were ever born (or would be born) were tainted with sin. By implication, this servant, though he was to have a human birth, could not be born in the normal way, for that would mean he would be tainted with sin like the rest of mankind. The servant could never be born of two human parents in the normal manner. Obviously there would be some radically different factor in the birth of the servant. The factor could only be a virgin birth.

(vi) Is. 53:12 NIV tells us that *"he poured out his life unto death"*. Clearly on account of his innocence he had no need to suffer death for sin, and could have walked away from such an experience. His innocence, which made it possible for him to be a victim, meant also that his sacrifice would be a willing gesture. He could not be compelled to make himself a sacrifice, but the purpose and desire of his Father, which he shared, was that he should take the *"body*

prepared for him" and replace the ineffective sin offerings of the Temple ritual with his own body (see Heb. 10:5-7). Thus Isaiah in recording that the servant "*poured out his life unto death*" speaks clearly of the fact that Jesus himself made the sacrifice willingly and of his own volition.

3. Beyond the Suffering

There is nothing more characteristic of the prophetic writings than the fact that they do not leave us at the point of death and judgement, and devoid of hope. They point to restoration. Certainly the Servant Song of Isaiah 53 does not leave the servant in death and judgement. Two great statements stand out toward the end of the message which speak of resurrection: "*he will see his offspring and prolong his day*" (53:10 NIV) and "*after the suffering of his soul he will see the light of life and be satisfied*" (53:11 NIV). They are, no doubt, the statements that enabled Jesus to embrace the suffering, and to "*endure the cross, scorning its shame*" (Heb 12:2 NIV). He knew of the glory beyond the cross as well as the prophetic word about his death.

Beyond the resurrection statements lies a great ascension statement: "*I will give him a portion among the great, and he will divide the spoils with the strong*" (53:12 NIV). As Paul the apostle, referring to Jesus, was later to express it: "*having disarmed the powers and authorities, he made a public spectacle of them, triumphing over them by the cross*" (Col: 2:15 NIV). The victory of the cross and the spoils of victory were received as the servant was made to sit at his Father's right hand.

Following the suffering would come, therefore, satisfaction for the servant (53:11). The satisfaction would come from the fact that he would make many "just" as they came to know and accept what he had done for them in bearing their iniquities. As Isaiah puts it, "*by his knowledge my righteous servant will justify many, and he will bear their iniquities*". It was in this way that the servant would start his great worldwide work of bringing justice to the nations, and restoring the Jewish nation. There could be no justice or righteousness without forgiveness of sin and a radical inner change of humanity. This could only be accomplished through a death for sin. There was no other way and there could never have been success in the servant's commission without his suffering. Thus **ultimate hope for mankind is to be found solely upon the death and resurrection of Jesus Christ.**

JESUS IN THE OLD TESTAMENT SACRIFICES

1.JESUS SEES HIMSELF IN THE OLD TESTAMENT BOOKS

Luke 24:13-47 NIV

"He explained to them what was said in all the Scriptures concerning himself"

1. Jesus Looks into the Mirror.
One of the most remarkable and formative bible studies ever experienced was that which Jesus gave to two of his disciples as they were walking along the Emmaus road on the afternoon of his resurrection (Lk 23:13ff.). It was remarkable because the resurrected Jesus was the expositor. It was given in a purely extempore manner. with no books or scrolls, coming out of a mind utterly stocked with scripture, and he spoke in power through the Holy Spirit (Acts 1:2). It was formative because it was wholly pertinent to the perplexities of the two who heard it, so much so that they seemed never to have even asked the unknown stranger who talked to them who he was or where he came from. The focus of it was in fact entirely on his recent death and his reported resurrection. It was the first coherent and comprehensive account from the scriptures ever given as to the reason and purpose of his death and the need of his resurrection (though Jesus had hinted at the nature of his death and resurrection before it happened). It was, therefore, a study and a revelation of immense importance, one on which the whole gospel was destined to be based. Finally, and most significantly for our purposes, it was a study that was expounded totally from the Old Testament.

It was not, of course, the only Old Testament bible study that Jesus gave after his resurrection. That very same evening of the resurrection day in the Upper Room he appeared to the disciples and once again showed them everything that had been written about him in the Law of Moses, the Prophets and the Psalms. Again he taught

them the need for his death and his resurrection, but on this occasion he added a whole new panorama of teaching, in which he showed them from the same scriptures a future preaching programme about repentance and forgiveness of sins that was to involve all nations (Lk. 24:45-47).

When we consider that this was only the first day of his resurrection, and that he appeared to the disciples over a period of forty days, teaching them a great deal more about the "kingdom", we can only begin to imagine how much of the Old Testament prophetic scriptures he caused to fall into place in their minds. This teaching truly was the basis of the fundamental truths proclaimed in the early church, and later collected in the shape of the New Testament.

For us to go, then, to the Old Testament and to explore there the same teaching Jesus gave his disciples about his birth, life, death, resurrection and world purposes is to go back to those heart burning studies of the early resurrection days. It is an invitation hardly to be missed! All the same, some might feel that, since all that insight has now been incorporated into the New Testament, there may be little point in such a laborious examination of the Old Testament. At least four very good reasons suggest themselves for correcting this impression.

2. Clarity from the Old Testament.

The first reason is that the Old Testament still brings much extra clarity to our understanding of Jesus, notwithstanding all that is presented in the New. Unfortunately, most people do not associate clarity with the Old Testament. Rather the reverse. Yet there was obviously no obscurity for the disciples as they were taken by Jesus through the Old Testament scriptures, only tremendous light. They could claim no real schooling like the priest or Pharisee, but what they were told made unquestionable sense. The reality is that there is in the Old Testament a tremendous foundation for understanding about Jesus (even if we do need a guide and the Holy Spirit!), and we need to avail ourselves of it. Imagery, symbol and picture, as well as simple statement, all contribute to this foundation.

To take an example: the New Testament teaching about the death of Jesus will tell us very clearly that *"he became sin for us"*, or that *"Christ died for the ungodly"*. It will tell us he was made an "offering" for us. However, this sort of language and these sorts of

concepts will be really comprehended only when we look at the whole pattern of Old Testament sacrifice as it was recorded in the Tabernacle (later the Temple). John the Baptist may have cried out that Jesus was the "Lamb of God who takes away sin", but the lamb sacrificed for sin can only be properly understood by what went on in the temple (facts which John's hearers would know only too well). It was the sin offering in the Temple that provided the full picture of what Jesus was doing when he hung on the cross. It is impossible to understand fully the cross without looking carefully at the Old Testament sin offering. Like the lamb in the Temple he carried our sin, his blood was spilt, he was "burned outside the camp" (the agony on Golgotha). Not only was he a sin offering as he hung on the cross, but he also represented there all the other different offerings that we see in the temple, and only as we see him fulfilling them can we fully grasp everything about what he was doing. There can be little doubt that Jesus would have expounded his death in relation to the Temple sacrifices, and, as he did so, the disciples would have been overwhelmed by the clarity with which they could now appreciate the need for his death. They would have made a very rapid connection, probably wondering why they had never seen it before! They learned very quickly that God had in fact given such a sacrificial system to Moses, and instructed him to adhere precisely to the pattern simply because it provided an educational foundation for the sacrifice of his Son. Such a survey, however slight, is hugely enriching. Old Testament teaching burned the truth of Jesus' sacrificial death on the minds and hearts of his disciples.

The death of Christ is not simply to be found in the Temple sacrifices. The great prophetic statement in Isaiah 52:13ff has no equal when it comes to speaking of the nature of Christ's death and the reason for it. There is clarity of statement here that is unsurpassed. There is here, moreover one of the clearest predictions of his resurrection (Is.53: 10-11). Many other images, "foreshadows" and statements could be added to the list.

However, as we have seen, Jesus was not only pointing to a clarification of his death when he taught his disciples after the resurrection. He wanted to involve them in his purposes for the future. He had died to redeem people from all nations, not just from among the Jews. The majesty of these purposes can frequently elude us, but it is impossible to read the Servant Songs of Isaiah and not

be taken up into such enlarged vision. The Psalms also particularly add to the grandeur of that vision.

3. The Prophetic Power of the Old Testament

There can be little doubt that one of the things that made the hearts of those two disciples on the Emmaus road "burn" was the fact that everything that had happened to Jesus at the cross, and was to happen after the cross, had been so clearly foretold in scripture. It was all a very startling fulfilment of prophecy. Though Jesus justly began his Emmaus road study with the rebuke, "How foolish you are, and how slow of heart to believe all that the prophets have spoken!" (Lk. 24:25 NIV), he left those two disciples with a totally new grasp on the whole issue of prophecy, its accuracy and its power. They could see with him that "the Christ had to suffer these things and enter his glory" (Lk. 24:26 NIV), because God had ordained it so, and spoken it through his prophets. They were face to face with the fact that God had spoken about what he was going to do, and then had actually done it. If there is anything that can make us come to life as we study the prophecies about Jesus in the Old Testament, it is that God really is a speaking God, a God of revelation and that what he speaks and reveals really does happen.

We need to understand this great truth about prophecy. It is fundamental to growth in faith. Amos speaks about it very succinctly: "Surely the Sovereign LORD does nothing without revealing his plan to his servants the prophets" (Amos 3:7). For Amos it was not even the case that prophecy comes true. It was rather that God would not act in major ways without first giving prophetic notice of it before hand. It was part of the express purpose of God that our faith in him should be stimulated by fulfilled prophecy (see later chapters of Isaiah. Is 48:3ff). Therefore he spoke prophetically through the Old Testament scriptures about the death, resurrection and world-wide proclamation of Jesus, so that when those events came to pass we should be assured of him and his promises. Not to appreciate the nature and power of the prophetic word is to be robbed of an extraordinary dimension which is both heart burning and motivating.

Such prophetic utterances give broad outlines, but what detail there is can be astonishing. Isaiah 53:9, for example, gives a precise statement about Jesus, the Servant, being "assigned a grave with the wicked and with the rich in his death". We see the fulfilment of this

statement when we see Jesus dying between two thieves, yet buried in a rich man's tomb! So we are left to meditate on Peter's words, "prophecy never had its origin in the will of man, but men spoke from God as they were carried along by the Holy Spirit" (2 Pet. 1:21 NIV).

4. The Impact of the Old Testament on Jesus
Listening to Jesus expound the scriptures concerning himself, the disciples would have seen not only his depth of perception, but also how crucial that perception had been for his own personal life and walk with his Father. When someone expounds the scriptures as Jesus did that day, it is almost always because the person has had to live by them. He was sharing with the disciples his own discoveries about himself and his work, discoveries he made as he grew up and immersed himself in the Old Testament books. He must have become acutely aware, for example, of the meaning of Isaiah's "Servant Songs", and that he actually was the "Servant" portrayed there. In particular, as he read through Isaiah 53 he would have become aware of the horrific death that lay in front of him, and the call to become a "guilt offering" for sin. This helps us to appreciate more profoundly the depth with which he embraced that call to die for sin. In a similar manner, the Holy Spirit would have revealed to him his kingly stature as he read both Isaiah and the Psalms, and would have made very clear to him that the nature of his kingship would be one of love, righteousness and justice. Even his earthly ministry as the anointed one preaching to the poor and releasing the captive would have become plain to him as he read through the same books, and especially Isaiah 61. The anointing that he received at the Jordan was not something that took him by surprise – he asked for it because he knew it must come to enable him to fulfil what his Father had called him to do by preaching and healing.

There can be few things as rewarding or edifying as seeking to understand the nature of Jesus' own ministry and how he came to understand it. We can come to grips with that when we follow Jesus into the pages of the Old Testament, and learn how powerfully and personally they influenced him.

5. The Old is the Essential Foundation of the New
What has been said so far will indicate that when the apostles began their proclamation and teaching about Jesus at Pentecost, they

taught what they had heard from Jesus, and consequently their teaching was full of Old Testament allusion and "proof". Thus what we read in the New is fundamentally an interpretation of the Old. Again, there is nothing more edifying than seeing how the tree of the New grew out of the roots of the Old. We can understand fully why the gospel comes to us so richly and so cogently, and why it lines up with the Old Testament. We are left with the assurance that only the extraordinarily interpretive mind of Jesus could have given the Christian faith the start that it had. Seeing all this is a final compelling reason for going into the Old Testament to see Jesus. An open bible, a listening ear to those who have already sought to explore this path, and the Holy Spirit are our essential aids for this task.

2. JESUS – A SIN OFFERING and A GUILT OFFERING

"God sent his Son to be a sin offering" Rom. 8:3 NIV

"The LORD makes his life a guilt offering" Is 53:10 NIV

The Tabernacle which Moses erected at God's direction was a tent covered in skins and divided into two parts, the Holy Place and the Most Holy Place. It represented God's dwelling place among the Israelites. It was set within an outer court marked off by a wall of screening material, and in this outer court stood the great brazen altar of sacrifice. The altar was situated at the entrance to the Tabernacle itself and its position indicated that there could be no progress into the actual holy dwelling place of God (and thus no real contact with God) without the offering of sacrifices. There were different kinds of sacrifice that were required to be offered on the brazen altar, and the nature of those sacrifices was revealed to Moses in great detail and had to be precisely adhered to. The reason for this was that God wanted to teach that he could only be reached through sacrifices of a quite specific nature and import. These sacrifices were in fact prophetically designed to express exactly the different aspects of the ultimate sacrifice Jesus was to make. They

were to be "types" of what was to happen on Calvary. These sacrifices numbered five in all, and all of them are important for any full understanding of what happened on the cross. They were the sin offering, the guilt (or trespass) offering, the burnt offering, the meat offering, and the fellowship (or peace) offering. Though having certain things in common, each one was quite distinct from the others in its intention. The sacrifice of Jesus is not fully comprehended if it is seen only, as it commonly is, as a sin offering, even though that aspect undoubtedly was the prime feature. Calvary presents us also with a burnt offering and a peace offering, features of great importance. However, the sin offering was pivotal and the proper place to begin.

The Sin Offering (Lev. 4:1 - 5:13 NIV).
"God sent his own Son ..... to be a sin offering". (Rom 8:3)
"Our old self was crucified with him so that the body of sin might be done away with". (Rom 6:6)
"... this priest offered for all time one sacrifice for sins". (Heb. 10:12)
"God sent his son as an atoning sacrifice for our sins". (1 Jn. 4:10)

The sin offering, burnt offering and peace offering were all offered daily before the Lord on the brazen altar. The sin offering was always the prior offering; the burnt offering and the peace offering had to be sacrificed on top of the sin offering, they could never precede it. In this way God made it clear that before he could receive any other kind of offering sin had to be dealt with, "atoned for" or removed. Thus the sacrificial system pointed immediately to man's greatest problem- his sin – and the need for it to be dealt with.

The person making the sin offering began by laying hands on the sacrificial animal to indicate transference of his sin to the animal. There is no question at all that this is the meaning of the act; everything that happens to the animal after hands were laid on it indicates that it had become sinful, and was carrying the sin of the one who was making the sacrifice. There is clearly a substitution of the animal for the person. The animal was then killed (the appropriate end for sin), and its blood, representing its life, was poured out around the altar. Nothing else could be done

with the blood for life belonged only to God and not to man. The sin bearer's life had been taken and returned to God at the altar.

One of two things could then happen to the carcass of the animal. If the sacrifice was made either on behalf of the congregation (as on the Day of Atonement), or for a priest, the carcass of the animal was burned, but never on the brazen altar. It was burned outside the Tabernacle court, the reason simply being that it was tainted with the transferred sin of the offeror, and nothing tainted with sin could be burned on the brazen altar before the Lord. God would not look upon such a burning, and it had no place near his dwelling. Only the fat of the animal was to be burned on the altar as a sign that God had received the offering. If an ordinary person (i.e. someone who was not a priest) made a sin offering then the carcass of their sacrificial animal would be eaten by the priests, not burned outside the camp. In either case, for priest or people, the offering was not burned "before the Lord" (on the altar) – it was sin tainted. It was not a *"fragrant"* or *"sweet smelling"* offering. It was necessary and received by God, but it was not something that God took any delight in.

The importance of this in understanding the death of Jesus is clear. If Jesus was a "sin offering" then his body which was bearing the sin of the world was bound to be taken "outside the camp", banished from the presence of God and "burned". So quite literally Jesus' body was taken outside the city, and at Golgotha it was "burned". The burning as he died on the cross was the burning up of sin, for he had literally *"become sin"*. The burning was of something utterly abhorrent to God, the burning of something by the wrath of God – the "fires of hell". Burning and banishment from the presence of God is the punishment for sin. The sin offering must bear that punishment. This is what we see taking place at Calvary – Jesus the sin offering burning under the wrath of God, and banished from God's presence. Much has been written on the hugely critical cry of Jesus, "My God, why have you forsaken me!" (Matt. 27:46 NIV), and many attempts have been made to minimize its meaning in the interest of theories which play down the consequences of sin, but the Old Testament "type" of the sin offering points unmistakably to the fact that in such a cry Jesus was expressing his moment of burning, his moment of banishment from the presence of his Father.

Great care was taken to choose for the sin offering an animal that was completely free of blemish. Quite clearly no animal could become an offering for sin if it already had imperfections. It is impossible to lay sin upon something or someone who is already tainted with it. Nothing could indicate more pointedly the perfection and innocence of Jesus. *"God made him who knew no sin to be sin for us"* (2 Cor. 5:21) is the way that Paul so clearly makes this point. Whilst the animal *"without blemish"* might be an approximation in reality for the purposes of a ritual, there could not be any approximation in the perfection of Jesus for the sacrifice at Calvary. He was in reality perfect. This perfection in the nature of Jesus immediately implies, of course, that Jesus in his humanity could not, like us, have been born of two sinful parents; his birth must have been unique. Anyone born of natural parentage can never be perfect but always bears the mark of the blemish of sin. Thus the demand for perfection in the sin offering has profound implications for our understanding of the person of Jesus: he cannot be merely human as we know it. His birth by the operation of the Holy Spirit, leaving him free from any stigma of sin in his nature, is an important corollary of his being "offered for sin" and a powerful pointer to his divinity.

A range of animals could be used in the sin and guilt offerings. A bull, a goat, a lamb or even pigeons could be used. Whilst the range may reflect the importance of the person(s) whose sin was to be atoned for, it is better seen as a way of making provision for everyone to avail themselves of the sacrificial process, rich and poor. There is, of course, no distinction between rich and poor in the provision of Jesus as our sacrifice.

Thus the sacrificial system of the Tabernacle first and foremost brought home the need for any person who wanted to draw close to God to confess and seek cleansing from sin. It taught that sin was something utterly abhorrent to God and could only be removed by another living creature taking it over and dying for it. Sin meant death, and death was avoided only through the substitution of another. God was willing to provide such a substitute, and for everybody. Here are the basic principles which underlie the death of Jesus. There could be no clearer "type" or analogy than this of the sacrifice of Jesus. No wonder Paul and the other New Testament writers described the work of Jesus in language directly taken from the tabernacle sacrifices! The process of animal

sacrifice may seem primitive, but the lessons being expounded were anything but primitive. At the very least it could be said that God, in using this sacrificial process, was taking something of the primitive behaviour of men and investing it with something profound and lasting. On the other hand, it could be maintained that it is hard to see how any "type" of the death of Christ could be pictured by something which did not involve a sacrificial death.

The sacrificial system was in fact an essential complement to the moral Law which the Israelites also received through Moses. The Law educated the people in the nature of sin so that they could not plead ignorance to it. The sacrificial system, particularly in its foremost offering – the sin offering - spelled out the fact that something other than mere confession of sin was required in order for it to be properly dealt with. Sin could only be removed by something or someone taking the punishment for it, namely death. Thus the sacrificial system was not advocating some grotesque sacrifice to some wayward, petulant, deity who was simply displeased and needed constant propitiation; it was teaching the devastating consequences of sin for humanity, and pointing to the only way for forgiveness, the provision of a sin bearer who was a propitiation for the justifiable wrath of God. The sacrificial system was abhorrent, but the necessary death of Jesus was much more so.

The Guilt (Trespass) Offering (Lev. 5:14 - 6:7 NIV)
"The Lord makes his life a guilt offering". (Isaiah 53:10)
"He was pierced for our transgressions; he was crushed for our iniquities and
the punishment that brought us peace was upon him" (Isaiah 53:5)

Isaiah makes a clear prophetic statement that Jesus (the Servant of the Lord) would be a guilt offering (53:10 above). In 53:5 he points to the nature of the guilt offering – an offering in which Jesus *"bore our transgressions"*, in other words took away our actual and specific trespasses. In describing the guilt offering the book of Leviticus always associates it with a person coming to make a sacrifice because of some particular sin he has committed, and it is frequently also associated with payment of amends to anyone defrauded by the sin. The descriptions of the sin offering proper, on the other hand, do not have any such focus on a particular

transgression but deal with sin in general. This is the only differential we have between the sin offering and the guilt offering. Both are offerings for sin, and the guilt offering could be seen as a particular form of the sin offering. Both sacrifices follow the same pattern in their ritual.

The suggestion has been made that whereas the guilt offering speaks of the need for our particular transgressions to be forgiven, the sin offering speaks of the need for each of us as a sinful person by nature to be forgiven. That certainly makes a comprehensive coverage of the sin problem in so far as it is both our very nature, not just our wrong deeds that need forgiveness and cleansing. In so far as the sin offering speaks of our inner heart need to be free from sin it addresses the greater need, but the guilt offering indicates God's readiness to address our specific and particular sins that make us feel guilty or distressed.

Paul, in Rom. 5:18 ff, speaks of Adam's "trespass", saying that *"the result of one trespass was condemnation for all"*. Paul sees Jesus, in making himself a guilt offering, as reversing the effect of Adam's transgression. Jesus' offering of himself was the "trespass offering" that atoned for the appalling trespass of Adam that brought so much prolonged pain to the world.

The Sin Offering and the Scapegoat on the Day of Atonement
The Day of Atonement took place once a year when the whole Israelite community made confession and sought atonement for its rebellion and sin. The High Priest first entered the sanctuary area with a young bull for a sin offering. He offered the bull to make atonement for himself and his household before he proceeded with any other sacrifice. He took the blood of the bull and sprinkled some of it with his fingers on the front of the atonement cover and then in front of the atonement cover in the Most Holy Place. Then from the community he took two male goats for a further sin offering. He cast lots over the two goats. One lot was for the Lord and that goat on which it fell was sacrificed as a sin offering on behalf of the people. He took the blood of both the bull and goat and sprinkled it on the horns of the brazen altar and before the altar. Thus even the sanctuary itself had to be "atoned for" by the sin offerings.

Finally he took the other goat, which was still alive, laid both hands on it and confessed over it all the rebellion and sin of the

community – so putting them on the goat's head. He sent the goat away into the desert so that the goat would carry on itself all the sins of the community to a solitary place (a God-forsaken wilderness). Though not a "type" indicating the need for the death of a sin bearer, the sending away of the goat nonetheless strongly reinforced the fact that sin meant banishment to a desert place. It underlines again the banishment Jesus experienced on the cross, the wilderness of his three hours of forsakenness.

3. JESUS - A BURNT OFFERING and A FELLOWSHIP OFFERING

Christ loved us, and gave himself up for us as a fragrant offering and sacrifice to God". Eph.5:1 NIV

These words of Paul refer to the death of Jesus as a "fragrant offering", a "pleasing sacrifice". This is a technical expression used of certain offerings in the Old Testament sacrificial system, and Paul's use of it clearly indicates that what he has in mind is either the burnt offering or the fellowship offering (or both). He is not referring to either a sin offering or a guilt offering, for neither of these two offerings was considered a "fragrant offering". The sin and guilt offerings took on the sin of the offeror and thereby became tainted. Consequently they were burned outside the tabernacle, away from the presence of God and not on the tabernacle altar. Whilst God accepted them, indeed required them, he took no "pleasure" in them, and they were never "fragrant". Although, elsewhere, the identification of Jesus with the sin offering was paramount in Paul's thought (e.g. *God sent his own son ... to be a sin offering".* Rom. 8:3), that was not in his mind here. He was far too well versed in Old Testament language and temple practice to use the word "fragrant" loosely. The "fragrant offerings" could only refer to the burnt offering and the fellowship or peace offering. We need, therefore, to consider what Paul was thinking when he saw Jesus' sacrifice in terms of these "fragrant" offerings.

The Burnt Offering (Lev. 1:1-17; 6: 8-13)

There were initial similarities between the sin offerings and the "fragrant" offerings. In both types of offerings, the offeror laid hands on the animal so that it might stand in his stead, and the blood of the animals was poured out around the altar. But in the fragrant offerings the laying on of hands was not associated with the transference of sin, and the disposal of the carcasses of the animals was markedly different. In the sin offering and the guilt offering the carcass was never allowed to be burned on the brazen altar since it had "become sin", was therefore unclean and had to be burned outside the Tabernacle. The burnt offering, however, was burned on the brazen altar before the Lord. The fact that it could be burned on the brazen altar in the tabernacle of God meant that the animal had not become a sin carrier for the offeror but represented something else.

The sacrifice represented, in fact, an act of absolute and complete dedication of the life of the offeror to the Lord: it meant he was ready to yield his life for whatever purpose God might wish to use it. This total commitment is typified by the fact that the carcass of the burnt offering was totally consumed and completely given over as a sacrifice to God. Thus, when the offeror initially laid hands on the burnt offering he was by that act offering his whole life in dedication to God. When Jesus went to the cross it was an act of total commitment to his Father, even though that commitment meant dying for sin. Thus, he gave himself as a "burnt offering", in total self-surrender. This was supremely pleasing to God, truly a fragrant offering, a sacrifice that could be burned on the altar before his presence. In this he is a pattern for us.

With Jesus, of course, such an offering of himself did not require any previous cleansing from sin for he was without blemish. The offeror in the Old Testament tabernacle, however, could not begin to make any offering of his life to God until his sin had been dealt with. For this reason, therefore, the burnt offering always had to follow on from the sin offering or guilt offering. In the same way for us there can be no satisfactory dedication of our lives as a "burnt offering" until we have availed ourselves of the cleansing of the "sin offering" in the person of Jesus. Moreover, that dedication of our self has to be offered through Jesus who is "our burnt offering". So, the Israelite, despite having had his sin dealt with by the sin offering, nonetheless had to use another

sacrificial animal for his dedication. Any presentation of our self in dedication, therefore, must be through the sacrifice of Jesus as a burnt offering. When we are in Christ, we confess our sin and identify that confession with our sin offering who is Jesus; when we offer up our lives with the mixed motives that always abound, we offer them through our burnt offering who is Jesus.

We can understand from the above why burnt offerings in large numbers were always offered among the Jews in moments that called for special affirmation of total commitment. A very clear example of this is to be seen in the dedication of the Temple by Solomon. On that occasion the numbers of burnt offerings were so vast that a whole new area of the temple had to be dedicated especially for them to be sacrificed. It was an unparalleled time of total commitment on the part of king, priests, and people to the Lord, and this was expressed, as God required, in burnt offerings. Likewise, when David bought the threshing floor of Araunah where God had stayed the plague in Israel, he immediately offered burned offerings there as a sign of his re-commitment to God (2 Sam. 24).

A remarkable example of the use of a burnt offering is found in the life of Abraham. When God called Abraham to sacrifice Isaac, he told Abraham to sacrifice him "as a burnt offering" (a "burnt offering" which actually pre-dated the Tabernacle sacrificial system). When eventually he stopped the sacrifice of Isaac God's words to Abraham were very significant: "*Now I know that you fear God, because you have not withheld from me your only son*" (Gen. 22:12). These words clearly indicate that the burnt offering was for Abraham a test of his willingness to give the best he had. The ram which God subsequently pointed to, and which was to be sacrificed instead of Isaac, was then offered as a "burnt offering". If the sacrifice of Isaac points to the sacrifice of Jesus, then it points not to Jesus as a sin offering, but to Jesus as a burnt offering.

The Sacrifice at Calvary was in fact a burnt offering just as much as it was a sin offering or a guilt offering. The full measure of Jesus' commitment as a burnt offering lay in the fact that he was ready to accept the call to be a sin offering. He embraced the agony of dying as a sin offering, because he wanted to embrace the will of his Father. Like Isaac, he allowed himself to be bound on the altar as a burnt offering, but unlike Isaac he himself had to remain there as a sin and guilt offering. The obedience of Jesus to the most appalling but absolutely necessary requirement of his Father's will,

is an example beyond parallel of a life offered as a burnt offering. It is this obedience that made this offering a "fragrant offering".

The Fellowship or Peace Offering (Lev. 3: 1-17; 7:11-36)

"Sacrifice fellowship offerings there, eating them and rejoicing in the presence of the LORD your God". Deut. 27:7 NIV

Though it was sacrificed like the other offerings with the laying on of hands and the pouring out of the blood, the fellowship offering differs from them in that the carcass of the animal was seen not as something to be burned up but as something that provided food. The fat of the animal's entrails were offered on the altar as a due portion for God, its breast and right thigh were waved before the Lord and then given to the "sons of Aaron" and the officiating priest, and the remainder was eaten by the offeror. The offering thus provided a meal for God, the priest, and the offeror. It was in effect a fellowship meal in which God, priest and offeror were at peace with one another. It is an offering that speaks not primarily of the removal of our sin (sin offering) nor of the dedication of our lives to God (burnt offering) but of our fellowship and feeding together on a sacrifice provided. This "peace-giving fellowship" could be nothing other than a "fragrant" offering.

The above verse from Deuteronomy refers to sacrifices offered on Mount Ebal at the time of the entry of the Israelites into the Promised Land and brings out clearly the nature of this fellowship offering as a time of joyous fellowship in the presence of God. The moment of entry, after such a long wilderness wandering, was obviously a moment of great joy and a time for great thanksgiving. It is this spirit that marks the fellowship offering; a time to eat and rejoice together. Significantly the fellowship offerings on that occasion were preceded by burnt offerings of dedication. The burnt offering always preceded the fellowship offering, for there could be no real fellowship apart from total commitment to God and his purposes. Mostly the two types of offering went together. We have noted the vast numbers of burnt offerings that Solomon made at the dedication of his Temple, but there were also on that occasion vast numbers of fellowship offerings, for it was as much a time of thanksgiving, joy and feasting as it was of dedication.

Jesus is the fulfillment of the "fellowship (or peace) offering" in the sense that, in offering himself, he has become the one on

whom we "feed" and the one who brings satisfaction to God. To explore the fellowship offering is to explore how we "feed" on Jesus. This is not to be seen, of course, in carnal terms; his is an offering which provides us with deep spiritual nourishment and strength. God's "food" is the deep satisfaction of contemplating what Jesus has done. Moreover, even Jesus himself finds satisfaction - *"he shall see of the travail of his soul and be satisfied"* (Isaiah 53:11 NIV). When we have confessed our sin and dedicated our lives through him, we are able to receive all his sustenance with great joy and with a great sense of thanksgiving, and in communion with a deeply satisfied God.

All animal sacrifices are "atonement sacrifices".
In all the animal sacrifices the blood was poured out on the altar. Leviticus 17:11 notes: *"the life of the creature is in the blood, and I have given it to you to make an atonement for yourselves on the altar"*; it is the blood that makes atonement for one's life. Thus, the pouring out of the blood on the altar makes all the animal sacrifices "atonement sacrifices", even though it is only the sin and guilt offerings which deal directly and exclusively with sin. They all involve a substitute whether they are sin, burnt or fellowship offerings. There is no such thing as an acceptable offering made without the death of a substitute. God has given the life of the substitute (i.e., allowed it to die) so that through that substitute a proper offering may be made. We first have to place our sin on a substitute (sin offering), then we have to dedicate our lives through a substitute (burnt offering), and we can only receive the spiritual strength and nourishment from God by means of a substitute (fellowship offering). At each stage we are totally dependent on something offered on our behalf, for everything we offer on our own, even our dedication and our desire for grace, is tainted. We cannot deal with our sin through a substitute and then in our own way make a dedication, for a dedication has also to be done through a substitute. At each stage something or someone "undefiled" has to present whatever we desire to offer. "Full" atonement can only be made when the Israelite has faced up to his sins, completely dedicated his life, and sat down to have fellowship with God, taking his provision. All three are necessary. All these offerings can only be properly done through "blood", that is through the death of another, whose death makes each offering acceptable. Unless they

are presented through one who is sinless and who has shed his blood on their behalf they cannot be received.

All this explains why Jesus is not only our sin and guilt offering but also our burnt offering and our fellowship offering. We must bring our sin to him and lay it upon him if our sin is to be removed, we must offer the dedication of our lives through him for such dedication to be acceptable, and we must seek the sustenance of God and the effective fellowship with others only through him. Self-effort has no place at any stage.

It is a salutary reminder that all the offerings were sacrificed every day, representing a daily cleansing from sin and a daily commitment to God and feeding from the sacrificed one. Nothing less is expected of a Christian in his walk with God.

The Grain (Meat) Offering and the Drink Offering (Num. 29:2, 25, 28, 31. Lev. 23:13)
"I am being poured out like a drink offering" Phil. 2:17 NIV

These two offerings were always additions to the burnt offering, and signified the same total dedication to the Lord. Whereas, however, the offeror offered up his life through the burnt offering, he offered up the fruits of his labour through the grain and drink offerings. A handful of the grain offering was burnt before the Lord, and the rest belonged to Aaron and his sons. This seems to indicate that there was a dedication of the work of his hands to the work of the tabernacle. The grain offering was made of flour (bruised), oil, salt and frankincense representing in turn a crushed and sifted life, the presence of the Spirit, freedom from corruption and fragrance in burning. All these were the features of the sacrifice of Jesus. The drink offering was wine, a further dedication of the offeror's labour. Paul, with humility, thought of the last stages of his life as a drink offering being poured out on greater sacrifices.

The Peace offering has additions of cakes and bread when it was either a thank offering or a vow offering, but without the salt and frankincense. It is called the "meat of the fellowship offering" (Lev 7:15). It is not burned however but eaten by priest and offeror. It adds to the concept of the fellowship offering as a time of mutual feeding.

4. THE SERVANT OF THE LORD *"A GUILT OFFERING"*

Isaiah 50:4-9 NIV; Isaiah 52:13 NIV - 53:12 NIV

Isa 53:3 "He was despised and rejected by men, a man of sorrows, and familiar with suffering. Like one from whom men hide their faces he was despised, and we esteemed him not.
4 Surely he took up our infirmities and carried our sorrows, yet we considered him stricken by God, smitten by him, and afflicted.
5 But he was pierced for our transgressions, he was crushed for our iniquities; the punishment that brought us peace was upon him, and by his wounds we are healed.
6 We all, like sheep, have gone astray, each of us has turned to his own way; and the LORD has laid on him
the iniquity of us all.
Isa 53:10 Yet it was the LORD'S will to crush him and cause him to suffer, and though the LORD makes his life a guilt offering, he will see his offspring and prolong his days."

1. Great Achievement through Great Suffering

Amid the human suffering, carnage and judgement that marked the nations of his own generation, Isaiah pointed forward in his prophecies to the great purposes which God yet had for blessing and restoring humanity. These were nothing less than bringing justice and salvation to the very ends of the earth and embracing both Jew and Gentile alike. The one who was to bring about this worldwide restoration was referred to by Isaiah as the "*servant of the Lord*".

However, the ultimate triumph of this servant in fulfilling these purposes would come only through a very bitter pathway of suffering. The first intimation of this theme of suffering in the Servant Songs is found in Isaiah 49:7 where the prophet, referring to the great things the servant would achieve, speaks nonetheless of "*him who was despised and abhorred by the nation*". This short reference to suffering is taken up at greater length in 50:5ff with the servant himself making a statement that "*I offered my back to those who beat me, my cheeks to those who pulled out my beard; I did not*

hide my face from mocking and spitting". Finally in Isaiah 52:13 –
53:12 we are given a detailed and graphic picture of the servant's
sufferings that makes clear for us not only their extent but also their
purpose.

These passages on suffering are, therefore, quite extensive. They
serve both as an astonishing prophetic validation of the sufferings
of Jesus and as an insight of great clarity concerning the reason for
those sufferings.

2. The Appalling nature of the Suffering

The servant depicted by Isaiah was to have a lifetime of rejection
and despite. He was a *"root out of dry ground"*, having *"nothing of
majesty or personal appearance that was attractive"* (53:2 NIV).
The servant was a person from whom others would turn away, and
they had the lowest possible estimation of him. The leaders of his
day dismissed him as a "rabbi" from Galilee! He was far too
ordinary to be considered of note. He spoke with the wrong accent,
and lacked the schooling of Jerusalem, being merely self-taught.

However the servant was to see even this rejection take a turn for
the worse and become bitter and implacable hatred. Eventually it
would lead to an appalling and vicious death. Isaiah spares no words
in describing the agony of his death. He states starkly that *"his
appearance was so disfigured beyond that of any man and his form
marred beyond that of any man"* (52:14). Such a statement of
comparison – marred and disfigured *beyond any man* – is not loose
exaggeration but sober matter of fact. This was to be the end of the
servant who was *"led like a lamb to the slaughter"* (53:7), was
"smitten", "afflicted" and *"crushed"* (53:4-5), and was *"cut off from
the land of the living"* (53:8) (implying sudden, unnatural death). It
was the hideous end to *"mocking and spitting"*, beatings and torture
(50:6). It was a death as horrific as could be conceived, and it was
the result of *"oppression and judgement"*, in other words gross
miscarriage of justice. In this manner the servant who would bring
so much blessing to the nations would meet his death.

Whilst crucifixion is not specifically mentioned by Isaiah, there
is so much here that is foundational to the crucifixion narrative as
we know it. Certainly all the horrors depicted here belonged to
Roman crucifixion. One of the most suggestive words used in the
descriptions of his suffering and death is the word *"pierced"*. (53:5).
This takes us immediately to the crucifixion story where the piercing

of his side is a matter of great significance to the gospel writers. There are, however, some other very clear pointers to the story: his *"wounds"*, *"the mockery and spitting"*, the *"assignment of a grave with the wicked, and with the rich in his death"* (53:9).

It is in this suffering that we see more perhaps than anywhere the essential humanity of the servant. The bleeding, broken body succumbing to intense pain and death links the servant unmistakably with humanity. The servant actually was to die just as surely as he was actually to be born, and thus as a human being was to fulfil God's purposes.

3. Suffering for a Purpose
Isaiah, therefore, clearly portrays the servant's suffering, and just as clearly he gives the reason for it. This is summed up in the expression, *"The LORD has laid on him the iniquity of us all"* (53:6). Six further statements expand and clarify this expression.

(i) Is. 53:10 NIV says, *"It was the LORD's will to crush him and cause him to suffer"*. This re-iterates the idea that the suffering and death were initiated by God himself: it was The LORD who *"laid on him the iniquity of us all"*. God was personally making the death of his servant consequential by laying sin on him. When *"we considered him stricken by God, smitten by him and afflicted"* (53:4), thinking that God was punishing him for his own sin, we failed to see that there was a much deeper purpose of God in the suffering the servant was bearing.

(ii) The idea that God was laying sin on the servant is further clarified by the expression, *"The LORD makes his life a guilt offering"* (53:10 NIV). God was fashioning the earthly life of his servant so that it became nothing less than an offering for sin. The "guilt offering" was a form of sin offering and we need to understand what happened to such an offering in the temple rituals of Isaiah's time. The sacrificial animal chosen for the guilt offering was brought to the altar, hands were laid on it as sins were confessed, and the sins were transferred symbolically to the animal. It was then killed, its blood poured out around the altar, and its carcass burned, not on the altar for it was a carcass polluted by sin, but outside the camp. The imagery is only too plain. The person's sin is confessed and transferred to the animal through the laying on of hands. The animal is killed, its life (the blood) is poured out making clear that death has taken place, and the carcass is destroyed

by burning, indicating the wrath of God on the sin. The animal took the sin of the offeror and died in his place. We are clearly meant to understand that this is precisely what was to happen to Jesus as the servant of the LORD: our sin was transferred to him and he died for it.

(iii) Is 53:5 NIV spells this truth out more clearly still: *"He was pierced for our transgressions; he was crushed for our iniquities; the punishment that brought us peace was upon him and by his wounds we are healed"*. Here the transference of sin is clearly written. He was not dying for his own sin but for our transgressions and our iniquities. They were to be transferred to him, and because they were transferred he would be pierced and crushed, but we would be spared. Clearly he became a substitute for us, and suffered what we ought to have suffered for our own sin.

(iv) Isaiah 53:5 also makes it plain that the servant *"was punished"*. Sin is seen to bring a punishment of suffering. The punishment was that he was *"crushed"*, *"stricken"*, *"cut off from the land of the living"* and tasted death. The word *"crushed"* is pregnant with meaning. There may have been inner crushing of the body in the process of crucifixion, but the main import would seem to be of the crushing of the inner person, the spirit and heart of the man. Such crushing would be reflected in the imagery of the sacrifice being burnt outside the camp, being banished from a holy place and from the presence of God. It was the image of the final effect of sin for humanity.

(v) Is. 53:9 makes it clear that though he was *"assigned a grave with the wicked"* the servant had *"done no violence, nor was any deceit in his mouth"*. This reminds us that a further important feature of the guilt offering imagery was that the guilt offering was to be without blemish. He was without sin himself so that he might properly bear the sin of others. The implications of this fact of the servant's innocence are enormous for our understanding of the nature of the servant. For what human being born in the normal human process could properly become sin for another human being? For all who were ever born (or would be born) were tainted with sin. By implication, this servant, though he was to have a human birth, could not be born in the normal way, for that would mean he would be tainted with sin like the rest of mankind. The servant could never be born of two human parents like the rest of mankind. Obviously

there would be some radically different factor in the birth of the servant. The factor could only be a virgin birth.

(vi) Is. 53:12 tells us that *"he poured out his life unto death"*. Clearly on account of his innocence he had no need to suffer death for sin, and could have walked away from such an experience. His innocence, which made it possible for him to be a victim, meant also that his sacrifice would be a willing gesture. He could not be compelled to make himself a sacrifice, but the purpose and desire of his Father, which he shared, was that he should take the *"body prepared for him"* and replace the ineffective sin offerings of the Temple ritual with his own body (see Heb. 10:5-7). Thus Isaiah in recording that the servant *"poured out his life unto death"* speaks clearly of the fact that Jesus himself made the sacrifice willingly and of his own volition.

3. Beyond the Suffering

There is nothing more characteristic of the prophetic writings than the fact that they do not leave us at the point of death and judgement, and devoid of hope. They point to restoration. Certainly the Servant Song of Isaiah 53 does not leave the servant in death and judgement. Two great statements stand out toward the end of the message which speak of resurrection: *"he will see his offspring and prolong his day"* (53:10 NIV) and *"after the suffering of his soul he will see the light of life and be satisfied"* (53:11). They are, no doubt, the statements that enabled Jesus to embrace the suffering, and to *"endure the cross, scorning its shame"* (Heb. 12:2 NIV). He knew of the glory beyond the cross. He knew the prophetic word about his death.

Beyond the resurrection statements lies a great ascension statement: *"I will give him a portion among the great, and he will divide the spoils with the strong"* (53:12). As Paul the apostle, referring to Jesus, was later to express it: *"having disarmed the powers and authorities, he made a public spectacle of them, triumphing over them by the cross"* (Col: 2:15 NIV). The victory of the cross and the spoils of victory were received as the servant was made to sit at his Father's right hand.

Following the suffering would come satisfaction for the servant (53:11). The satisfaction would come from the fact that he would make many "just" as they came to know and accept what he had done for them in bearing their iniquities. As Isaiah puts it, *"by his knowledge my righteous servant will justify many, and he will bear*

their iniquities". It was in this way that the servant would start his great worldwide work of bringing justice to the nations, and restoring the Jewish nation. There could be no justice or righteousness without forgiveness of sin and a radical inner change of humanity. This could only be accomplished through a death for sin. There was no other way and there could never have been success in the servant's commission without his suffering.

5. JESUS OUR GREAT HIGH PRIEST

"We have a great high priest who has gone through the heavens, Jesus the Son of God" Heb. 4:14 NIV

The Letter to the Hebrews stands out as the major New Testament example of the detailed way in which the evangelists and apologists of the early church used the Old Testament to demonstrate that Jesus truly was the Messiah. In this they were following the approach which Jesus adopted with his disciples after his resurrection, when he expounded to them *"all the things written in the Law and the Prophets concerning himself"* (Lk 24:27 NIV). Paul also adopted this approach, as, for example, in his work at Thessalonica where he *"went into the Synagogue and on three Sabbath days reasoned with them (the Jews) from the Scriptures, explaining and proving that Christ had to suffer and rise from the dead"* (Acts 17:2-3 NIV). It was an approach that had immediate and particular relevance, of course, to Jews, and Hebrews is clearly written for Jews. These were Jews who had embraced Jesus as the Messiah, but who for one reason or another were in danger of turning back from their faith, and needed their faith under girding. The author of Hebrews methodically and biblically shows them how superior Jesus was to the leading persons and institutions of the old Jewish faith, that is to say how superior he was to angels, Moses, Abraham, Joshua and the Tabernacle with its High Priesthood, sacrifices and covenant. It is with the exposition of the High Priesthood and the Tabernacle that this pamphlet is concerned.

The Tabernacle and the Letter to the Hebrews

All Jews would naturally have been conversant with the structure and arrangement of the Tabernacle and with the duties of its priesthood. God had ordered Moses to construct the Tabernacle as a moveable place of worship which the Israelites were to take with them throughout their wilderness wanderings. It became the basis in all its essential details and arrangement for the permanent Temple built by Solomon and later, in the time of Jesus, rebuilt by Herod. God strictly warned Moses to make it exactly as he was told, for its structure and its priesthood were intended from the very first to enshrine important truth for the Israelites and to point to an ultimate spiritual fulfilment.

The Tabernacle was really a very simple structure (see diagram), and is sketched out in some detail in Hebrews 9:1-10. The Tabernacle area was enclosed by a screen of curtains, and divided into three distinct parts. There was an open outer court in which was situated a great brazen altar where the sacrificial animals were to be offered. There was also a covered section divided into two parts, the first of which was accessible from the outer court and called the "Holy Place", and the second part accessible only from the "Holy Place" and called the "Most Holy Place". In the "Most Holy Place" was the Ark of the Covenant which contained the ten commandments of God and which was covered with a Mercy Seat guarded by two carved Cherubim. God "dwelt" in the Most Holy Place by his "inner presence", and no one was allowed into that Most Holy Place on pain of death. The only exception was the High Priest who was allowed into it once a year on the Day of Atonement. The adjacent Holy Place represented the "outer presence" of God and housed the Altar of Incense, representing the prayers of the saints, a candlestick representing the Light of God, and a table of Showbread representing the provision of God. Only selected priests were allowed into the Holy Place to attend to these three symbols of the "outer presence" of God. In the outer court sacrifices of numerous kinds were held daily on the altar– sin offerings, burnt offerings, thank offerings, peace offerings etc, all of which were performed by Levitical priests. These were the sacrifices through which alone it was possible to gain access to the two Holy Places and to the presence of God. **The whole scheme was designed to represent the process by which humanity could come into the**

presence of God, or, better, by which the presence of a holy God would come close to humanity.

This was the basic picture that forms the background to chapters 4 to 10. The main estimate of the Temple/Tabernacle as the author of Hebrews saw it in his day, however, was that it revealed not "access" but, on the contrary, a restriction of access to God: *"The Holy Spirit was showing by this that the way into the Most Holy Place had not yet been disclosed as long as the first tabernacle was standing"* (Heb. 9:4 NIV). What he meant was that though the Tabernacle was certainly a picture of how access to God could be made, the reality was that the animal sacrifices never prevailed for real forgiveness, and the High Priest was never able to open the Most Holy Place permanently. Direct access to God, therefore, actually remained closed. What the Tabernacle and its priesthood represented was only a shadow of the real thing: *"They (the priests) serve at a sanctuary that is a copy and a shadow of what is in heaven"* (Heb. 8:5 NIV). The object of the author of Hebrews was to show that in Jesus, the new and heavenly High Priest, the real thing had arrived – in Jesus full access to God had been obtained once and for all through a new sacrifice that was fully adequate. The shadow gave way to reality.

It was this kind of thinking of which Hebrews was such a conspicuous example, that brought to the Christian church the recognition that the Temple and its sacrifices had had their day, and left the church with an indelible image of the High Priesthood of Jesus in heavenly places: *"we have a great high priest who has gone through the heavens, Jesus the Son of God"* (Heb. 4:14).

The High Priesthood

It is with the High Priest that Hebrews is particularly concerned. It is the High Priest who typifies Jesus. This was not simply in the fact that he is able to *"sympathize with our weakness"* and understand us (Heb. 4:15 NIV), but more significantly in the fact that it was the High Priest alone who could make atonement for the sin of the whole people and enter the inner sanctuary. He alone could meet with God at the throne of grace and at the mercy seat. It was important to demonstrate to the Jews that they needed to see Jesus as the one who perfectly fulfilled this High Priestly role. He was the one to whom every previous earthly High Priest pointed. It was important also that they saw that the Most Holy Place which Jesus

entered was a heavenly sanctuary, the true fulfilment of the Tabernacle, and that as a result of his resurrection and ascension he dwelt there permanently, eternally alive to make intercession.

Hebrews anticipates an objection that might be raised by a Jew, namely that Jesus did not come of the high priestly line of Aaron. Lineage was important to the Jews. The author takes hold of a crucial Messianic psalm which indicated that, as priest, the Messiah would come from a different line. Psalm 110 was thoroughly recognized as Messianic by the Jews, and that psalm stated categorically, *"The Lord has sworn and will not change his mind, 'You are a priest for ever in the order of Melchizedek'"* (Ps110:5). In its brevity, sheer clarity and authority it is, on any reckoning, an astonishing prophetic word . It refers back to a very brief episode in Genesis 14:18-20, and it delineates conclusively, and in majestic manner, a type of priesthood infinitely greater than Aaron's Levitical priesthood. Hebrews expounds the significance of this lineage from Melchizedek at length in Chapter 7, for its significance is not restricted simply to explaining why Jesus was not of Aaron's line.

The very name, Melchizedek, is significant for it means "King of Righteousness" (Heb. 7:1ff NIV). Melchizedek was also the ruler or king of Salem, and "Salem" means peace, so making him "King of Peace". King of Righteousness and Peace, therefore, by name and rank, he was, as Hebrews also points out, at the same time "Priest of God Most High" (7:1). He was in fact both King and Priest, and was a true symbolic figure of the great Messianic Priest/King who was to come. It was of this order of priesthood that Jesus came. There are, however, further implications to be seen in the nature of the Melchizedek order of priesthood which Hebrews unfolds. Melchizedek was the priest to whom even Abraham, the founder of the Jewish race, paid tithes (Heb. 7:4), and indeed from whom even Abraham received a blessing. There was, therefore, a majesty and an authority in this Priest/King to which Abraham (and, in Abraham, the whole Jewish race, including Aaron,) dutifully bowed. He stands towering in his authority over the nation from its very inception, pointing to the spiritual Priest/King to come.

Perhaps the most astonishing implication that Hebrews sees in this priesthood derives from the fact that no genealogy of Melchizedek is presented in Genesis. From this fact Hebrews draws the following conclusion: *"Without genealogy, without beginning of*

days or end of life, like the Son of God he remains a priest for ever." (Heb. 7:3 NIV). Thus Jesus, fulfilling the fact that Melchizedek had no mention of forebears, *"became a priest not on the basis of a regulation as to his ancestry, but on the basis of the power of an indestructible life"* (Heb. 7:16 NIV). Jesus *"has a permanent priesthood"* (7:24), and *"Therefore he is able to save completely those who come to God through him, because he always lives to intercede for them"* (7:25). There is a divinity in his priesthood.

The High Priest and his Sacrifices

The sacrifices on the Day of Atonement, for which the High Priest personally was responsible, were comprehensive. The object of the sacrifices was that *"atonement is to be made once a year for all the sins of the Israelites"* (Lev. 16:34 NIV). On that day the High Priest entered twice into the Most Holy Place. On the first occasion he entered with the blood of a bull offered as a sin offering for his own sins, and on the second occasion he entered with the blood of a goat offered as a sin offering for the whole Israelite community. As he did so no other Israelite was allowed in the Holy Places. Even he, however, was not allowed to see the mercy seat, it being expressly covered by the smoke from the incense altar; he simply sprinkled the blood on it and before it. Having sprinkled the blood on the inner sanctuary, the High Priest sprinkled it on the altar of sacrifice. After this he confessed the sins of the people over a second goat and released it into the wilderness to carry away the people's sins (the "scapegoat"). Finally he offered burnt offerings, indicating total commitment, for himself and for the people. So he *"made atonement"* for himself, the people and the Holy Place.

Hebrews stresses that all these sacrifices were subsumed in one infinitely greater sacrifice, the body of Jesus himself: *"he entered the Most Holy Place once for all by his own blood"* (Heb. 9:12), that is to say, *"the blood of the Messiah who through the eternal Spirit offered himself unblemished to God"* (Heb. 9:14 NIV). The only sacrifice not subsumed was Aaron's sacrifice for his own sin, for Jesus was *"unblemished"*, and this fact Hebrews makes plain. It was a once for all sacrifice (9:28), and Jesus, our High Priest remains within the heavenly and true sanctuary pleading our cause with his own blood, thereby securing full, continuous and open access to the throne of God for all who come through him.

The High Priest and the New Covenant

The author of Hebrews has yet another perspective. He reminds us that the tabernacle expressed regulations appropriate for the first covenant God had made with his people, the Mosaic covenant: *"Now the first covenant had regulations for worship and also an earthly sanctuary"* (Heb 9:1 NIV). He goes on from there to establish the fact that with the superseding of the earthly sanctuary by the heavenly sanctuary, there also came the superseding of the first covenant by the inauguration of the new covenant. Our new eternal High Priest, Jesus, is, therefore, the mediator of the New Covenant.

Once again the author of Hebrews draws on Old Testament scripture to show that such a new covenant had been prophesied, quoting from Jeremiah 31:33-34 NIV. *"This is the covenant I will make with them after that time, says the Lord. I will put my laws in their hearts and I will write them on their minds"*. This new covenant promise of God was that he would give those who came to him through the Great High Priest a heart on which there was indelibly written a deep desire for and understanding of his laws. Though not specifically mentioned in Hebrews, the agent of this was to be none less than the Holy Spirit himself, a truth that becomes evident in the parallel passage on the New Covenant in Ezekiel 36:24. Thus Jesus becomes the High Priest of the new Covenant of the Spirit.

Hebrews, therefore, not only profoundly shapes our understanding of Jesus' role in his ascended ministry, but profoundly shapes it by Old Testament exposition. It underlines just how crucial Old Testament understanding is for our faith.

THE MEANING OF THE CRUCIFIXION

CONTENTS

Introduction

It is not without reason that the cross has always been the acknowledged sign of the Christian faith. Every aspect of that faith finds its source in the death of Jesus; the incarnation itself was needed in order for such a death to take place; Jesus' resurrection (and ours) came out of God's acceptance of the sacrifice of Calvary; it is due to the forgiveness and cleansing that came from Christ's death that the Spirit of God is now able to indwell believers and empower them for a holy life; our hope in the priceless promise of eternal life rests on the fact that he was willing to pay the penalty of our sins. All roads come to and lead from the cross.

The crucifixion speaks of the depth of God's love for us in a way that nothing else can, for the propitiatory sacrifice of Jesus, purposed and provided by God himself, has removed the wrath and judgement of a Holy God. The crucifixion also speaks to us of the depth of

Jesus' own love for us and it is in that love that we find the source of his ready obedience to the Father's will. It is at the cross that the awesome righteous judgement of a holy God and the love exemplified in the grace of God are seen together acting on our behalf.

It is critically important that we adhere to the biblical presentation of the cross as we find it, and do not allow any secular or liberalised concepts to modify it. That is the purpose of this short summary. The scripture presents a clear picture of Jesus bearing our sin and our punishment for sin in his own body as a substitutionary sacrifice of atonement. His death was a great example of obedience, but it was more than just exemplary. It served a definite purpose in that it enabled a holy righteous God to forgive us our sins and at the same time do so in a manner which vindicated his own righteousness.

1. THE DEATH OF JESUS IN THE GOSPELS

The Witness of John the Baptist

The first act of Jesus when he began his ministry was to seek out John the Baptist by the river Jordan. His intention was that John should baptise him. But John objected. John was a prophet, and it is no surprise therefore that on meeting Jesus he should instantly in his prophetic spirit have recognised him as the "*Greater One who is to come*", about whom he had been preaching. When Jesus asked for baptism, John said it was Jesus who should baptise him (Matt. 3:14). John proclaimed a baptism of repentance and he knew that Jesus did not need to repent; there was no sin in him. Jesus, however, insisted on being baptised and explained why; it was "*to fulfil all righteousness*". What did that mean? It meant that his baptism was an act of identification with those who did need to repent; he wanted to stand in the water with them and allow himself to be "*numbered with the transgressors*" (Is. 53:12 NIV). Unless that identification took place, God's plan to bring righteousness in full measure to people could not happen, and such identification was only properly fulfilled when Jesus took the place of sinners on the cross.

On another occasion, possibly just before Jesus' baptism, John the Baptist saw Jesus *"coming toward him"* and said to his followers, *"Behold the Lamb of God who takes away the sin of the world"*. The next day he repeated the expression *"Behold the Lamb of God"* (Jn. 1:29, 35 NIV). This was an extraordinary prophetic utterance by John. The expression "Lamb of God" can only refer to a sacrificial lamb, whether the Passover Lamb or some other sin bearing sacrifice. That much is clear from the expression *"who takes away the sin of the world"*. The prophetic words indicated that Jesus would take away sin and do so by being himself a sin offering of some sort. The Cross was to be the earthly fulfilment of those prophetic words.

These early pointers to Jesus' death are very important. It would be absurd to think that John's words took him by surprise and that Jesus himself was ignorant of his destiny as the sacrificial lamb for sin. On the contrary his insistence on being baptised against John's reluctance showed his commitment to being the sacrificial lamb and identifying with sinners. It certainly didn't show that Jesus was confused about whether he needed to be baptised. He knew better than John that he was innocent of sin, and that his innocence was the very thing that could make him the "Lamb of God". Thus Jesus, at the very beginning of his ministry, embraced the fact that his life would finish as a sacrifice for sin, and he dedicated himself to that end. When this revelation first came to Jesus it is impossible to say. But we know that he was of course a "Prophet" in his own right, and, perhaps even more significantly, he was, at the age of thirty, hugely aware of the prophetic scriptures and what they had to say about the death of the Servant Messiah. He knew he was born to die. He would have wrestled with this thought for some considerable time before he came to John. John's ministry was the moment of challenge for him to explicitly embrace his destiny, and he gave himself to his ministry in the full knowledge of an appalling death.

Early Ministry

Jesus was not long into his ministry before he was giving veiled indications of his death. Speaking to John the Baptist's disciples about fasting he told them that the proper time for fasting would be when the *"bridegroom was taken away from them"* (Matt 9:15). John had himself called Jesus the *"bridegroom"* (Jn. 3:29), so the application was obvious. But the expression *"taken away"* in reference to a bridegroom was very

unusual and has clear connotations of a violent happening. Such indications were not made simply to the disciples, however. Jesus made a very pointed reply to the Pharisees who early on wanted to know his authority for cleansing the Temple. He said he would give them a sign of his authority, namely *"Destroy this temple and in three days I will raise it up"* (Jn. 2:29). He was, of course, speaking of his own body and his death and resurrection – and his disciples would recall it vividly after those events had taken place. Again, in the conversation with the Pharisee Nicodemus, Jesus said, *"Just as Moses lifted up the snake in the wilderness, so the Son of Man must be lifted up, that everyone who believes may have eternal life"* (Jn. 3:14). Sometime later, and once more in conversation with Jewish religious leaders who were challenging his claims, he said, *"When you have lifted up the Son of man then you will know that I am he ..."* (Jn. 8:21). The phrase *"lifted up"* resonates loudly with the cross. Clearly his death (and resurrection) never left his mind and such allusions could have been numerous.

The Transfiguration
As far as his own disciples were concerned there were at least three times during his ministry when he spoke to them plainly and directly about his death. One of these was immediately before the transfiguration and the other two shortly afterwards. This is not surprising since the transfiguration itself was a turning point in his ministry and marked the time when he finally set his face to go to Jerusalem and meet his death. Luke's gospel tells us that when Jesus met with Moses and Elijah on the mount they spoke of his coming "departure" or death. We do not know what was said at that point, but we do know that on those three occasions surrounding the transfiguration Jesus spoke in detail about what would happen to him. On the first occasion he told them, *"he must suffer, be rejected by the religious leaders and be handed over to the Gentiles who will mock him, spit on him, flog him and kill him"* Mk. 10:33ff NIV. He also added, *"Three days later he will arise"*. The other two occasions repeated (as though for emphasis) what he had said. But the disciples simply could not or would not grasp what he was saying, and on the first occasion Peter even roundly challenged Jesus, only to earn himself a sharp rebuke.

There were other more oblique comments about his death which the disciples heard (e.g. *"I am the good shepherd. The good shepherd*

lays down his life for the sheep"). But the main feature of his remarks lay in simply stating the fact that he was to suffer in his death. It was one way of disarming his disciples of any idea of a worldly triumphal Messiah. There was also an increasing sense of compulsion about his coming death, and especially after the transfiguration; Jesus' comment that *"he must suffer"* indicates there was a real sense that he had to do this, that there was a deep inner compulsion and that there was a definite purpose in his death. He must present himself for death. But apart from one notable exception he did not at this point speak out about the purpose of his death. That exception was very significant: speaking after the transfiguration he said to his disciples *"the Son of man did not come to be served but to serve, and to give his life a ransom for many"* (Mk. 10;45). His death was not purposeless but would pay the price of freedom for many. He did not enlarge on the kind of freedom he had in mind, however. At the beginning of his final Passover feast, when being sought by the Gentiles, he would volunteer the remark that *"a corn of wheat does not bear fruit unless it falls into the ground and dies, but if does die it bears much fruit"* (Jn. 12:24 NIV). His death would produce a harvest, but he once again did not specify what sort of harvest.

From the Last Supper to the Cross
It is when we come to Jesus' last supper with his disciples that the purpose of his death is much more openly and clearly expressed: he would die for the forgiveness of sins. Matthew records the words of Jesus as he gave the cup to his disciples during that supper; *"This is my blood of the new covenant which is poured out for many for the forgiveness of sins"*. (Matt. 26:28 NIV). The purpose of his death was now plain. It was for the forgiveness of sins. The blood he speaks of is *"poured out blood"*, spilt blood, blood that speaks of death. It was sacrificial blood, therefore. Its immediate background was, of course, to be found in the sacrifice of the Passover lambs. Whether or not Jesus was crucified at the actual time of the sacrifice of the Passover lambs (as some suppose) the symbolism is clear. As Paul was to write later, *"Christ our Passover is sacrificed for us"*. Here was John the Baptist's cry of *"Behold the lamb of God"* very precisely fulfilled. The sacrifice of the Passover lambs and the putting of their blood on the Israel's doorposts had delivered the Israelites' from the most devastating judgement that God visited on

the Egyptians, namely the death of their firstborn. It was such a deliverance that was the necessary seal of the new covenant.

How much the disciples understood Jesus' actions and words at the supper it is difficult to say, but Jesus was adamant about them repeating the meal he had instituted. His words were direct; *"do this in remembrance of me"*. Here in simple symbol was the essence of the new covenant; he died that our sins might be forgiven. Jesus did not expand further on the nature of his death as he went on to give his lengthy teaching during the last supper, but John's gospel records that he did say a great deal about the coming of the Holy Spirit, for the gift of the Holy Spirit would be fundamental to the new covenant which his blood established. He wanted them to know that those for whom his sacrifice brought forgiveness would also experience a whole new inner dynamic toward holiness planted within them by the presence of the Holy Spirit.

Gethsemane

Supper having ended, Jesus made for the Garden of Gethsemane to pray. During his ministry he had spoken about his coming death and had doubtless struggled with the prospect. At one point he had said, *"I have a baptism to undergo, and what constraint I am under until it is completed"*, (Lk: 12:50). But now the final struggle had come and he *"began to be deeply distressed and troubled"*. Luke, the medical physician, speaks knowledgeably of him *"being in anguish"* and *"sweating drops of blood"*. Jesus himself cried out, *"My soul is overwhelmed with sorrow to the point of dying."* He had reached the point of human extremity and *"an angel came to strengthen him"*. All the time his prayer was, *"My Father, if it be possible let this cup be taken from me"*. The level of anguish depicted here was clearly much higher than that of simply facing death, even if it was by crucifixion. We cannot think of Jesus as lacking in the fortitude that has characterised many others in the face of such painful death. The "agony in the Garden" was no ordinary agony. The explanation for it is best found in the words from Jesus' own lips, *"if it be possible let this cup be taken from me"*. What was that cup? Biblically the most obvious application is that of the *"cup of wrath"* which God pours out on sin. That application here is in perfect harmony with his last supper statement when he presented himself as "the lamb of God" whose blood was shed for the forgiveness of sin, the sacrificial lamb which at the very first

Passover took the full brunt of the wrath of God on behalf of the early Israelites. Jesus knew himself to be facing not just death but the wrath and judgement of God in that death. No one knew more clearly what the wrath of God meant than Jesus himself. Bearing that wrath was the central fact of the crucifixion.

The Crucifixion

When Matthew and Mark go on to describe the actual crucifixion they go straight to the scene which speaks most clearly of what is was that Jesus dreaded. They speak of the darkness which fell over the whole land for the final three hours and the great and startling cry which Jesus uttered toward the end of that time, "*My God, my God, why have you forsaken me*". For them this was the most important moment in the crucifixion; it speaks of the agony of forsakenness. Any attempts to soften the implications of this cry are misguided; this is not Jesus losing his mental grasp under the delirium of being crucified. He had been genuinely forsaken; God had withdrawn his presence from Him and Jesus knew it. Had it been a sense of temporary forsakenness it might have been bearable, but the real bitterness of the forsakenness was found in the feeling that it was permanent. With the withdrawal of God's presence Jesus also lost his spiritual grasp of the fact that it was only temporary. He could no longer count on the truth that he would eventually "*see the light of life and be satisfied*" (Isaiah 53:11). The fact was that when the Father withdrew his presence from Him, so also the Spirit of God and His illumination withdrew. Jesus was experiencing the ultimate of God's wrath – the loss of God's presence and love (not imagined, but real). Matthew and Mark do not alleviate the scene. They leave it there in all its darkness, as though whatever else we might know of the cross this was the essential factor to grasp. It was left to Luke and John to remind us that Jesus, shortly after his great dereliction cry, released yet another cry, "*It is finished*" and finally, "*Father into your hands I commend my spirit*". These two cries need to be taken together. The final cry is addressed to His Father and indicates that fellowship was restored as he died. The cry of "*it is finished*" can only refer to the moment when that fellowship which he had lost was restored and when he knew the "sacrifice" had been accepted.

See NOTE A.

2. THE EARLY CHURCH and the PREACHING OF THE CROSS

The Teaching of the Resurrected Jesus

Luke's gospel gives us an enlightening picture of the period between the death of Jesus and his ascension. He has a vivid focus on the resurrected Jesus. He stresses the fact that Jesus was actually very much alive in bodily form. He was recognisable, he could eat, he was "tangible", he could speak and he spent time with his disciples. For Luke this was no "spiritual" or mere "inner visionary" resurrection. It was real, bodily and active. He was at work with his disciples, teaching and enlightening them. His disciples had witnessed both the crucifixion and the resurrection, and they were now open to understanding the cross in a way that they could not have been before. His resurrection teaching was in fact vital for their proper understanding and proclamation of his death, and what they learned was of the utmost importance.

This ministry of teaching began on the very first day of his resurrection and lasted through forty days until Jesus' ascension. It was thorough. On that very first day he explained from all the Old Testament Scriptures why it was that the Messiah had to die. He did this first for the two disciples on the Emmaus road (Lk 24:13ff) and later for the disciples who met together in the Upper Room (Lk 24:36ff). Doubtless he continued the teaching in the days that followed until they had thoroughly grasped it. They would have had the extraordinary opportunity of asking him questions and discussing issues. This means that the gospel that the apostles went on to proclaim after Pentecost was fundamentally and firmly rooted in nothing less than the teaching of Jesus himself. It was not the creation of his disciples or the early church or of Paul. We have, therefore, a gospel that has the highest authentication.

What is of great significance is the fact that it was on the Old Testament Scriptures that Jesus grounded his teaching about the need and purpose of his death. Here was a textbook "par excellence" ready to hand and profoundly and prophetically enlightening and stimulating. When he had ascended that textbook would remain with the disciples and become a ready tool for them in their own teaching

and personal refreshing. In doing this Jesus was, of course, simply passing on to his disciples a process of learning and understanding that he himself had gone through in his own life and ministry. Taught by the Spirit he drank deeply from the Scriptures right from his younger "hidden years"; Luke depicts him at the age of thirteen *"about his Father's business"* and learning in the Temple. From the moment he started his ministry he was already well aware that he had come as a *"the lamb of God"* and was to be *"numbered with the transgressors"*. So deeply in fact were the Scriptures embedded in his own consciousness that even in his moment of dereliction his cry took the form of the Psalmist's *"My God, why, have you forsaken me?"* We are on very good ground, therefore, whenever we look for the purpose of Jesus' death in the Old Testament.

Peter's Preaching
When Peter, the predominant spokesman in the very early days of the church, preached on the Day of Pentecost, he made two things very clear about the death of Jesus. First, it was no accident but had happened *"by God's deliberate plan and foreknowledge"* (Acts 2:23). Jesus' teaching had showed Peter just how much the Old Testament had pre-figured the death of Jesus and was God's purpose from the start. Second he preached that Jesus was the Messiah, risen from the dead by the power of God, and was calling for people to *"repent and be baptised in his name for the forgiveness of sins"* (Acts 2:38). The resurrected Jesus had insisted on the baptism of believers when he was giving his instructions to his disciples, and baptism spelt out the death of Jesus and his forgiveness. For Peter the death of Jesus was in essence a *"deliberate plan"* for the *"forgiveness of sins"*.

At Pentecost Peter did not enlarge on the actual sacrificial nature of the death of Jesus, and Luke reporting his other preaching sticks simply and primarily to the fact that the death of Jesus was for the forgiveness of sins. However, he does recount one story at length which has a very important bearing on the nature of Jesus' sacrifice: the conversion of the Ethiopian eunuch (Acts 8:26 ff). He records the Ethiopian, an official of substance, travelling in his chariot and reading from Isaiah 53:7-8 the words, *"He was led like a sheep to the slaughter ....."* Hearing this, Philip the Evangelist ran alongside and asked him if he understood the passage. Invited by the Ethiopian to explain what it meant, Philip immediately applied it to Jesus. The

Ethiopian responded and was baptised there and then. Luke does not tell us much of what would have been quite a lengthy conversation, but it must have involved an exposition of both the Suffering Servant passage in Isaiah 52:13-54:12 and of the meaning and need of baptism. We do not need any clearer proof than this of the fact that the Isaiah passage about the Lord would have been part of the early church's understanding of the meaning of the Cross. It is one of the most lucid of the prophecies of the meaning of Jesus' death. In verse after verse it spells out with unsurpassed clarity exactly what Jesus accomplished on the cross:

"He was pierced for our transgressions ....(53:5 NIV)
The punishment that brought us peace was on him ...(53:5 NIV)
The Lord has laid on Him the iniquity of us all. (53:6 NIV)"

What this scripture implies is that Jesus did not simply identify with us and suffer mere exposure to sin, but that he bore the penalty and punishment of all our sins in a substitutionary sacrifice. His death was a sin offering. It was this prospect of experiencing the judgement of God on sin that was the real cause of the agony in Gethsemane. It was this that gives full meaning to the great anguish of being *"forsaken"* as he hung on the cross. Jesus had walked with the knowledge of this scripture throughout his ministry, he had fulfilled it, and without any doubt it would have been prominent in his resurrection teaching of the disciples. (See NOTE B)

Peter's First Letter
Fortunately Luke's sparse account of Peter's preaching and understanding of the cross can be filled out from Peter's own writing, particularly from his first letter. This letter is, of course, very much later than the early days of that first Pentecost, but there is every reason to think that what he wrote in the letter was substantially what he had learned from Jesus in his resurrection teaching, especially since his concepts are utterly based in Old Testament Scripture. Peter's "gospel" did not develope or change over the years. He makes three striking comments on the cross:

"You have been chosen ...... to be obedient to
Jesus Christ and sprinkled with his blood"

1 Pet. 1:2 NIV
"You were redeemed not with corruptible things ...

but with the precious blood as of a lamb without
blemish or without spot, even the blood of Christ."
1 Pet. 1:17-18 NIV

"He himself bore our sins in his own body on the tree,
so that we might die to sins and live for righteousness
………… by his wounds you have been healed".
1 Pet. 2:22 NIV

These passages all embody Old Testament concepts belonging to sacrificial offerings. The first speaks of the covenant blood from Jesus' sacrifice sealing the New Covenant (which is precisely the way in which Jesus described the "cup" which he instituted at the last supper); the second speaks of our being bought out of slavery (of sin) by the death of Jesus as a spotless lamb. The third speaks of Jesus "*bearing*" (that is taking on himself the full consequences) of our sins as he died under the curse of God (Ex. 24). These are very strong and clear statements that Jesus died a sacrificial death for our sin, in which he paid to the full the penalty of sin. It was in other words a "sin offering".

John's First Letter

Though Peter was the foremost speaker in the early church, his close companion was the apostle John. Luke records nothing of John's preaching in Acts, but we do have three of John's letters, also written much later in life. Often called "the Apostle of Love" he writes in his first letter,

"This is love, not that we loved God but that he loved us
and sent his Son as a propitiation (atoning sacrifice) for our sin"
1 Jn. 4:10 NIV

This is one of the most important statements on the crucifixion. John sees the death of Jesus primarily as an act of love on God's part, and, at the same time, a "*propitiation*" of wrath. He puts together two things which many in our modern age find impossible to reconcile: love and wrath. "Propitiation" is a word associated with averting wrath, in this case God's wrath. For many a God of love cannot be a God of wrath and they prefer the alternative expression "*atoning sacrifice*" in an attempt to soften the meaning, and leave room for an interpretation which does not necessarily countenance any wrath

on God's part. John's meaning, however, is that it is in providing a sacrifice which takes the punishment of the wrath of God that God shows the true depth of his love. It is extremely difficult to imagine that the Jews of Jesus' generation who were so steeped in the Old Testament would shy away from the concept of the wrath of God as the punishment against sin. The wrath of God was plain to see in book after book of the Old Testament. It was not difficult for them to accept that the wrath of God, which was always directed at sin, was directed at Jesus in his death as a sin offering; he bore the wrath, the judgement and the penalty of sin (death, physical and spiritual) for us. Paul, as we shall see, has more to teach us about this fundamental perspective.

3. PAUL THE APOSTLE AND THE CRUCIFIXION

Paul the Apostle was not among those early apostles who heard the resurrected Jesus explaining in person from the Old Testament Scriptures the reason for his death. In fact Paul was the great persecutor of the early church. It was only after his conversion on the Damascus road, when he met Jesus the divine Son of God risen from the dead that he had to come to terms with a crucified Messiah. As their persecutor undoubtedly he would have been aware of what the early Christian preachers were saying about Jesus' death, and would have known something of their biblical perspective. But he was really indebted to the early church for a full understanding of the cross, a fact he made clear in writing to the Corinthians; *"For what I received I passed on to you as of first importance that Christ died for us according to the Scriptures"* (1Cor.15:3 NIV). So Paul received from the church and its apostles a biblically based understanding of the purpose of the cross in the direct tradition of Jesus' teaching. What had been to him the insurmountable offence of worshipping a crucified criminal now became the very centre of his faith. He had nothing essentially to add to that apostolic tradition. But in drawing out the full implications of Christ's death in his letters and in his preaching of the gospel, he added immensely to our grasp of what it meant.

The Letter to the Romans

In his letter to the Romans he lays out this "gospel" of Christ's death in depth. He begins (chapters 1 to 3) by showing the desperate plight of humanity. He affirms first that *"God's wrath is revealed against all unrighteousness of men"* (1:18 NIV), and he then goes on to demonstrate that all human beings are guilty of this *"unrighteousness"* and are therefore under the wrath of God: *"There is none righteous, no not one"* (3:10 NIV), *"all have sinned and fall short of the glory of God"* (3:23 NIV). This is true both of the Gentile world and of the Jewish world. The Gentile world had rejected the witness of the creation to the fact of a Creator God, and had deliberately given itself over to idolatry and the lusts of the flesh. The Jewish world, though having the Law of God through Moses, had been unable to keep its requirements and had indulged in the same lusts as the Gentiles. The wrath of God was on both Jew and Gentile, and that meant God had *"given them over"* to their lusts and to the dire consequences of those lusts. There was no way in which humanity could present itself as righteous or escape the wrath of a holy God. Paul saw all human beings as *"slaves to sin"*, and the wages of sin was death. Paul makes precisely the same point as he proclaims the gospel in his letter to the Galatians, *"But the Scripture declares that the whole world is a prisoner of sin"* (Gal 3:22 NIV). There was no way out for humanity on its own.

Paul's great discovery, however, was that in the Christ that he had met on the Damascus road God had provided a way for people to be declared righteous and to be justified before God. He summed the matter up in a few precise words:

"All are justified freely by his (God's) grace through
the redemption that came by Jesus Christ.
God presented Christ as a propitiation (an atoning sacrifice)
through the shedding of his blood – to be received by faith". (3:24-25
NIV)

God himself, Paul writes, provided a sacrifice that would atone for sin, and the benefits of that sacrifice could be received by faith in the one who made the sacrifice - Jesus. What man could never achieve, God by his grace had achieved in the death of his Son. This was the gospel that Paul gloried in, and he vigorously defended it against all attempts to dilute it (cf. esp. Letter to the Galatians). He

put aside all "worldly wisdom" in the proclamation of this gospel, writing to the Corinthians, *"I resolved to know nothing while I was with you except Jesus Christ and him crucified"* (1 Cor. 2:2 NIV). This gospel was not the fruit of any earthly intellectual thinking, but was the outcome of divine revelation.

Fundamental to Paul's statements about the cross is the reality of the *"wrath of God"*. Paul would have been appalled at the idea so common in our own era that "wrath" was a concept irreconcilable with the idea of a God of love. For him it is precisely this wrath of God that we are saved from, and it is in a salvation from such wrath that Paul found the very depths of the love of God. At great cost God had taken the initiative in reconciling those who through sin were at enmity with him, and of redeeming (buying back) those who were slaves to sin and whose end could only be death. In talking about wrath Paul is not describing "pagan" wrath, which is fickle, selfish, impetuous or tormenting. He is speaking of the anger of a holy God solely directed against the destructive power of sin and evil. It is the anger that ultimately bars from his Presence those who choose to follow evil. For Paul God's wrath is not, as some have suggested, an impersonal force built into the world in which we live but a wrath that is an active part of God's holiness. He makes all this clear:

"God demonstrates his own love for us in this;
while we were yet sinners Christ died for us."
"Since we have been justified by his blood how much
more shall we be saved from God's wrath through him."
Rom 5:8-9 NIV

Paul also makes it clear that the sacrifice of propitiation in which Jesus suffered the wrath of God on our behalf demonstrated the righteous nature of God. That *"righteousness of God"* could not overlook our sin; God could not forgive simply because he is a "forgiving God". It was far too serious a matter for that. A penalty for sin had been decreed, and it must be paid or justice had not been done. Man must pay the penalty of his sin or else a sinless substitute must pay it if man was to be justly forgiven. The man, Christ Jesus, "the second Adam" was that substitute and made the necessary sacrifice out of his love for his Father and his love for humanity:

"God presented Christ as a sacrifice to demonstrate his

righteousness so as to be just and the one who justifies
those who have faith in Jesus" (3:25-26 NIV)

Paul was well able to hold together the two concepts of the Wrath of God and the Love of God. Far from being in any sense incompatible they belong together; holy love must burn with fire in the face of sin.

Thus Paul elucidates what Jesus has done in his death in order to bring us forgiveness. It is not our relying on our own good works of the law, but entirely on the merits of a perfect sacrifice made on our behalf by one who was sinless. But Paul pushes on further than just forgiveness. He is very concerned that people should not think that faith in what Christ as done on the cross should lead to any idea of cheap forgiveness and an easy attitude to sin (Ch. 6). He calls for a fully holy life. Jesus' death not merely justifies us and brings forgiveness of sin; it also makes possible our sanctification and a genuine holy life. His words are

"We know that our old self was crucified with him, so that the
body ruled by sin might be done away with,
*in order that we should **no longer be slaves to sin** – because*
anyone who has died has been set free from sin. (6:6 NIV)

"All of us who were baptised into Christ Jesus were baptised into
his death. We were buried with him through baptism into death in
order that, just as Christ was raised from the dead, through the
glory of the Father, we too may live a new life" (6:3-4 NIV).

*"But now **you have been set free from sin** and have become slaves*
of God,
the benefit you reap leads to holiness, and the result is eternal life"
(6:22 NIV).

Paul is saying that the sacrifice of Jesus has actually set us free from the curse of sin; we are no longer in bondage to it. It has lost its grip. We are to grasp that freedom by faith and act on it. At the same time we are to live in the new positive power of the Spirit of Jesus indwelling us and enabling us to keep the Law. In Ch. 8 he writes,

"For what the law was powerless to do in that it was weakened
by the sinful nature, God did by sending his own Son in the likeness

of sinful man, in order that the righteous requirements of the law might be fully met in us, who do not live according to the sinful nature but according to the Spirit" (8:3-4 NIV).

At this point Paul has reached a description of the New Covenant of the Spirit which the death of Jesus has now inaugurated. We can say that not only did his death break the power of sin working in our lives, but by making us righteous or justified he enabled the Spirit of God to take up residence within us and work holiness within us – and all this by faith, by believing on Jesus.

Paul's other letters
This same "gospel" consistently emerges in Paul's other letters. In 2 Cor. 5:21 NIV he writes, *"God made him who had no sin to be sin for us, so that in him we might become the righteousness of God"*. This is precisely what he wrote in Romans, and has been described as "one of Paul's most important statements about the death of Christ". The statement that *"God made him who knew no sin be sin for us"* is a majestic summary of what happened on the cross. The cross was God's plan, Jesus was sinless but was treated as a substitute for sinful humanity, and he was a "sin offering" bearing our sins. Nothing could be plainer than this.

With similar plainness Paul writes to the Galatians (3:13 NIV),

> *"Christ redeemed us from the curse of the law, having become a curse for us: for it is written 'cursed is everyone who that hangs on a tree'"*.

Anyone who failed to keep the Law came under the curse or judgement of that same law, and Paul insisted that all had indeed failed and had therefore come under the curse of the Law and therefore God's wrath. The Law decreed that everyone who hangs on a tree is under such a curse (Deut. 21:23). Jesus had hung on a "tree" at Calvary and there he suffered as a curse on which God's judgement fell. But he suffered the curse "for us". For early Christians who were being besieged by others to turn back to the "Law" this was a particularly appropriate way of stating what Jesus had done on the cross. And it meant exactly the same as the

comment to the Corinthians: Jesus was our substitute and paid the penalty of sin for us.

4. THE DEATH OF CHRIST IN THE LETTER TO THE HEBREWS

We do not know who wrote this letter, though there have been many suggestions, and neither do we know when it was written. But we can discern that the main aim of his letter was to *"exhort"* Christians of Jewish background not to fall away from Christ and go back into their old Judaism. We can also say that whoever wrote Hebrews was, like Apollos, *"mighty in the Scriptures"*. Though it is highly unlikely that he heard Jesus himself teach, he had the same mind set as Jesus and searched the scriptures because he knew that they "spoke of Him". His letter is full of exposition of Old Testament Scripture from a great variety of sources. Very methodically he sought to show his readers from these sacred writings the superiority of Jesus to every figure and person that they looked up to in their Judaism. He began by showing them that Jesus, as Son, was superior to angels in his revelation of God. He goes on to show Jesus as superior to Moses, for if Moses was a servant in God's house Jesus was actually the Son and heir and builder of the house. He was superior to Abraham the founder of God's people, and his priesthood was superior to Aaron's. As high priest he was the instigator of a new and better covenant than Moses.

It is particularly in his exposition of the High Priesthood of Jesus (4:14 to 10:18) that the author gives us his own understanding of the nature and purpose of the death of Jesus. He builds his treatment of Jesus' High Priesthood on one part of a verse from a recognised Messianic psalm, Psalm 110:4b NIV, *"You are a priest forever, in the order of Melchizedek"*. Its appearance in the New Testament, however, is unique to this letter to the Hebrews: no other writer mentions it. It remains none the less one of the most striking and instructive examples of the Old Testament's prophetic witness to Jesus, and critical to understanding his death.

The name Melchizedek means "king of righteousness". He was also king of Salem (which means "king of peace"), and was

therefore both priest and king. As priest he actually blessed Abraham and received tithes from him, showing his superiority to Abraham the father of the chosen people (and, therefore, to the priestly line of Levi and Aaron, as yet unborn). Very unusually in Genesis (where he first appears in Scripture, Gen. 14:18) he is given no genealogy or forebears, and so the author of Hebrews sees this as pre-figuring the Son of God "*without beginning of days or end of life*". He is "an eternal figure", and it is this eternal nature that vindicates his priesthood; he has no need to be part of the earthly tribe of Levi. This great High Priest, moreover, did not serve in the earthly temple as did Aaron, but served in the "*heavenly sanctuary, the true sanctuary*" of which the earthly temple was only a "*copy and shadow*" – a "type". His sanctuary was the heavenly sanctuary of the eternal God himself.

One of the earthly high priest's most important tasks was to enter the "Most Holy Place" of the earthly Tabernacle once a year with sin offerings for the atonement of the sin of the whole nation and to sprinkle the blood of the sin offering on the Holy Table. No other person was allowed into that Most Holy Place and the high priest himself only once a year. Hebrews stresses the fact that "*he never went in without blood*". This blood was the shed blood of an animal on which the sins of the nation had been laid and which had been killed for the atonement. In contrast to this earthly ritual the new High Priest, Jesus, after the order of Melchizedek, has now gone "*through the curtain*" and into the Most Holy Place in heaven itself. He did not go in, however, as the earthly high priest went in, "*with the blood of bulls and goats*" but "*with his own blood*" (9:11-2 NIV). He himself was the atoning sacrifice and by his sacrificial death obtained "*eternal redemption*". Moreover Jesus has done it once and for all, and he does not need to do it again: "*Unlike the other high priests, he does not need to offer sacrifices day after day ... he sacrificed for their sins once for all when he offered himself*" (7:27).

Thus for our author, Jesus was in a sense the supreme sin offering for the whole people for all time. The implication of the sin offering is plain from Scripture. The animal had to be without blemish, and the high priest laid his hands on the animal as a sign that the sins of the nation were transferred to it. It was then killed and its blood (a sign of life shed) sprinkled on the altar. Its carcase, still bearing the stigma of sin was then burned outside the camp, a carcase that had

become grossly sinful and fit only for destruction. Though some have sought avoid the term, the sin offering was very much a case of a substitute taking away our sins.

Hebrews has much to say about the fact that Jesus through this atoning death was "the mediator" of a new covenant "*much superior to the old one since it is established on better promises*" (8:6 NIV). Not only does his death take away sin and bring forgiveness but it ushers in the promise that God will write his law on the hearts of people and enable them to live a truly holy life (8:3-13). In this way Hebrews parallels Romans, in which Paul is anxious to write about the new covenant that Jesus brought into being.

This is how the author of Hebrews expresses it:

"How much more will the blood of Christ who through the eternal Spirit offered himself unblemished to God, cleanse our consciences from acts that lead to death, so that we may serve the living God. For this reason Christ is the mediator of a new covenant, that those are called may receive the promised inheritance – now that he has died as a ransom to set them free from the sins committed under the first covenant." (9:14-15 NIV)

Hebrews, like its own Melchizedec, may well seem to come from nowhere, but one thing is very clear: in every way, and with a unique perspective, the author brings to us precisely the same "gospel" that echoes throughout the rest of the New Testament. Jesus suffered as a sin offering, bearing the punishment of sinners so that they may be forgiven and go on to serve a living God under a new covenant. There is no conflict in the New Testament as to this core gospel.

NOTE A. Jesus' Words from the Cross

There are seven "words" recorded from the cross. The first three (*"Father, forgive them"*, *"Today you will be with me in Paradise"* and *"Woman behold your son ......"*) seem most likely to have been spoken in the first three hours of the crucifixion. They reveal the love, compassion and grace of Jesus for others even in the midst of his suffering. They say nothing, however, of the depth of his own personal suffering. The last three (*"I thirst"*, *"It is finished"*, and *"Father into your hands I commit my spirit"*) were spoken at the very end of the crucifixion and follow in swift succession. They

speak of a painful composure as he dies. It is only his fourth "word", (*My God, My God, Why have you forsaken me?*"), which speaks directly of the depths of Jesus' own personal agony. It was also spoken toward the end the end of the second three hours. This "word" stands alone in the first two gospels as though to compel our attention. It is the key "word" for understanding the nature of Jesus' real spiritual suffering on the cross.

"Forsaken": the word must be taken literally. Jesus had been abandoned by God. God's presence was no longer there. Communication had gone, both from the Father to the Son and vice-versa. The fellowship so real to Jesus throughout his life and ministry was utterly absent.

"Why?" This small word has a huge implication. It means that Jesus had lost the perception of any purpose in the cross. In the course of his ministry he made it clear that *"he would give his life a ransom for many"* but *"he would rise from the dead"*, that was *"going to prepare a place"* for his disciples and *"they would follow"*. As Hebrews puts it, *"For the joy that was set before him he despised the cross"*. The continuance of these thoughts would have given comfort to his pains and agony of body and mind, but instead there was only an agonising "why?" This can be explained. If God had forsaken him, that meant not only the Father but also the Holy Spirit had left him. He was, however, completely dependent on the Holy Spirit for his grasp of his destiny as a sacrifice for sin and for the reward it would receive. Without the Spirit the revelation of the purpose of the cross was lost. Only one thing could have brought about such abandonment by God – sin! That is exactly what happens when people sin – abandonment is God's judgement on sin. Since Jesus himself was without sin his agony points unmistakably to the fact that he was bearing the sin of others. This is the point at which he became a "sin offering" – in Paul's words, *"God made him who had no sin to be sin for us"* 2 Cor. 5:21; in Peter's words, *"He bore our sins in his body on the tree"* 1 Pet. 2:24

"My God, My God ... " Even in the midst of abandonment Jesus did not lose the consciousness of God: he knew he was there. His agony lay in the fact that he was forsaken by God. True forsakenness, as he undoubtedly felt it, has the profound agony of it seeming to be

for ever. The Father's love would or might not ever come back to him. Though he made the cry toward the end of the second three hours there is every reason to believe that he felt the abandonment throughout those three hours. The depth of this agony was graphically portrayed by the happenings in the physical world during that period. The sun ceased to shine and darkness was everywhere. That remarkable natural physical event was a crucial divine witness in the eyes of Matthew and Mark

NOTE B. The Suffering Servant - Isaiah 53:13 – 54:12

The Old Testament background for our understanding Jesus' death and sacrifice is to be found mostly in the sacrificial system that was instituted with the Law. It is there we find the guilt offering, the sin offering, the Day of Atonement, along with burnt offerings and the peace offerings. All these have great relevance to our perception of the offering of Jesus: they are the "types" which pre-figure his death. There are other "occasional types" such as *"As Jonah was in the belly of the whale 3 days and nights, so will the Son of Man be"* (Matt. 12: 40 NIV), and *"Just as Moses lifted up the snake in the wilderness, so the Son of Man must be lifted up"* (Jn 3:14 NIV). These are very few, however, in the Gospels.

The prophet Isaiah, however, gives us a series of profound prophetic utterances which come under the general title of the Servant of the Lord, and unmistakably they point to Jesus. They are "mountain peaks" in our understanding of what Jesus has done and has yet to do; they describe his Messianic ministry both prior to and after his death and resurrection. The final prophecy of the series is of the Servant who Suffers. It's relevance to the crucifixion is without parallel; it is comprehensive and it is clear.   It depicts his humble origins, the despite in which he was held, his unbearable sufferings and the composure with which he met them. It speaks even of his being assigned a grave with rich and of his resurrection. But, more important, in verse after verse it provides an abundance of explanation as to why he suffered and died, culminating with the words,

"It was the Lord's will to crush him and cause him to suffer"
and though the Lord makes his life an offering for sin

He will see his offspring and prolong his days" (Is. 53:10
NIV)

It is not possible to read Isaiah's words without recognising that the death of Jesus was purposed by God himself: he came as a sin offering and took our punishment on himself. The glory of Jesus is in his obedience to his Father's will. Our glory is in accepting what he has done.

SPIRITUAL FOUNDATIONS IN THE LIFE OF JESUS

CONTENTS

Introduction

A study of this nature, "the spiritual foundations in the life of Jesus", is possible only because Jesus was fully human. It is only because we can watch him as a true human being that we can find anything relevant for our own lives and draw parallels for our benefit between him and us.

Throughout its long centuries of considering the person of Jesus the Christian church has maintained an essential viewpoint, namely that Jesus was fully man and fully God. There was nothing that made his life short of manhood, and nothing that made him short of Godhood. There are difficulties in understanding and explaining the precise working of this duality, but the truth of his complete manhood and divinity is something from which we cannot depart without serious error.

The reason for this is simply that no other understanding will do justice to the picture that the New Testament gives us, the gospels in particular. Only a disregard for the validity of the New Testament record allows other constructions to be made.

When it comes to his divinity then the massive record of John's gospel permits no alternative viewpoint. Jesus is seen to be

constantly making claims of the highest order, and frequently coming under the threat of stoning for the blasphemy of making himself equal with God. John's prologue sums up the viewpoint of the gospel perfectly - "*in the beginning the Word ..... was God*".

The testimony of the gospels to his full humanity is equally clear. His human origin goes back exactly to where ours began - to a conception in the womb, to a human period of gestation and then to a normal human birth. Nothing can bear better testimony to his humanity than that. He became part of a normal family and well known to neighbours and friends. Through childhood he grew normally, and though it seems he had a very perceptive and intelligent mind, he had to learn things and think through things. He "*grew*" in wisdom.

Later on the crowds and the Jewish leaders certainly did not find him unnatural, though undoubtedly unusual. Neither did his disciples. They saw themselves as following a Rabbi and, living and travelling with him, knew him as a human person, not a spiritual phantom. They never had to learn that he was human, but their pilgrimage was rather that of coming to a realisation of his divinity. They saw his deep struggles in prayer, they saw his tiredness, his hunger, they saw his need of fellowship, and they tasted his companionship. It was on this account that a commentator like William Barclay could write. "*Any Christology must begin from the historical fact that those who lived and walked and ate and talked with Jesus saw absolutely nothing unnatural and abnormal about him. His manhood was complete*".

Consequently Jesus encouraged his disciples to watch him and listen to him, to seek to walk as he walked. He wanted them to know the spiritual foundations of his life, and he wants the same for us.

1. JESUS - MAN OF THE SPIRIT

At the heart of Jesus' spiritual life was his relationship with his Father. He knew Him intimately; he knew His will and what He wanted doing. Jesus walked in the closest proximity to his Father and he knew he had come to reveal the Father. For that relationship with his Father, however, he was, as a human being, totally dependent upon the Holy Spirit. It was the Spirit that brought it into being. We can rightly say, therefore, that the central spiritual

foundation in the earthly and human life of Jesus was his dependence upon the Spirit of God. It was the Spirit of God who brought him in his humanity into relationship with the Father and gave him his knowledge of the Father and the Father's will. It was the Spirit who gave him his ability to carry out the will of the Father and enabled him to reveal the Father to his disciples. The Spirit of God impinged on Jesus in every way, making genuine spiritual life possible. Similarly for us the Spirit has to be the pre-eminent foundation for our spirituality. Not only is the Spirit essential to us in order to relate to the Father, but also to relate to Jesus himself.

This work of the Spirit in Jesus can be conveniently looked at in more detail under two heads - Jesus born of the Spirit, and Jesus anointed of the Spirit.

Jesus - born of the Spirit

The very humanity of Jesus, the incarnation, was the work of the Holy Spirit. This is abundantly clear from the angel's words to Mary, explaining how Jesus would be conceived; *"The Holy Spirit will come upon you and the power of the Most High will overshadow you."* (Lk. 1:35 NIV). These words were confirmed later to Joseph when the angel, speaking about Mary's pregnancy, said to him that *"that which is conceived in her is of the Holy Spirit"* (Matt. 1:20 NIV). Thus the Spirit operated on the humanity of Mary to bring about the birth of the human child, Jesus. He was born of the Spirit from Mary's flesh. This means that he was genuinely Mary's child, flesh of her flesh. The Spirit did not simply make use of Mary's womb for a totally new creation of flesh. Paul affirmed this when he wrote of the origin of the Son, *"as to his human nature (he) was a descendant of David"* (Rom 1:3 NIV). He was truly a descendant of David, not an intruder into the physical line.

There is, of course, much more to the idea of a conception of a child than the creation of a physical body. The conception of a person is something of which the body is only one part. Along with the body there also grows a mind, feelings, a unique identity, a will, a soul, a spirit. These other parts also have their origin at the moment of "conception", and together make up the human person. If we are to see Jesus as fully human, therefore, we have to allow in the human nature of Jesus all these other things that make up the totality of our humanity. This means that when we talk of the conception of Jesus by the Spirit of God we are talking not simply about the creation of

a physical human body but about the human spirit, the mind, the emotions and all the other features that go to make us human beings.

In the normal process of human conception all these different attributes, though retaining something of their original beauty and wonder, are marred or tainted. The central problem of that fallen nature is that the spirit in particular has lost its full contact with God through sin; the human being starts off with a spiritual blindness. The consequence of this is that all the other features are impaired; the will is rebellious, the mind is wrongly directed, the emotions lack self control etc, and destructive behaviour follows. This, however, did not happen in Jesus. If such spiritual blindness was latent in Mary, as undoubtedly it was, it was not passed on to Jesus; he was described by the angel as that "*holy one*" (Lk. 1:35). This can only mean that the humanity that came from Mary to form the human origins of Jesus must have been purified and regenerated by the work of the Holy Spirit. Put another way, the eternal Son of God, in taking on human flesh through the working of the Spirit, could not but regenerate that flesh. Thus whilst it remains true that the human flesh of Jesus bore the mark of our humanity and was therefore subject to all the temptations and natural limitations of our humanity, it is equally true that because it had been given its life by the Spirit it became regenerated humanity and therefore able to receive from God and respond to God in a full unimpeded flow. *"The humanity that he takes is the old humanity of Adam ..... now taken from Mary and given a capacity and an ability that are not native to it. It is the capacity and ability to be so united with God that it becomes the means of his (God's) self-expression and self giving to the world"* (T. Smail, Giving Gift)

It was this sanctification of the humanity of Jesus by the Spirit that made all the difference. It meant that Jesus grew up as a fully human person but with a spirit that was fully open to the reality of God and to his ways. It was a humanity that was aware of and in contact with God because it had been born of the Spirit. The growth and development of that intense awareness of God was due to a continued intimate fellowship with the same Holy Spirit that had brought about his birth. This was the foundation of his early years of childhood and manhood - a regenerated humanity in touch with his Father through the Spirit and a humanity constantly fed by the presence of the Spirit.

What does this have to teach us about our own spiritual foundations? The answer is simply that our own human nature (our spirit in particular) must have the same touch of the Holy Spirit on it if we are to have a full flow of spiritual fellowship and knowledge of God. This is precisely what Jesus spoke of in his conversation with Nicodemus. He drew Nicodemus' attention to the need for a "new birth" for any human person who wants to see or enter the kingdom of God, and this new birth he describes as being *"born again of the Spirit"* (Jn 3:3-8). In other words, Jesus was saying that, if we are to begin a life of true spiritual understanding and awareness, something has to happen to our human nature - it has to born of the Spirit. More precisely our human spirit has to have restored to it the ability to be in tune with God and aware of Him. He was pointing to the fact that something of what had happened in his own conception has now to happen in our human lives. The same point is underlined by a statement that John makes in the prologue to his gospel. There he describes those who receive Jesus and believe in his name as being given the right to become children of God, saying that they are children *"born not of natural descent, nor of human decision or a husband's will, but born of God"* (Jn 1:13 NIV).

Further consequences of being born of the Spirit

A very important aspect of the spiritually unclouded humanity of Jesus was that he was able to perceive through the Spirit his true nature as a person and his standing with God. As he grew, he developed an awareness that God was his Father in a very profound way, that he and his Father were "one" in divine nature, that he was the "only begotten and unique son". This awareness was the work of the Spirit. Thus, though in every way human, he became aware at the same time of his divinity. The first intimation that we have of such a realisation was his remark to his parents in the Temple when he was in his early 'teens, *"... I must be about my Father's business"* (Lk. 2:49). Later on, in the midst of his ministry, the full force of that consciousness broke out in the words, *"Before Abraham was born, I am"* (Jn 8:58). The Spirit, in other words, enabled him to realise who he was in relation to God. It is very important for us to know that the Spirit seeks to do exactly the same for us. He does not, of course, reveal to us that we are divine, but he certainly reveals us that we are his sons and daughters. As Paul says, *"The Spirit*

bears witness with our spirit that we are sons of God" and so we cry, "*Abba, Father*". There is no greater spiritual foundation than our awareness of our standing as children of God, for it is at that point that we also become aware of being loved with an everlasting love. We have really found ourselves; our foundation is secure.

Another characteristic of Jesus' spiritual nature was the inner imperative or compulsion from the Spirit to make God's concerns his central interest. This comes out very clearly in the remark already quoted from his youth, "*I **must** be about my Father's business*". Two further important aspects of the Spirit's work in him were the impulsion to study the scriptures and to engage in conversation with his Father (prayer), aspects to be considered in more detail in separate chapters. These are all crucial aspects of the life we are led into when, like Jesus, we become born of the Spirit. Without that new birth nothing of real consequence can be built. That is why the Spirit is the central spiritual foundation of our life. Without Him and his work we remain unrelated to God.

Anointed with the Spirit.
All four gospels make mention of the fact that the Holy Spirit came down upon Jesus after his baptism. All speak of the Spirit coming upon him as a dove, and John notes that it remained on him. Matthew, Mark and Luke all record a voice from heaven re-iterating the truth of which Jesus had become deeply conscious, "*You are my Son, whom I love; with you I am well pleased*" and John the Baptist bears this out in John's gospel (Jn 1:34). This episode introduces us, therefore, to a further working of the Spirit in the life of Jesus, and one of tremendous importance for his human mission.

Two words in particular are associated with this coming of the Spirit on Jesus after his baptism and help us to understand it. The first is the word "*anointed*". This is a word Jesus himself used in connection with this episode. In Luke's gospel we are told that Jesus himself, preaching in the synagogue at Capernaum, used as his text verses from Isaiah 61 in which came the words, "*The Spirit of the Lord is upon me for he has anointed me to preach.....*" (Lk 4:16ff NIV). Luke transposes this preaching event at Capernaum and puts it at the start of the ministry of Jesus simply in order to make the point that for Jesus the event at the Jordan was a fulfilment of the promise of the anointing of the Spirit as prophesied in Isaiah and the means whereby he could undertake his ministry. Obviously this

event reveals that Jesus saw the coming of the Spirit on him at the Jordan as an anointing.

The second word associated with this coming of the Spirit is one which occurs in John's gospel and is the word *"baptise"* (Jn 1:33). John the Baptist had a direct revelation from God that the one on whom he saw the Spirit descend would *"baptise with the Holy Spirit"*. It seems only too evident that there is an implication here that this giving of the Spirit to others by Jesus, described as a "baptising in the spirit", had a close affinity to the way he was receiving the Spirit himself. It would not be out of place to say that he was "baptised in the Spirit" at the Jordan.

The context of this coming of the Spirit, this anointing or baptism is quite clearly the context of the start of Jesus' active ministry. The context must be allowed to determine the nature of the coming of the Spirit on Jesus as something necessary for his ministry. It is Luke who picks up the expression "baptise in the Spirit" in the opening chapter of Acts and applies it to a similar context, one in which the disciples receive "power" (enabling) for the purpose of witnessing or ministry. Such a usage in Acts fits perfectly with the usage when Jesus received the Spirit at the Jordan. It was through the baptism or anointing that Jesus was enabled to minister. He did not engage in active ministry before this time, but he certainly did afterwards, and what we witness here is the Spirit of God coming on Jesus for the purpose of adding a new dimension to his life - the work of ministry. The Spirit had not rested on him like this before.

The preaching and the mighty works of Jesus were the obvious outcome of this anointing, but it is important to see that it involved something other than powerful works of service and expressions of gifts from the Spirit, crucial though they were. This other aspect is primarily indicated by the symbolism of the dove which came to rest on him. We need to recognise that such a visionary symbol was of great importance in communicating the nature of the Spirit that came to rest on Jesus. His was to be a ministry which was to bear the marks of gentleness, graciousness and compassion. The coming of the dove pointed to the heart attitude that was to underlie all the mighty works. Compassion was to be their starting point. The love and mercy and grace of his Father were now to fill the human frame of Jesus in full measure through the Spirit. They were to be the river in which the gifts of power were to flow and operate. When he saw the poor, the needy, the widow woman, the sick, the demonised, the

outcast and the oppressed then compassion and pity would flow from him initiating again and again healing and comfort. In his own heart as Son of God he would find an immense inner response to these powerful gracious urgings of the Spirit.

In the light of this we need to recognise that true anointings, true baptisms of the Spirit are as much an impress on the heart as they are on the actions of those who receive them. They can be equally described as a baptism of love as well as a baptism of powerful works. The expression *"full of the Spirit"* which Luke uses in such contexts is an apt description. Any analysis of Jesus as man of the Spirit without taking this Jordan episode into consideration would be incomplete.

Jesus, then, was born of the Spirit and anointed with the Spirit. In every department of his life the Spirit had sway. That needs also to be our experience. It is a call to be constantly open to the Spirit, doing all we can to *"go on being filled with the Spirit"* seeking his fellowship in praise and worship of Jesus and the Father, watching lest we should grieve or quench him with unrighteous attitudes and behaviour. He is the source of our spiritual life and our link to Jesus and the Father He is the other "Comforter" that Jesus has so graciously given to us. His presence is our first foundation.

2. JESUS - MAN OF THE WORD

Everything in the spiritual life of Jesus came from the work of the Holy Spirit. This is nowhere more evident than in the way he used the Scriptures, and, more significantly, in the way they impacted him. If the Spirit himself working in Jesus provided the fundamental foundation of his spiritual life, the scriptures were a major tool of the Spirit for doing what he wanted to do in Jesus. This should not surprise us since the scriptures are consistently portrayed as having the Spirit as their author, and constitute a revelation of God and his purposes. They "spoke of him", Jesus, prophetically and comprehensively. Under the influence of the Spirit what he read about himself in the scriptures was bound to impact him, therefore, and it was inevitable that Jesus would become a man of the "Word".

Searching and understanding the scriptures would become another fundamental spiritual foundation of his life.

It is no different for us. If we do not allow the Spirit to make us committed students of the scriptures then we will neither understand nor grow into that degree of spiritual maturity in the purposes of God that the Father intends for us.

A selection of scriptures will help to understand this need.

1. *"Sitting among the teachers, listening and asking questions"* Lk 2:46 NIV

In his providence the Father made sure that from his birth Jesus not merely had access to the scriptures but was surrounded by a culture in which the study of them was central and in which they were deeply reverenced. So from earliest boyhood he was taught them, with much of his schooling at Nazareth centred on the synagogue. This was the start God gave to his Son. There can hardly be a greater affirmation of the value of the scriptures for human living than this. By the age of twelve he was astonishing the religious teachers of the law in Jerusalem by the depth of his knowledge and the perception of his questions. He clearly had a very able and penetrating mind and was giving a great deal of attention to the study of the Old Testament books, even if it was the "Spirit of wisdom and the Spirit of the knowledge of the Lord" that gave him his spiritual perception. He went on throughout the "hidden years" reading, learning and growing in the knowledge of the scriptures, and it is worth noting that Jesus seems to have combined his studies of scripture in his young adulthood with a very busy working and family life. These years remind us that an early and deep education in scripture remains a priceless privilege and an essential foundation for spiritual growth. They were extremely informative years in which the Spirit was his teacher and the scriptures his text book.

2. *"Did not the Christ have to suffer these things and then enter his glory" Lk. 24:26 NIV*

It is abundantly obvious, therefore, that by the time he reached the age of thirty and presented himself at the Jordan ready for baptism Jesus had gained a massive biblical understanding. The gospels reveal his very wide grasp of the Old Testament as well as a very profound use. The essential foundation for his ministry was laid. There can be no doubt that, at the Jordan, he understood not only the

nature of the ministry that he was about to embark on, but also that the culmination of that work would be a sacrificial death on the cross followed by a resurrection. The notion that Jesus entered his ministry without such an understanding is quite absurd. John the Baptist's cry of *"Look, the Lamb of God who takes away the sin of the world"* (Jn 1:29) would certainly not have taken him by surprise but merely have confirmed to him what he already knew from his reading of the scripture, namely that he was ordained to be *the* sacrificial lamb. Without such an awareness in his heart the baptism would have been a pointless exercise, rather than the powerful dedication of himself to sacrificial death that it actually was.

The important thing to grasp is that it was through his studies of the scripture that he came to such a definitive and clear perception of what lay in front of him. In his human growth and spiritual development it was the scripture that mapped out for him his destiny. The gospels give us clear indications of how the Old Testament pointed to where his ministry would finally end, as, for example, his remark early in John's gospel; *"Just as Moses lifted up the snake in the desert so the Son of Man must be lifted up so that everyone who believes in him may have eternal life"* (Jn 3:14). He knew he had *"a cup to drink"*, a *"baptism to be baptised with"*; he knew that he was indeed to become the true Paschal Lamb, that Passover pointed to Him; he knew that he was the *"guilt offering"* of Isaiah 53, the servant who was to suffer though he was without fault; he knew he was to have a Jonah experience of three days in the belly of Hades.

All this, and much more, he later made clear to his disciples after his resurrection. The truths about his sacrifice that he had lived with, that he had openly given voice to, that he had wrestled with and allowed to guide his path to the cross he made intensely illuminating to his puzzled disciples. As it had been for him so now it was for them that the scriptures should give the essential enlightenment that they so desperately needed in their moment of despair and confusion immediately after the crucifixion. It would be quite impossible to conceive of Jesus going through with his destiny without the Spirit taking the prophetic scripture and illuminating and undergirding him in that destiny. Clarity and understanding of calling were the priceless contribution they made to the work he came to to accomplish.

For us they do exactly the same. Our own lives are not so precisely delineated, of course, as the One of whom the scriptures primarily spoke, but those same scriptures record our destiny as well as his, they record our own sonship by adoption, and they speak to us of the good works that are set before us. They give reality and expression to the inner longings of the heart and that sense of hope that the Spirit prompts within us. They speak of heaven and constantly re-assure, as no doubt they constantly did to the Son of man.

3. *"Today this scripture has been fulfilled in your hearing"* (Lk 4:21 NIV)
The nature and direction of his earthly ministry was equally well laid out for Jesus in the scriptures and must have been very much with him as he stood at the Jordan. He knew that it was not only a moment of dedication for his sacrifice but a moment also in which he would receive the anointing of the Spirit for his preaching and healing. The coming of the dove was no surprise for him, for he was praying for the Spirit at that very moment (Lk 3:21). He knew, as was evident later from his preaching in Nazareth (Lk 4:16ff.), that the anointing was to be a fulfilment of Isaiah 61:1ff and would be his empowerment for that preaching and healing. As he preached in the synagogue at Nazareth he had no difficulty in finding the text in Isaiah and no difficulty in expounding it. He was also aware of another passage in Isaiah, Isaiah 9:1ff, and its prophetic word about a great light in Galilee. He knew he was that light, and he was clearly led by that scripture to choose Galilee for his ministry. Certainly the Spirit would also have given him a sovereign impulse to focus on Galilee, but it was all so much more clear in his mind and heart when it was so remarkably undergirded by the word of his Father.

So it should be with us; the Spirit prompts and leads us into different experiences, but then the scriptures come again and again to provide a strong and necessary undergirding. With the scriptures enlightened by the Spirit it is possible to walk through life with open eyes rather than simply on impulse, even though the impulse may be God given. Whatever the Father requires of us becomes much more clearly outlined by meditation in the scriptures. It is, of course, this remarkable relevance of scripture for the pattern of our lives that stamps those writings as being of more than human origin.

4. *"I know where I came from and where I am going"* Jn 8:14 NIV
As his ministry developed the question arose in people's hearts, *"What manner of man is this?"*. Jesus already knew the answer. John's gospel reveals that Jesus had a profound self-awareness of the fact that he was much more than an ordinary human person. There was a compelling and magnificent authority about him, as of one who knew he had origins that were unique. The statements that came from his lips were unequivocal, such statements as, *"Glorify me in your presence with the glory I had with you before the world began* (Jn 17:5), *"You are from below; I am from above"* Jn 8:23, *"I and the Father are one"* (Jn 10:30), *"Before Abraham was, I am"* (Jn 8:58), *"I am the resurrection and the life"* Jn 11:25). These statements show him to have been aware of a previous and eternal existence. If Mary did speak to him of the nature of his birth, that alone would not have brought about the full serenity or the depth of this self-awareness. It is the direct revelation to Jesus of this pre-existence by the Holy Spirit that accounts for its depth, but that revelation would have come undoubtedly in large measure through his reading of the scriptures. From them he would have learned for example, that he was the one of whom Isaiah spoke as being *"Wonderful Counsellor"* and *"Mighty God "* (Is. 9:6); he would know that in his kingship he was a *"greater than Solomon"*; he would know that he was the heavenly *Son of Man* depicted in Daniel 7:13, and he told his accusers as much when he was on trial (Mk 14:62); he would have seen the pointer to divinity in Psalm 45:6 which said of the coming Son of David, *"Your throne, O God, will last for ever."* It is not difficult to see him pouring over such scripture and finding immense enlightenment. Thus the collusion of inner revelation on the one hand and the illumination of the scripture on the other brought about a majestic certainty concerning his own divine being.

All this explains why Jesus put so much store on the scriptures in all he did and said. He knew that as far as he was concerned they bore the imprint of God; they could not be anything other than divine testimony. That is the value we should also place upon them. They will not only show us him but will convey to us our own standing with God, our own divine adoption as children of God, our own life yet to come. It is a poor spiritual life that does not have a deep sense of its standing and status with God through deep meditation in the scriptures.

5. *"It is written, 'You shall not test the Lord your God"* (Matt 4:7 NIV)

Certain books and passages of scripture become from time to time a clear mirror of the events of our lives. They are intended to do so. They encapsulate our anxieties, temptations and difficult situations; they provide necessary strength and guidance. This is precisely what happened to Jesus in his temptations. He responded to Satan consistently from Deuteronomy, for he saw the trials of the wilderness wanderings in scripture as a mirror of his own trials. He found that of immense value. It is very unlikely that he had the scroll of Deuteronomy with him, however! He had mastered the book, and it was part of him - the Spirit was bringing its message to his memory, something Jesus later said his disciples would experience (Jn 14:26).

6. *"Do not think I have come to abolish the Law or the Prophets"* Matt 5:17 NIV

Jesus totally endorsed the great moral statements of the Old Testament revelation. That much is very clear from his own teaching. But his own grasp of them was very different from the teachers of his day. They worked at codifying every detail for every situation, producing huge burdens for behaviour, whereas he worked on the great principles underlying the Law and released people into the freedom of genuine moral behaviour. No greater example of this can be found than his day to day attitude to the Sabbath, which he interpreted in the greater perspective of genuine love for our neighbour. He exposed the greed, envy, ambition and violence which underlay the behaviour of those most concerned to cavil over the codified law, the Scribes and Pharisees. From the priests he demanded *"mercy, not sacrifice"* (Matt 9:13). He showed forgiveness, not condemnation to an adulterous woman, he showed compassion not arrogance to a poor widow. He was not satisfied with outward behaviour but with the wellsprings of the heart, which should be clean of impure and violent thoughts.

Here was the essence of his great teaching programme - it was a programme deeply rooted in the Old Testament law. It was a programme that had the same perspective as that of the prophets when they vainly tried to call Israel back to the real meaning of the Mosaic legislation. There is in fact very little that Jesus taught that cannot be grounded in the Old Testament scripture. His basis was

the basis of the ten commandments to which he had been accustomed from a boy. There is little doubt that he spent a great deal of time meditating over such a massive foundation for moral and godly living or that it gave him his essential starting point in his teaching. Like David he would have said *"your word is a lamp to my feet"*. He knew *"the fear of the Lord"*.

7. *"He showed them in all the scriptures the things that belonged to himself"* Lk 24:27 NIV
The best commentary on the value of scripture for Jesus can be seen in the way that Jesus taught his disciples to base their "gospel" on what he taught them "in all the scriptures the things about himself" (Lk 24:27). The scriptures were foundational. He was a man of the word; they must follow. To have the scriptures to hand (in our case both Old and New Testaments) is a profound blessing, therefore, and not to have them is a profound loss. Not to use them when they are to hand, and when the Spirit is constantly prompting us in that direction, is an appalling failure. To seek to provide the scriptures for those who do not have them is a work of immense significance.

3. JESUS - MAN OF PRAYER

Jesus led a busy life. We may infer this about his early years from the fact that he was born into a typical Galilean home in which he would not have been allowed, and neither would have wished, to shirk the responsibilities of providing for family needs. When eventually he gave himself to his ministry the busy nature of his life is written all over the gospels. He had a ministry which involved a lot of preaching, a lot of healing, a lot of discipling and a lot of walking and travelling. He was given the whole of Galilee to cover as well as frequent activity in Jerusalem. All this was to be accomplished in some two or, at the most, three years. So time was short. Its ultimate success was due to the fact that everything was envisioned by the Spirit and undergirded by a mind saturated in Scripture. However, one other factor also kept his life and ministry together - his constant seeking of and conversation with his Father. This was the glue of his spiritual life. Despite the incessant busyness, prayer was never short-changed. Prayer was work, and

this fellowship with his Father was the primary work on which all other work was built. Prayer was the third spiritual foundation of his life.

We know nothing from the gospels of Jesus' "daily routine" of prayer. Tired, hungry, living with disciples and pressured by crowds he doubtless found such a "routine" difficult. He may have prayed as he travelled from one village to another, taking whatever chance offered itself. What the gospels do show us, however, is a series of blocks of time which Jesus dedicated to prayer and fellowship with the Father and which he kept well away from all distractions. These "block times" can be seen to be absolutely crucial for him and his work, and they represent a pattern which gives a very practical solution for putting a solid prayer foundation into any busy life. An examination of those occasions indicates how varied and suggestive they are in their nature.

1. The Forty Days - Praying and Fasting (Lk.4:1 ff)
The first of these "block times" was the longest, and an occasion of immense importance It took place immediately after his baptism and anointing, at the very beginning of his ministry, and its importance lay in the fact that he was praying through the nature of the ministry which he was now about to start. This seems evident from the fact that Satan's temptations at this time were clearly intended to misdirect his ministry and give it a worldly flavour. This indicates to us how important it is even though we have both the envisioning of the Spirit and the undergirding knowledge of scripture that we should take time to prayerfully reflect at depth, unhampered and unhurriedly on whatever lies before us. We need to think things through in his presence, praying until they are deeply embedded and fully clarified in our hearts. It was the Spirit of God himself who impelled him into the desert for precisely this purpose, and we should expect such impulsions also in our own prayer life. When he emerged from the desert, Jesus had found great clarity of purpose and firmness of resolve, fully grasping the principles of ministry that were to guide him, and having fought off very powerful temptations to act in ways contrary to those principles. Luke describes him as returning from the desert "*in the power of the Spirit*". Thus it is precisely in the place of prayer, where we have time to wrestle and overcome the darker thoughts of Satan, that the work of the Spirit and the word is established, albeit recognising at the same time that

such wrestling deeply involves both the Spirit and the scripture. Prayer and fasting have a key role in the warfare of overcoming Satan's attacks and securing depth of faith and conviction. **This period in the desert secured the integrity of his ministry.**

2. Early Morning (Lk. 4:42 ff & Mk. 1 35:ff)

This early morning block of time followed immediately after intensive ministry in Capernaum, ministry that was very effective and widespread. There was a great hunger in the city for more of such ministry. However, despite the draining effects of his work, Jesus rose very early for prayer in order to assess the situation. As previously in the desert, he obviously felt the Spirit's impulsion to such a review. In those quiet and undisturbed hours he reached a clear decision that he would turn his back (at least for the time being) on all the seemingly legitimate calls in Capernaum and move on to *"the other villages"*. The reason he gave his disciples for this was simply, *"because that was why I was sent"* (Lk 4:43). Thus he made a critical decision in which he accepted the Father's plan that he should cover all Galilee, a plan which he saw clearly outlined in Is 9:1ff, and so did not allow himself to get tied down in his strategy. It is very instructive that such a decision cost him several hours of early morning sleep and several hours of prayer. He would have felt deeply the needs that there were in Capernaum and was doubtless rejoicing in the response of the people there. He would have struggled with these feelings over and against an impulsion of the Spirit, through the scriptures, to press on to meet other needs in other parts of Galilee. The early hours of prayer enabled a right decision before the situation overtook him. It was, of course, a great challenge to his physical, mental and spiritual strength, a challenge that will come our way also. But, happening as it did at the beginning of his great Galilean ministry, **this secured the right direction and full extent of his ministry.**

3. Frequent Withdrawal (Lk. 5:16)

Luke, who is the main chronicler of Jesus at prayer, notes that he often withdrew to *"lonely places"* and prayed (Lk 5:16). This comment comes right in the midst of his great ministry of mighty works and teaching, and clearly indicates the place of prayer in sustaining it. He reminded his disciples of the need of such prayer when later he had to tell them that their failure to heal a demonised

boy was because, *"this kind comes out only by prayer and fasting"*. Such works called for sustained faith, and time in the presence of his Father alone could nurture that. Constantly he refreshed himself in the truth that he was doing the Father's works and that they would be effective. Such times provided the spiritual food which was so crucial to him. The enabling of the Spirit and the strengthening of the scripture were the stuff of these times, but he still had to apply himself in prayer. **These times secured the power of his ministry**

4. All Night (Lk. 6:12 ff)

One of the most important decisions Jesus made was in his choice of his apostles. As the ministry grew, he knew that he needed to send into ministry some of those who had been with him for some time in order both to extend and to consolidate the work. The choice was all important, particularly since they would become the future leaders of the church. Once again he found a lonely place to pray, this time a mountainside. Once more it was in the midst of a ministry flow, calling for personal discipline on his part and making big demands on all his resources. It is frequently the case that praying calls on our human resources in a way more demanding than any other activity - as many have experienced.

It is not difficult to imagine the process of that night of prayer: First he had to get assurance that it was the right time to branch out with his disciples, and then he had to choose the apostles, each candidate no doubt being offered to the Father and held up before him. Perhaps there was also a process in which he needed to receive confidence to entrust them with the work, accepting their limitations and counting on the Father to keep them. This was, once again, therefore, a process of careful thought, reflection, praying and waiting to hear. By the morning the process was complete, the choice made. **This secured the Apostolic band and the Leadership of the church.**

5. A Week Away (Lk. 9:28 ff)

After many months of ministry with his disciples Jesus challenged them to say who they thought he really was (Lk 9:19ff). Peter declared him to be the Christ. Jesus immediately began to speak to them of a Christ who, contrary to prevailing belief, must suffer, be killed and rise from the dead (9:21). Clearly such events were in his mind when he posed the question. He knew the moment for such

happenings in his life was fast approaching and it was time both for himself and for his disciples to face up to this next stage. Eight days later he took Peter, James and John with him for a journey on to a mountain to pray over the issue. As he prayed two remarkable things happened: Jesus was totally transformed by the bright glory of God, and he discussed with Moses and Elijah, also gloriously attired, the events of his last days that were to come in Jerusalem. The disciples witnessed all this, and it was undoubtedly the most remarkable experience of prayer that they ever had - for Jesus it may not have been unknown, but still remarkable. It was all well worth the long and hard journey (it is always worthwhile taking time to get away and alone!). Being transformed by prayer and being given revelation through prayer - these were the massive gains of that journey. Jesus knew the divine glory rested in and on him, but here it became wonderfully manifest; Jesus knew he had to face the cross in Jerusalem but here fresh contact with that truth was given to him in the most astounding and strengthening of ways. The whole scene concluded with a manifestation of the divine cloud and a voice affirming Jesus' Sonship and calling for the disciples to listen to him. **This episode secured his final and most important ministry direction.**

6. The Last Supper John 17
In John's record of this occasion we have something that is quite unique in the gospel records. Whereas in most of the sequences that show us Jesus at prayer we only have the story of him praying and are obliged to infer what he was praying from the context, here in John's account of the Last Supper we actually listen in to his praying. We hear the prayer with which Jesus concluded the supper. He had spent a great deal of time teaching them and preparing them for the coming of the Comforter and the lifestyle of love he expected from them, but then he prayed. It was an intimate occasion, secluded and unhurried and powerfully focused on the disciples. The prayer began with a petition asking that the Father would glorify him, and enable him to complete the work that would glorify the Father. He then interceded for the disciples. He acknowledged they were the Father's gift to him, and that they had heard and received the Father's word. He prayed for them because, unlike him, they were to remain in the world. He prayed that they would remain as one, united; and he prayed that they might be kept from the evil one. He

was deeply aware of the dangers they faced , much more so than they. He prayed for those who were to believe through their witness, and he prayed that they all might come to be with him and see his glory. It was direct, methodical, earnest and necessary. Here was Jesus through his intercession bringing down upon his disciples everything that the Father wanted to give them. **This secured his disciples survival.**

Luke records (22:31) a further moment when Jesus, aware of an oncoming sifting by Satan that would accompany his death, prayed specifically that Peter's faith would not fail, but that he would be able to strengthen his brother disciples. This prayer is the reason why Peter, though denying his Lord, survived to exercise leadership in the church.

7. Gethsemane (Lk. 22:39 ff)

Jesus' struggle at Gethsemane was the ultimate struggle of humanity - he faced the horror of complete spiritual darkness and separation from God. Every fibre of his human frame shrank from such a prospect, but he knew this was the price that had to be paid on the cross for humanity's salvation. It was prospect that made him sweat blood. There was only one place to face it and that was in his Father's presence. There he wrestled with it, desperately seeking another way out *("if it be possible")*. This was a real, genuine, human struggle. His Father was deeply aware of the struggle and its depth and importance. An angel came to strengthen Jesus. We little realise how much we need (and how much we receive) such strengthening. Angels hover in the Father's presence as we seek it. His disciples could not keep pace and slept, but the angel did not. The struggle was resolved, Jesus accepted the cup and he set his face unflinchingly toward the cross. Thus **Gethsemane secured the victory of Calvary.**

The lessons are clear from the above incidents. **Every major step in the life of Jesus was secured by prayer.** It was prayer with space and time providing an uninterrupted focus. It had to be built into a busy life. It involved much thought, meditation, petition, intercession and thanksgiving. It was an absolutely essential spiritual foundation in the life of Jesus. We neglect such at our peril.

FACE TO FACE with the RISEN JESUS

"Their eyes were opened and they recognised him" Lk. 24:31 NIV

CONTENTS

GROWING IN AWARENESS

At the very heart of the Christian faith is the fact that Jesus rose from the dead. Whatever else we may believe about Jesus, if we have not grasped this truth in our hearts we do not have an authentic faith, indeed our faith is meaningless. Paul the Apostle made this point very clearly when he wrote to the Corinthian church: *"if Christ has not been raised' our preaching is useless and so is your faith"; "if Christ has not been raised, your faith is futile and you are still in your sins"* (1 Cor. 15:14, 17). For Paul all hope of sins forgiven and resurrection to glory is pinned on the fact that Jesus rose from the dead, bodily and actually.

What this means for us as Christians is that we need to have a profound grasp of this truth at the deepest level and not an uncertain acquiescence in an inherited doctrinal formula. We need to walk

increasingly in the reality of this truth and we must constantly wipe away anything that dulls a clear apprehension of it and robs us of the warmth, joy and hope that it releases in our spirit.

It is important to recognise, however, that in grasping this truth we are not simply left to believe in the resurrection of Jesus as a matter of blind faith, as many people, Christians included, often suppose. The contrary is true. There are very definite ways in which we can know that Jesus is indeed alive and walking with us. We need to be aware of these different ways and learn to walk in the assurance that they bring. These ways are clearly shown in the gospel stories of how Jesus revealed his resurrected presence to his disciples. In addition to these Jesus himself had some very definite things to say about how he would manifest himself to his followers after his death and resurrection. It is the purpose of this study to outline these different ways and Jesus' teaching, and thereby to strengthen and stimulate our faith in his resurrection. These ways are not focused on any historical discussion of evidences for the resurrection; they are focused on what we can and should be experiencing of the risen Jesus in our lives now.

1. JOHN and PETER – OUT FISHING

"It is the Lord" Jn. 20:7 NIV

There are two different ways in which Jesus encountered his disciples after he rose from the dead. There are some encounters which could be called direct encounters: he suddenly appears in a full physical resurrection body and is immediately recognisable. Such a direct encounter is described for us on the evening of the day of resurrection when he suddenly appeared to the disciples in the upper room, showed them his hands and side and actually ate with them.

There are, however, other encounters in which he does not initially reveal himself in such stark and clear physical manner. These we might call indirect encounters: Jesus engages with his disciples but they do not immediately recognise him physically. It only becomes apparent that he is Jesus after he actually does

something for them or to them which makes them realise who he really is. In this sort of encounter the disciples recognise the living Jesus by what he does, not by physical sight. It is these "indirect" encounters which are important for us to study for they show Jesus clearly revealing himself in certain ways but without necessarily manifesting his physical appearance. His risen presence can be known, in other words, by things that happen to us that mark out his touch or his presence.

One of these "indirect encounters" is recorded for us in John's gospel (21:1-4). It took place some days after the direct Easter Day encounter and it reveals how a group of disciples recognised the presence of the risen Jesus with them not by physical recognition but by an unmistakably significant happening that occurred to them. In this episode Peter decides to go fishing. He knows that Jesus has risen but he doesn't know quite what lies ahead of him or quite what to do in the present. Puzzled, frustrated, and tense he decides that fishing was at least something he could do! Accordingly, he and a few other disciples went back for the night to the job that had been their trade for years. It was, however, a very disappointing night; they caught absolutely nothing, and their frustration doubtless deepened considerably.

In the early dawn a figure, whom they did not recognise, called out from the bank asking if they had caught anything. When they replied, "No!" he told them to cast their nets on the other side of the boat and said they would find fish. They did so, possibly thinking that the stranger could see something they could not see from the boat. Immediately they found their nets filling up with large fish in such numbers that the nets were too heavy to be hauled into the boat and would need to be pulled directly to the shore.

It was at this point that the "beloved disciple" (John) recognised intuitively that in this catch of fish they were witnessing something that had a unique touch about it. He had seen exactly this happen before when Jesus had been around. For him this was no ordinary catch; it betrayed the hand of Jesus. He called out to Peter, "It is the Lord!" Peter responded immediately to what he knew was true; he appears to have forgotten the fish and jumped into the water to go straight to Jesus.

It was, therefore, in the catch of fish that John recognised the presence and power of Jesus. The point of illumination lay in seeing the fish rather than the figure on the shore. It was a moment of

profound spiritual awareness, even of revelation. An ordinary and disappointing night's work was suddenly stamped with a divine touch; Jesus was there. It would not have mattered if, at that point, Jesus had simply disappeared and gave them no chance to recognise him physically. They did not need to recognise him physically; they knew that what they had witnessed in the boat was the result of him being present.

Why the "indirect" revealing of Himself?
We have to ask some questions at this point; "Why did Jesus manifest himself in this particular manner? Why keep his identity secret whilst he worked such a miracle? Why did he not just appear as the risen Jesus and then give his instructions about the fish?" The answer to these questions clearly seems to be that Jesus chose this way so that the disciples would know that, though his physical presence would be taken from them, his actual presence and power would remain with them and would be manifest in all sorts of life situations and happenings. It would be a lesson they would not be likely to forget, and it would be invaluable for the future when he had ascended into heaven. There are a number of points about this encounter which need to be kept in mind.

1. It happened in the middle of ordinary everyday life, it was a manifestation of the risen Lord in the "work place". Its context was not one in which they were engaged in spiritual exercises, such as prayer; it happened whilst they were fishing. There is something immensely comforting in this. It reveals how closely Jesus is involved in the very fabric of our ordinary work-a-day lives and how ready he is to manifest himself in the midst of it. After all, he was a carpenter for most of his life and walked with his Father as much in his vocation as a carpenter as in his teaching and healing. We should in no way be surprised if the touch of the risen Lord is made apparent in our lives in such an ordinary context. On the contrary we should look for it and expect it.

2. It happened at a time of frustration, stress and uncertainty. There was an immediate frustration in that they had caught no fish after many hours of working and waiting. There was, however, a deeper and more important sense of unease and bewilderment which concerned their future. They knew Jesus was alive but they were utterly dependent on him manifesting himself and showing them the nature of that future. Such manifestation was unpredictable, and

they had no control over the situation that faced them. It is not surprising they were somewhat nervous. The catch of fish came to them as an enormous relief both to their present and their future needs. The catch of fish in fact became a prelude to breakfast and to Jesus speaking to them of their future commission, and especially Peter's. We need to learn, therefore, that this sort of "Jesus touch" is likely to come at times of real difficulty. It is when we feel broken, desperate or in crisis and need real contact with the Lord, that we are most likely to meet with some "happening" which reveals the presence of Jesus and which straightens things out.

3. This catch of fish is an event that moves over into the miraculous. It is not a blatant miracle with Jesus creating fish out of nothing. The probability is that such large shoals of fish would have been both seen and landed from time to time in Lake Galilee, noted as it was for teeming with fish. The miracle lay in the fact that such a large shoal was so close at precisely the time of such deep frustration and need. It was totally unexpected and against the run of things. The disciples could scarcely believe what they were seeing. It is for that reason we can use the expression "the event moves over into the miraculous". Though the event could be dissected and rationalised there was an element in terms of time and place clearly beyond the ordinary in what happened. At the same time it took an inner alertness to recognise that; it took a spiritual intuition to recognise that it was not simply an extraordinary piece of "good fortune". When Jesus had ministered with his disciples he had constantly led them into situations of such miraculous happenings. They had come to expect this miracle touch, and were encouraged to expect it. And now they were able to recognise it. The important point here is that like the disciples of Jesus we do need to recognise that in our own journey with him he can and does work miracles of this nature as he deems fit and that he is wanting to school us in the miraculous. We need to recognise that he can radically change circumstances and situations for the better by some happening, some event which "moves over into the miraculous". This leads us to a further point to notice.

4. Peter initially failed to make the connection between the catch and the presence of Jesus. It was only when John said to him, "It is the Lord" that he realised what was happening and that Jesus was manifesting his presence. It is very possible, therefore, even for a close follower to be in the middle of a happening that is witnessing

to the active, live, real presence of Jesus and yet be blind to it. Peter's eyes and attention were totally on the catch and how to land it, and at the same time, perhaps, already working out just how much it would be worth. That was very natural. However, concentration on surface (but important) issues can blind us to deeper factors. The deeper factor has to be "seen"; it's not automatic. Thankfully when John called his attention to the fact that Jesus was at work Peter responded immediately. This means we have to maintain on our part an awareness, and an attitude which is actually ready and prepared for Jesus to make his presence felt in the "miraculous" happenings of daily life. It also calls for a readiness to listen to fellow disciples when they give their testimonies about the experiences they have had in meeting with the risen Lord in this way.

5. In the very nature of a happening like this catch of fish there is always room for disbelief and cynicism. The most extraordinary event of this kind can always be insisted upon as being just a "coincidence" or an "accident". This is particularly so in a "rational" age like our own which discounts any notion of the miraculous. Unfortunately this tendency to unbelief is likely to be present even among committed Christians. We need to avoid being gullible but we need also to be in tune with what a risen Jesus may choose to do in the events of our life and other people's lives.

Conclusion and Personal Testimony

These miraculous touches of Jesus in our lives are not normally an everyday occurrence. But neither are they a great rarity. They happen far more frequently than we might think, and if we were alert and expectant we might well recognise a great many more such moments in our own lives. It is very important that we do recognise them and take note of them; they are part of our living testimony to a living Lord, and they constitute our "spiritual capital".. They can be drawn on in difficult and needy times and as they are recollected can give a boost of essential faith. They also fuel a life of thanksgiving and praise. Indeed it is a very worthwhile exercise to literally take note of them and record such touches in a notebook or journal. My notebooks have many such moments recorded when the touch of the living Jesus has been evident.

Shortly after I became a follower of Jesus I became engaged to my future wife. We planned for and looked eagerly toward the wedding. Then after a few months I felt a profound call into the

ordained ministry (we both shared the call). This produced a time of struggle when we realised that we had now to postpone the wedding (already planned) indefinitely. I needed to go for training and marriage was not considered appropriate and was hardly practical. Life became very clouded and uncertain. We battled through the first year of training with frustration and dashed hopes. Towards the end of the year the Principal of my theological college called me into his office. He simply said that a lady had come into the college from close by and who was planning to go live in Scotland for the coming year. She wondered if there might be a student who was married and could live in her house and take care of it whilst she was away. She would gladly let the couple have the place rent free. The Principal looked at me and said, "I think this is for you, and you ought to go ahead with your marriage. For me (for both of us) this happening was exactly like pulling in a mighty catch of fish after a very long and bleak night. It had all the hallmarks of the Jesus touch in the exquisite timing of the offer and the sheer bounty of the offer (a free house in London for a year when we had no resources to house ourselves). It spoke to us the words, "It is the Lord". The marriage was quickly arranged and it came exactly at the right time to give us a year together before we went to our first post.

This is only one of a long list of such similar happenings which now span more than a half a century of ministry. Crucially important is the fact that the cumulative impact of many successive similar happenings at critical times has powerfully cemented the knowledge that the living Jesus has been at work in the ongoing everyday fabric of life. The recollection and meditation of such events has built up an increasing resonance of faith. Many of us would doubtless describe such occurrences as an answer to prayer. That would not be wrong. But beyond the prayer is the living Jesus very much actively at work as the head of the church and involving himself (as he did in Acts) in the active, working lives of his disciples and followers. It is this extra perception of the risen Jesus that we need to walk with. He is very much alive.

2.TWO FRIENDS – WALKING and TALKING

Did not our hearts burn as he opened up the Scriptures?"

Lk. 24:31 NIV

After describing the events of the early morning of Easter Day, Luke's gospel goes on to record two very different types of encounter with the risen Jesus, one of which happened on that same afternoon and the other later that evening. The evening encounter was a direct encounter. The apostles had gathered together in Jerusalem and were listening to the testimony of two other disciples who had met with the risen Jesus earlier in the afternoon. As they were talking Jesus simply appeared in their midst. It was a direct, immediate, physical and recognisable appearance. For a moment they thought they were seeing some kind of spirit, but Jesus quickly showed them that he was indeed Jesus, risen from the dead. He let them touch and feel him, and actually ate food with them. Thus they came in the most direct and literal of ways face to face with the resurrected Jesus bodily. All the doubts and confusion that had accumulated during the day gave way to mingled joy and amazement. Having physically established his identity, Jesus then went on to turn their attention from his physical presence to the Scriptures. He showed them from Moses, the Prophets and the Psalms all the prophetic Scriptures that spoke of himself, his ministry, his death, his resurrection and his future intentions for all the nations. He wanted to "earth" everything that had happened to him and the disciples in the prophetic word of Scripture. It would be invaluable for their future ministry.

It is the earlier encounter in the afternoon with the two disciples, however, which is our main concern. Here we have what we have previously called an indirect encounter. It is very different from the direct encounter that has just been described. Luke relates Jesus travelling with them and doing things with them, but not revealing himself until the very end of the encounter, and then only in the briefest of moments. There is no prolonged physical revelation. This encounter shows him speaking to them at length from the very same Scriptures as mentioned above, and with the same intent, so that the purpose of his manifestation was identical. But the whole approach

of Jesus is very different. Whilst the evening revelation majored on a direct physical appearance as a starting point, the afternoon revelation did precisely the opposite. It is this very indirectness, however, that yields vital lessons about the different ways he can choose to reveal his risen presence without being physically seen.

Luke writes the story with care and at length. These two disciples set out from Jerusalem to go to Emmaus, a distance of some eight miles and about two hours walking. They were not part of the original band of twelve but were obviously close to Jesus. As they walked they were talking together about the events of the early morning when the womenfolk had reported that the tomb was empty and that they had seen a vision of angels who had said Jesus was alive. Both of them were perplexed and uncertain. The risen Jesus approached them and started to walk with them. However, in contrast to what would happen later than evening with the larger group of disciples, he did not immediately reveal to them who he was. As far as the two disciples were concerned he just happened to be an ordinary fellow traveller. They were deeply absorbed in their conversation when Jesus joined them and asked them what they were talking about. Surprised that the stranger didn't seem to grasp the subject of their conversation they stopped and told him about Jesus of Nazareth, that he had been publicly crucified, that his body had disappeared from his tomb and that there had been visions of angels and reports that he was alive.

At that point in the conversation Jesus might well have chosen to reveal his identity, as of course he could well have done. Indeed it might seem to have been an ideal moment for such a disclosure. But he did not; he chose to remain still unknown by sight. The eyes of the two companions remained closed as to who he was. Instead, Jesus chose to turn their attention to the Scriptures (precisely as would do with the larger group later that evening). So, on that Emmaus road *"beginning with Moses and the prophets he explained in all the Scriptures what was said about himself"*. We do not know at what point in the journey Jesus joined the two disciples but the explanation must have been long and thorough. They do not appear to have been in any hurry; as we have noted the two disciples actually stopped to give Jesus the account of their concern over Jesus. At no point during that time did they have any idea who the stranger was. Not until they had actually reached Emmaus, and they had pressed him to stay with them for supper did he disclose his

identity. It was as he broke bread with them at supper that they suddenly recognised him, but immediately he disappeared. They had no time to really take in his revealed physical presence. But together they agreed on one thing; *"Were not our hearts burning within us while he talked with us on the road and opened the Scriptures to us"*. There was recognition in these words that they ought to have realised who the stranger was in the very way he taught them and the profound understanding and conviction that he brought to them. He had brought new hope to them in the midst of their perplexity and disillusionment. All their confusion and bewilderment had been answered as Jesus enlightened their minds and hearts. They ought to have recognised who he really was.

What was Jesus doing here in this delayed revelation? Why did he choose to reveal himself so indirectly? It seems reasonably clear that Jesus was giving to these two disciples an abiding lesson that even if he was not physically recognisable, or indeed physically present, his voice could none the less be unmistakably heard in the way he would make the Scriptures burn in them. He wanted them to understand that in the reading and studying of the Scriptures they would actually hear that voice of clarity and power at times of bewilderment and need. He also wanted them to realise the importance of the prophetic Scriptures because the Scriptures would remain when he had ascended and they were intended to be the rock of their faith and understanding as they carried on as his witnesses. Jesus was underlining in a very pertinent way the imperative need of Scripture and the voice of Jesus making those Scriptures understandable and relevant.

The scriptures are full of truth. It requires, however, a "voice" to make that truth come "alive" and burn into the apprehension of the reader. That voice is the voice of revelation. It is the voice of Jesus. It is at the same time the voice of the Holy Spirit for the voice of the Spirit is the voice of Jesus. Without that voice the Scripture remains pedestrian, obscure and ineffective. The Scripture will always be a document of interest for the scholar simply by being a great literary and religious document of such long standing and historical consequence, but it can never be what it was intended to be, namely an instrument to reveal divine truth, without the divine voice speaking. It was that voice which those two disciples heard on that afternoon. He wanted them to recognise that voice again whenever their hearts began to burn in the reading of the Scriptures.

It is not that Christians in reading Scripture always have or should have an experience of Scripture burning with immediate and relevant meaning in the very powerful way those disciples experienced it that afternoon. For the most part the Scripture is read in a manner which brings a quiet refreshing of truth and for the purpose of a gradual gaining of new understanding. And such quiet reading is always edifying. But it is a fact that most Christians have experienced moments when the Scripture has had a very real sense of burning about it, and that this has been generally at moments of very great need or when some very important new truth about the Kingdom has been revealed to them. At those moments the words they read (or hear!) become very much alive. The "burning" is actually due to the depth of the relevance of what they read and the depth of conviction of the truth of what they read. What we read and hear at such moments always becomes fundamental revelation and directs and steers our lives in a powerful and lasting way. Such moments are very clear markers on our Christian journey. And they are in essence the presence of the voice of the living Jesus. We need to be quite clear in our minds that on such occasions we are with the resurrected and living Jesus.

These "burning" moments also become a very powerful part of our living testimony to Jesus, and we should always be ready to offer them to others whenever they can bring guidance and comfort. They need to be noted down also for our own personal refreshing in the same way as "lakeside" experiences need to be. I certainly seek to do so.

A striking example of Scripture "burning" came to me when I was deeply exercised about the question of speaking in tongues. I had had an experience of being filled with the Spirit but could not resolve whether speaking in tongues was right and something to seek or ignore. One morning at that time I was walking round a park and praying, and the subject of my praying was not the question of tongues but a simple request that Jesus might become more real to me. As I walked the Scripture flashed into my mind, *"He that speaks in an unknown tongue builds himself up"*. It brought immediate and powerful illumination. I realised at once that my request about Jesus was a request that I might be "built up (edified)", and this was a burning voice telling me that tongues was an important gift because it would do exactly that - build me up in perception and faith. All the confusion over tongues abruptly vanished and I simply knew that

in pursuing tongues I would be pursuing something that would be of great benefit to me. The different arguments and viewpoints concerning speaking in tongues had been completely overridden by a voice which burned with truth. Without more ado I went to a friend who prayed with me, and I broke out speaking in tongues. This poured out of me for a solid hour. That hour of constant uninterrupted praying in tongues fully confirmed the reality and truth of the value of tongues. Later a further simple truth of Scripture became acidly clear, namely that when I speak in a tongue it is my spirit having direct fellowship with the Holy Spirit. No wonder I was edified!

I think this testimony makes clear to me the fact that "ordinary" reading of Scripture stocks up important knowledge in our hearts and is of great value, and at the same time showed me what could happen to such Scripture when Jesus takes hold of it and makes it burn and resolves our inner wondering and doubts simply by making it burn or underlining it in the way only he can.

A still more remarkable experience for me was at a time when I was desperately seeking to understand the nature of the fight we have with powers of darkness. I was pushed into this by a very unpleasant experience of such forces, which really left me very dismayed and with no doubt of their reality and power. I went to my bible with a great need to find answers and I was immediately given several passages from the Old Testament in which the whole struggle became very clear. This was very much a "burning" time for me, when new truth poured out from different places in my bible and gave me the light, assurance and resolve that I desperately needed. Those Scriptures had never meant very much to me before but at that time they were indelibly underlined. The fact that they came out of the Old Testament rather than the New Testament gives me a sense of affinity with those disciples who listened that afternoon to a survey of Old Testament prophecy and found profound understanding of the very events that were creating the New Testament. The Old Testament can burn just as much as the New when the living Jesus himself speaks through Scripture. We should expect and anticipate such times.

3. TWO FRIENDS – THE BREAKING OF BREAD

"Jesus was recognised by them when he broke the bread"

Lk. 24:35 NIV

The journey of Jesus with the two disciples to Emmaus was significant not only for his "burning" exposition of Scripture but also because of its significant ending. After keeping his identity hidden from them for the whole of the journey, Jesus finally disclosed who he was in the act of breaking bread over supper. And then he disappeared. This implies very clearly that his presence is to be found in the breaking of bread just as much as in the tone of his voice as he expounded the Scriptures. Whilst the latter is widely appreciated and raises expectation, the former, perhaps, can all too easily be overlooked and neglected. This calls for some serious consideration of the act of breaking bread.

The final episode of the story, therefore, strongly underlines the breaking of bread as a matter of great importance, an act in which we should expect the presence of Jesus to be revealed. Jesus had previously broken bread with his apostles at the Last Supper and had enjoined them to remember his death by repeating the act. Now, on the first day of his resurrection he endorsed his injunction by breaking bread himself and making it the focal point of personal revelation.

It is an interesting question as to whether the two disciples on the Emmaus road were in anyway aware that Jesus had broken bread in the solemn manner that he had at the Last Supper. The two certainly did not belong to the apostolic band – one of them was called Cleopas, a name not listed among the apostles, and the two of them went straight back to Jerusalem after their encounter in order to tell the apostles that they had seen the resurrected Jesus. It is doubtful, given the fear and flight that followed the arrest and crucifixion, that the apostles had shared with anyone else what had happened at the Last Supper. Thus the probability is that the two only learned of the significance of the breaking of bread when they told their story to the eleven later that evening. The fact that Jesus had revealed himself to the two other disciples in the act of breaking bread would certainly have resonated powerfully with the apostles, and

reinforced in their minds how important Jesus' injunction to break bread was. It would have resonated in similar fashion with the two who had now been enlightened.

Why was the breaking of bread so important to Jesus? Why was it given such prominence at the Supper and the day of resurrection? The obvious answer is because this act pointed up in the simplest and clearest of ways the absolute centrality of his death on the cross. The act of breaking bread at the Supper was invested with the words, "This is my body given for you"; it was also accompanied by sharing a cup of wine which spoke of his blood as the blood of a new covenant for forgiveness. This sacrifice on the cross was what Jesus wanted remembered since everything depended upon it. The long bible study that took place on the Emmaus road had equally emphasised the death of Jesus as it had been prophetically foretold in the Scriptures. Here in the breaking of bread was the same emphasis in an act of remembrance in the midst of a meal. If the calling to mind of his death through the Scripture could attract his presence, so equally could the symbolic act of breaking bread.

What are we to learn from this? It is a call to engage with the breaking of bread with alertness and with expectation of it being a moment of revelation of the presence of Jesus to us. There has to be an attitude to it which has a true solemnity. This does not mean we should abuse its extraordinary simplicity and obscure it by some sort of magnified "mystique" or magnified ritual. Its setting in the early church was in the homes of the believers when they worshipped and prayed together in intimate fellowship together. Their mind set was one of seeking the presence and power of Jesus.

If we are to expect Jesus to make himself present at the breaking of bread then we must be ready for that presence to be manifest in a great variety of ways. It could be in some encouraging word from a fellow believer, it could be in the healing of a sick person, it could be guidance, warning and much more. Praying for each other in the context of the breaking of bread should be seen as one of the most powerful of acts.

4.MARY MAGDALENE - THE INNER VOICE

Jesus said to her, "Mary!" She cried out, 'Rabboni'"

Jn. 20:16 NIV

The two friends on the Emmaus road heard the "burning" voice of Jesus in the Scriptures. Mary Magdalene heard the same voice in a much more direct and personal manner. This personal voice can still be heard.

Mary Magdalene was very possibly the first person to see Jesus risen from the dead. When the other women and the disciples had left the empty tomb on the morning of the resurrection Mary remained there alone, weeping inconsolably. She thought that someone had removed the body, and she was deeply distressed. The grief of his death had been much aggravated by the absence of the body. After two angels had spoken to her to no avail Jesus himself approached. She did not recognise him, and when first he spoke she thought he was the gardener. It was then that Jesus broke into her consciousness by simply calling her name in personal tones. This immediately revealed to her who he was and brought instant relief to her distress. Once again, in this encounter we have Jesus revealing himself by something other than a recognisable bodily appearance, something intangible but very real - his voice. It is this same voice that can be heard today, and especially, as with Mary, in times of distress or perplexity.

Several such moments of hearing this voice stand out for me personally from my early Christian life and in connection with my calling into the Christian ministry. I struggled against that call, but it kept coming to me through a very direct and personal voice. Waking up at night I could hear the voice saying, "Go into the ministry". I remember listening to a preacher in a small Methodist chapel and sensing some unseen person behind the preacher saying directly to me, "Go into the ministry". The voice stayed with me for twelve months until I obeyed. My wife and I had intended to marry but, sitting in a college library one day after I had accepted the calling, I sensed yet again a person come and this time sit next to me saying quietly, "Postpone your wedding". A further struggle and then further compliance. All this was very direct and personal. It

was all a time of considerable distress. But I do not think anything less than this direct, personal hearing of his voice would have been sufficient to reach me in my reluctance and get me into the ministry It is now many years since this occurred, and I can see clearly now that this inner voice experience was nothing less than a major work of grace by Jesus to enable me to enter into a life's work for which I am increasingly more thankful, and which I was so foolishly near to rejecting.

5. THE APOSTLES – A PROMISE OVER SUPPER

If anyone loves me, I will show myself to him" Jn 14:21 NIV

We have seen how Jesus manifested his living presence through his resurrection appearances to his disciples, but did so in indirect ways that are still very relevant for us today. He showed them how to recognise his presence not simply in terms of a physical manifestation but in terms of significant and miraculous happenings in their lives, and in the detecting of his voice, both in the Scriptures and inwardly. However, he also gave them some clear and direct teaching about how they would be able to recognise his living presence when he was no longer physically with them. It came during the course of the Last Supper on the night before his crucifixion, and is recorded for us in Jn. 14:15-23.

When Jesus met with his disciples at that Supper he knew exactly what would happen to him later that night and on the following two days; he would be betrayed, tried, crucified, buried in a tomb and then rise from the dead. Such a train of events would seem, however, inconceivable to the disciples as they met for the meal, and so Jesus gave them no specific details of what the next hours would bring. However, he did make extensive general allusions, though necessarily enigmatic, as to what lay ahead. He told them he was going to leave them, going to prepare a place for them where in due course they would follow. He told them not to be afraid but to go on believing in him. He told them he would appear to them but not to the world. The disciples were very much perplexed by all this, as their questions indicate, but the events that were to follow would bring clarification.

At one point Jesus made a definite statement of promise; *"Whoever has my commands and obeys them, he is the one who loves me. He who loves me will be loved by my Father, and I too will love him and show myself to him"*. 14:21. This is a stark and unambiguous statement that Jesus would show himself to those who loved him. Three important features are immediately apparent in this promise. First there is a timeless quality about the promise and it is not to be confined to the immediate days of his observable physical resurrection. This timeless quality is underlined by the second feature, namely that, though spoken to the disciples, the promise is much more inclusive in scope than just the disciples; it is a promise that he would show himself to "whoever" loved him and showed that love by obedience to his commands. It is in fact a promise which we may take and embrace for ourselves today. The third feature is that the Greek word for "show" is strong and emphatic; it means Jesus would show himself in a clear and obvious manner, even in an intimate manner. It would be appropriate to use the expression "in an objective manner". This is not a promise about a vague appearance, but something definite and real.

In v. 22 one of the disciples, Judas (not Iscariot), listening to him, asked him a direct question about this promise, the substance of which was *"How are you going to do that? You say you won't show yourself to everybody, but just those who love you. How are you going to do that? Tell us more about how you are going to show yourself"*. Remembering that this conversation was taking place before the crucifixion and the resurrection, we might think that Jesus would have answered Judas by saying that he was going to die, but would be resurrected and would appear bodily to his disciples but not to anyone else. That would have course been absolutely true. But that is not the answer Jesus gave him. He made no mention of his resurrection body. In v. 23 we read what Jesus actually replied; *"If a person loves me and keeps my word then my Father will love him and we (i.e. the Father and Jesus) will come and make our home with him"*. The answer to the question *"how are you going to manifest yourself?"* was that Jesus was going to come and live with and inside a person permanently, and, not only that, but the Father's presence would also come in like manner. That is how he would show himself. The language here makes it very plain that when Jesus was speaking of manifesting himself he was not talking about a physical presence but a spiritual presence.

Before examining the meaning and nature of this spiritual indwelling in more detail, we need to note that this conversation had actually followed on from a previous promise Jesus had made, a promise about the Holy Spirit in Jn. 14:15-17 NIV. Again speaking of those who would love him and keep his commands, Jesus had said that they would receive the Holy Spirit, the Spirit of truth, and that he would live with them and be in them always; *"If you love me, keep my commands. And I will ask the Father and he will give you another advocate to help you and be with you for ever – the Spirit of truth"*. It was in that context that Jesus went on to say that He would manifest himself to them and that he and his Father would come to live in them. This all fits together very naturally simply because when the Spirit of God comes into a person, then the Father, Son and Holy Spirit all come together into a person, for the Spirit of God is both the Spirit of the Father (God) and the Spirit of Jesus. When the Spirit comes into us he does not leave the Father or Jesus behind, they are indivisible. As with the previous verses we have looked at, this promise of the Spirit speaks not of a physical manifestation of a risen Jesus but once again of a spiritual manifestation. We should also note that when Jesus is speaking of the Spirit of God coming into a person he is emphatic once more that this would be a definite and recognisable manifestation: *"**You know him,** for he is with you and (will be) in you"* 14:17.

Understanding a "spiritual manifestation"
So when Jesus says *"I will show myself to him"* he is speaking of a spiritual manifestation, a manifestation that will be very clearly experienced within the person's own being. It will be a manifestation of nothing less than God and Jesus himself, and for that very reason we are hardly going to be unaware of it! God living in us is not going to be "hidden". What, then, is that manifestation going to be like? What should we expect to see, or feel? If we seek answers to those questions and look out for his manifestation it will undoubtedly be hugely significant for our growth as Christians and a great source of comfort and enlightenment. Many Christians go through life as though Jesus and the Father were distant and even uninterested, with no concept of a close and inner impact. That is not how Jesus wants it.

To understand the nature of a spiritual manifestation we can take a human analogy. If my spirit were to come into you, that is to say

if my essential being (that part of me which I am conscious lives in my body but which is different from my body), came into you, you would change. You would feel the impact of the desires and motivations of my spirit; you would feel the strength and vitality of my spirit or conversely the weakness of my spirit. The things that are of interest to me would become of interest to you, or at least you would find new inclinations in your life that were really mine; your desires would change. My spirit in you would become apparent and would begin to affect your behaviour. If you were alive to your own inner promptings you would become aware of this. I would be making my home with you. This is very much like the change that begins in you when Jesus comes into you by his Spirit and begins to manifest himself – you begin to change, there is a new dynamic of change. You change unmistakably and profoundly in the direction and desires of your heart. You would be different from what you were before.

Let's go further and ask the question, what sort of changes would be likely to take place? The answer to that question simply lies in knowing what sort of person Jesus or the Spirit of Jesus is, his character and his motivations. We have an abundance of information on that. First and foremost the Spirit of Jesus is a "Holy" Spirit. In him there is an intense dislike of evil, even a "hatred" of evil. He abhors uncleanness, lying, selfish covetousness, violence and abuse, anger and malice, stealing and corruption, pride and arrogance. On the other hand there is a great love of all that is righteous, true, loving and gracious. These fundamental and intense motivations constitute an incredibly powerful dynamic at the heart of Jesus. When Jesus (and the Father) makes his home with us this dynamic will be life-changing for us, this will make us really a "new creation". This heart for holiness will be above everything else the way in which Jesus manifests himself to us if we follow him. It will be a profoundly objective manifestation and we shall be very aware of it.

Personal experience
In my own personal experience this powerful new dynamic of a desire for godliness first flowed through me when I gave my life to Jesus. He accepted my life and immediately came and made his home with me. My whole desire was immediately fastened on walking with God in the way that God wanted it, the way of

holiness. It released profound joy and well-being. It was an amazing discovery. It was extraordinarily deep and powerful. The day before I yielded to Jesus it was not there, but the day after, it was intensely real and life changing. It replaced an increasing and uneasy conviction of sin which had been growing for some months before. I recognised in my spirit the beauty of a righteous life and felt compelled to pursue it. In itself it had great "enabling" power toward living a godly life.

The fact remained none the less that I still retained something of my old "sinful" nature. The new dynamic was in conflict with an old dynamic- the tendency to do what was not righteous, the tendency to self-seeking, to inappropriate fleshly pleasure etc. At times there was (and still is) a struggle between the new and the old nature. But the new dynamic was allied to a new fact, and that was that the grip which evil had on my life had been broken by the conquest of sin at the Cross of Christ. This was a spiritual fact and could be accessed by holding on to what Jesus had done and by presenting sinful tendencies to the cross. Thus intense desire for righteousness was allied to what Jesus had done on the cross to break the hold of sin, and so a new righteous life was not just an eager desire, but also a real possibility. My first grasp of this was that in giving my life to Jesus I felt I was forgiven and had had a spiritual bath leaving me clean.

Paul the Apostle testifies with great power to this transforming dynamic of the Spirit of Jesus in his own life. In Romans 7 he speaks of his personal experience of trying to fight the power of sin in his own strength. Though he was keen to obey and follow the law of righteousness he found himself incapable of achieving that goal. In Romans 8:2 he gave this experience of his inner inability to cope with sin a name, a full description. He called it "*the law of sin and death*"; he was describing a law or a principle in humanity as we know it, that sin is always too strong for unaided humanity. This was a profound experience that caused him much suffering, and a desperate longing for release. But in the same sentence in Romans he affirms that this power was broken by another law – "*the law of the Spirit of life in Christ Jesus*". Here was something else acting right inside his humanity but with an opposite result to the law of sin; it was a principle of new, godly life and it set him free from the law of sin and death. He was deeply aware of a new inner law and

that law was the life of the risen Jesus working in and through the spirit of Jesus.

The Spirit of Jesus is an enabling Spirit in many other ways, and in discovering this we find more confirmation that Jesus has come to live in us by his Spirit. It is not simply in matters of righteousness that we find a new dynamic entering our lives when he takes up residence within us. In all sorts of ways what had not been possible for us without Christ becomes possible once we have committed ourselves to him and to his commands. He brings new inner resources. These are very real, objectively real. Paul wrote "I can do all things through him (Christ) who gives me strength" (Phil.4:13 NIV), and he wrote it from the midst of all the struggles and needs of life. He became a contented man as he trusted Jesus to see him through. Paul recognised that when life became too difficult for him to cope with there was another power within him helping him to handle the most impossible situations. He became aware of the peace and joy which belonged to Jesus, and which would invade him at moments of great need.

If we seek to serve and witness for Jesus (in obedience to his command and out of love for him) we find a whole new set of "enablings" become evident in our lives through his Spirit. Personally, as a minister, I have found a very powerful "enabling" in preaching - something that is much more than any human ability. Many have found that in their personal witness to others, in their praying for others etc. Many have found it in the release of "gifts of the Spirit". In all these experiences it is so important to recognise the living, risen presence of Jesus. Without him and without our personal union with him these things simply do not happen. This Jesus, who lives in us, manifests his presence again and again by taking us into realms that belong to God himself. He abundantly fulfils his promise to reveal himself to those who love him and seek to be obedient.

JESUS and THE SEAL OF THE SPIRIT

INTRODUCTION

One of the greatest gifts which God has given to his people is the presence of his own Spirit in their hearts. We have become those in whom God himself has come to dwell. Jesus made that fact very clear when he said to his disciples at the Last Supper, *"If anyone loves me, he will obey my teaching and My Father will love him, and* **we will come to him and make our home with him"** (Jn. 14:17 NIV). When the Father and the Son come into our hearts they come of course through and with the presence of the Holy Spirit.

God in us is the true glory of the Christian. It is something that can happen to anyone, the only stipulation being that we fully commit ourselves to following Jesus and putting him at the centre of our lives. This is an utterly life changing experience, living with God in us. It is very important for our Christian life that we have a deep awareness of that indwelling Spirit and can recognise His Presence in our own lives. It is fundamental to our assurance and our joy. Unfortunately the fact is that many who would call themselves Christians seem scarcely aware of that Presence, and are somewhat mystified by talk of the Spirit. It is the purpose of this booklet to show how we can recognise the presence of the Spirit in our lives so that our joy may be full.

1. THE SPIRIT AS A SEAL

"Having believed, you were marked with a seal, the promised Holy Spirit, who is a deposit guaranteeing our inheritance until the redemption of those who are God's possession".
Eph. 1: 13-14 NIV

He anointed us, set his seal of ownership on us, and put his Spirit in our hearts as a deposit, guaranteeing what is to come."
2Cor. 1: 21-22 NIV

"Now it is God who has made us for this purpose (to have a new body eternally) and has given us the Spirit as a deposit, guaranteeing what is to come"
2 Cor. 5:5 NIV

In these verses Paul makes it clear that it is the presence of the Holy Spirit in our lives that is the true source of our assurance that we belong to God and that we will inherit eternal life. The Spirit, now living in our hearts, is the confirming *"seal"* and *"guarantee"* of everything God has planned for us in Christ.

In Eph. 1:13 Paul points us to the moment when this sealing took place; it was *"when we believed"*, that is at the time when we believed in Jesus and committed ourselves to following him, when faith was born in our hearts and we gave a heart response. In whatever way we may have made such a personal commitment it was that act of faith that caused us to be *"sealed"* with the gift of the Spirit. Paul, moreover, implies that all who make such a genuine confession of faith are marked in this same manner.

Thus we are saved by faith, and that salvation is sealed by the Spirit of God. The seal of the Spirit is a mark of the fact that we are now "owned" by God, that we belong to him, we are his possession – *"he has set his seal of ownership on us"*. Not only is the presence of the Spirit the mark of God's ownership, but it is at the same time a *"deposit"*, (a *"first instalment"*, a *down payment"*, "an *earnest"*) of what is to come. Three times Paul uses this expression (Gk. arrabon). A *"deposit"* is indicative of the fact that, though an impartation of the Spirit has been made, a great deal more of the same is yet to come. His presence in us now by his Spirit is an immensely rich gift (nothing less than God living in us!) but it is yet to be followed by an infilling of the Spirit and an open revelation of the glory of God that will transcend even this precious seal. That will be when we finally stand before God, and our redemption is completed. Thus the nature of this *"first instalment"* speaks loudly of the nature the great glory which is to follow. The word for "deposit" is the Gk. *"arrabon"*. In Modern Greek the same word still exists and means "an engagement ring". A bride's engagement ring is a seal (a deposit) of great beauty and value, but it remains but a token of what is yet to come to her when her marriage is finally completed. So it is with the seal of the Spirit.

In 2 Cor. 5:1-5 NIV Paul gives some definition of this greater glory that is to come. He states *"We know that if the earthly tent in which we live is destroyed we have a building from God, an eternal house in heaven not built by human hands"* 2Cor 5:1. He is speaking here of the new resurrection body and the totally new life and existence that is part of our inheritance in Jesus. He is contrasting our present existence as a life lived in a temporary "tent" with an eternal life lived in a permanent "building". This is God's purpose for us. He continues, *"Now it is God who has made us for this purpose (to have a new body and a new life eternally) and has given us the Spirit as a deposit, guaranteeing what is to come"*.

2. THE SPIRIT AS A RECOGNISABLE SEAL

"You know him for he lives with you and will be in you".
Jn 14:15 NIV
"We (I and my Father) will make our home with him".
Jn 14:17 NIV

It is not in the nature of a seal to be unrecognisable or invisible or obscure. On the contrary a seal is intended to be something that is clear, evident and unmistakable. But the Holy Spirit is "Spirit"; he is not tangible or visible or audible in the way that the seals of this physical world are. An engagement ring can be seen and fingered and displayed, but this is not the case with the heavenly *"arrabon"*. Here we are dealing with "Spirit", not the flesh or the physical. How, then, do we recognise that which is "spirit"? Jesus answers this question when, speaking about the Spirit to his disciples at the Last Supper, he said *"The world neither sees him nor knows him ....* ***But you know him, for he lives with you and will be in you. "*** Jn. 14:15. In that statement he acknowledged that the "world would neither see him nor know him (the Spirit)" with ordinary human faculties, but the disciples would know him because he would come to live in them. Jesus repeated the substance of this statement shortly afterwards with the words, *"If anyone loves me, he will obey my teaching and My Father will love him, and **we will come to him and make our home with him"*** Jn. 14:17. The "seal", therefore, is not something to be recognised by our physical being but by the

recognition of something that happens in and to our hearts – the seal is that of a new and living Presence at the very depth of our being. In other words, the seal will be recognised in the fact that as he comes into our hearts there will something of a radical change at the core of our being. To take a simple analogy, if one person were somehow to come into the heart of another person and be at the spiritual centre of their life, there would be a recognisable change in that second person: the second person's outlook would start to reflect the first person's aspirations and personality. They would begin to think the thoughts and feel the impulsions of the first person. They would be aware of this new presence. Essentially, therefore, when we are looking for the seal of the Spirit we are looking for a spiritual seal, an unmistakable influence on our own spirit, a mind-set, an outlook that is not native to us, but is seeking to direct us or re-direct our lives. Indeed we are looking for something that is essentially of the mind-set of God and heart of God. Even though it may be humanly intangible, if God's Spirit came into our own heart it would be so impacting that it would be actually very difficult not to be aware of it.

We need to ask the question, "What impact would the Spirit be likely to make on our own hearts?" What changes is He likely to make, and how can we recognise them? The answer to that question is to be found in what we know of the nature and heart of God himself, for it is God's desires and God's purposes that he would begin to press into our hearts. We would begin to want what he wants and we would begin to seek to be as he is for he would be seeking to transform us into his likeness. It is critically important that we know what we are looking for and how to recognise such an impact in our own lives if we are to walk in the full assurance that the presence of the Spirit is intended to bring to us. Above all other characteristics he would seek to make us holy people, full of righteousness.

3.   RECOGNISING THE SPIRIT OF HOLINESS

"I will give you a new heart and put a new spirit within you;
I will remove from you your heart of stone and give you a
heart of flesh....... And I will put my Spirit in you and move you
to follow my decrees".   Ez. 36:26,27 NIV

"This is the covenant I will make with the people ..... I will put my Law in their minds and write it on their hearts". Jer. 31:33 NIV

"If the ministry that brought condemnation was glorious (Moses and the Law*), how much more glorious is the ministry that brings righteousness* (the ministry of the Spirit*) .... and we are all being transformed into his image with ever increasing glory, which comes from the Lord who is the Spirit."*
2 Cor. 3:9 & 18 NIV

God chose you to be saved by the sanctifying work Of the Spirit

In the texts above Jeremiah and Ezekiel speak prophetically of a new covenant in which God would fundamentally change the hearts of people. This change would be so profound that it is described as receiving a *"new spirit"*. It would be brought about by God putting his own Spirit in them. The hard, unresponsive heart *("a heart of stone")* would become sensitive and responsive *("a heart of flesh")* as it was touched by the presence of the divine Spirit. The particular nature of the change would be that the desires of the hearts of those so touched would be fully focussed on walking in the way of the righteous commandments of the Lord; people would love and seek godly behaviour in a way that had not been possible before. In the language of Jeremiah he would *"write the Law on their hearts"*, meaning that the Law would become central in their thinking and desires. It is in this way that the Spirit would *"move"* people (energise, motivate, inspire, enable) them to the godly life which is enshrined in *"his decrees"*.

This is precisely the new covenant which Jesus brought into being through his death, resurrection, ascension and his consequent gift of the Holy Spirit to all who believe. In the quotation from 2 Cor.3 Paul starkly reminds his readers that the old Mosaic covenant whereby people were given the "commandments" and told to obey them was actually something that could only bring *"condemnation"* because the hardness of the human heart would not allow them to be obedient to those decrees. This *"ministry of condemnation"* he vividly contrasts with what he calls *"the ministry which brings*

righteousness", namely the ministry of the Holy Spirit. This new work of the Holy Spirit is a ministry which is bit by bit *"transforming"* us into the image of Christ with *"ever increasing glory"*. The Holy Spirit is at work in believing people enabling them to be righteous in a way that was impossible before.

This change of heart, this profound desire and love for righteousness, is eminently recognisable when it happens to a person. It is this that makes us realise we have been given a *"new spirit"*. A true reception of the Holy Spirit is a life-changing experience, felt in the heart but as real as anything in the physical realm. The New Testament elsewhere refers to people being *"born again of the Spirit"* and *"becoming a new creation"*. These are both graphic and vivid alternative ways of expressing this same essential experience. They speak of a very deep re-direction of life.

The people who most obviously recognise this "seal" on their lives are people whom God has rescued from the depths of depravity, and there have been many such people. For them the *"new birth"* comes as a startling, total transformation and as a huge new beginning. For them the memory of the change remains very deep and energising, leading in many cases to powerful and enduring ministry. But radical change is not just for those whose lives have touched such a low. Sin in its many forms is the universal experience of all humanity. Greed, lust, pride and the like beset us all in varying degrees. Waking up from what might be described as the pleasures of a "normal" life to find that it is actually much more polluted than we had thought, and then tasting the delights of a truly godly life should be normal to a Christian, though it may not necessarily come about in a startling or sudden manner.

The Holy Spirit rested on many people in the Old Testament even though they were not living under the all-embracing new covenant, and his influence in their lives can be seen clearly. David was one such example, whose heart feelings are portrayed in the book of Psalms along with many others. Psalm 119 NIV is remarkable for the expressions of the author's sheer *"delight"* in the Law of the Lord and the commandments of God. These are expressions which betoken the influence of the Spirit: *"your commands give me delight"* (v.143), *"See how I love your precepts"* (v.159), *"I hate and detest falsehood, but I love your law. Seven times a day I praise you for your righteous laws"* (v.164), *"I obey your statutes for I love them greatly"* (v.167). Where these sentiments of love of God's

word genuinely exist in our hearts we may be sure that we have the seal of the Spirit.

Paul expresses the same thing in a more doctrinal mode: *"Through Christ Jesus the law of the Spirit who gives life has set you free from the law of sin and death"* (Rom.8:2 NIV) He had experienced in his life the fact that even though he wanted to do good he could never achieve it fully in the strength of his own natural self (Rom. 7:14ff NIV). This was because of the *"law of sin and death."* But he also knew what it was to be free from sin by living in the power of a life under the control and influence of the Holy Spirit. This was *"the law of the Spirit who gives life"*.

Jesus expresses it in picturesque style: *"If any man believes in me out of his innermost being will flow rivers of living water"* (Jn.7:38 NIV) to which John the Apostle added, *"By this he was speaking of the Holy Spirit which those who believed in were to receive"* (Jn. 7:39 NIV). The river of the Spirit is a gushing of holiness and righteousness. When the Holy Spirit takes up residence in us there pours out of our own spirit the same holiness and righteousness.

4. RECOGNISING THE SPIRIT OF REVELATION

"I pray that the God of our Lord Jesus Christ may give you the Spirit of wisdom and revelation that you might know him better" Eph. 1:17 NIV

"... having the eyes of your heart enlightened that you may know the hope to which you are called..."Eph. 1:18 NIV

"God sent the Spirit of his Son into our hearts, crying "Abba, Father". Gal. 4:6 NIV

"The Spirit will take what is mine and make it known to you". Jn.14:15 NIV

"The Holy Spirit will teach you all things". Jn. 14:26 NIV

In the first of the quotations above Paul prays for the Ephesians that they may receive the *"Spirit of revelation in order that they may know God (and Jesus) better or more fully"*. The word *"revelation"* means an *"unveiling"*, a removal of a cover to see something which is hidden. Paul earnestly wants his readers to grasp the hidden reality of God and his purposes. In the second quotation he vividly illustrates what he means by *"revelation"* by using the expression, *"having the eyes of your hearts enlightened that you might know ..."* Here the idea is of light shining on the eyes in order that something not seen can be seen – in other words a removal of blindness. Paul recognises that God is in a very real sense "hidden" from wayward humanity, and that humanity is "blind" to God in its waywardness. This is the case even though there is sufficient evidence in the created world of his existence, and even of his character (Rom:) This hidden ness and blindness is removed only by the Holy Spirit himself working in the human heart. There is no other way that it can happen. Hence the revelation of God is a spiritual thing that can only come from God himself. It cannot come from purely human thinking, no matter how intellectual it may be. This is made clear in 1 Cor. 1:21 where Paul makes the comment *"In the wisdom of God the world through its wisdom did not know him"*.

Revelation, therefore, for Paul is not just the mind coming to know something; it is **the heart** (the essential spiritual being of a person) perceiving the ultimate truth that God is real and seeking relationship with people. It is a "seeing" of something at the deepest level. It is a self-authenticating knowledge. It is much deeper than mental knowledge about the concept of God. Genuine revelation is in a real sense a meeting with God, even, indeed, a personal meeting with God. People can know about God conceptually, even believe there is a God, and yet not know him with that degree of certainty and warmth which comes when the eyes of our hearts have been opened to His reality and person. Revelation is thus much more than simply to know about something; it is an encounter. It is something which enables our "hearts" to cry out *"**Abba, Father**"*. Reading a biography will teach us much about a person, but actually meeting that person takes us into another dimension and enables us to say we really "know" them.

The *"**eyes of the heart**"* is a phrase which points us to something more than the function of the mind, beyond normal mental knowledge. In fact, for the eyes of our heart to be enlightened does

not necessarily call for a high intelligence or intellect. The process is fundamentally a "spiritual" perception, an acknowledgment and recognition of truth through a profound depth of conviction in our spirit not just our minds. To bring about such a conviction is precisely the work of the Holy Spirit as Jesus himself depicted it: *"When he (the Spirit) comes he will convict the world of sin righteousness and judgement"* (Jn.).

Luke, a close travelling companion of Paul, provides us with an example of this happening to a person when he recorded the conversion of Lydia at Philippi (Acts). He relates, in typical Pauline phraseology, that as she listened to Paul speaking *"the Lord **opened her heart** to respond to Paul's message"*. That message would certainly have centred in some way on the need of forgiveness of sin and the righteousness that comes through Jesus, and it was her heart that was opened to the truth by the Spirit. Such was the depth of her revelation or conviction that she immediately submitted to baptism and offered her home as a base for Paul and his companions.

The Spirit of Revelation and the Scriptures
Lydia's conversion also points to another very important aspect of the work of the Spirit of Revelation: He opens the eyes of people particularly through the illumination of the Scriptures. The women who met by the riverside in Philippi were either Jews or proselyte believers in the God of the Jews, Lydia being among the latter category. It was Paul's normal procedure to speak about Jesus from the Old Testament prophetic scriptures when talking to such a Jewish audience. It was as she listened to his exposition of those scriptures that her heart was opened. This is indicative of the common experience of Christians throughout the ages that on receiving the Spirit the bible becomes a "live" book, a genuine tool of understanding and guidance in faith and following Jesus. What at one time was a dull, lifeless and meaningless book becomes alive and relevant in an astonishing manner. This is not surprising given the fact that the Scriptures claim divine origin through the inspiration of the Spirit himself. Not only does the bible give a full overview of God's nature and purposes, but it has the ability to speak again and again directly and personally to the needs of individual Christians in all situations in life. This is a fact known only too well to genuine believers, but remains baffling to the disinterested and unbelieving. It is for this reason that the believer

who has the Spirit is drawn irresistibly to reading the bible. By this appetite we recognise the presence of the seal of the Spirit.

5. RECOGNISING THE SPIRIT OF POWER

"You will receive power when the Holy Spirit comes upon you; and you will be my witnesses ….. to the ends of the earth"
Acts 1:8 NIV

"in a few days you will be baptised with the Holy Spirit".
Acts 1:5 NIV

"He will baptise you with the Holy Spirit and fire".
Lk. 3:16 NIV

"The Spirit of the Lord is on me because he has anointed me to proclaim good news to the poor …. to set the oppressed free".
Lk 4:18 NIV

"The man on whom you see the Spirit come down and remain is the one who will baptise with the Holy Spirit"
Jn. 1:33 NIV

Luke was a close colleague of Paul the Apostle and worked alongside him in some of Paul's later missionary activities. He had first-hand experience, therefore, in the spread of the early church, and in writing the book of Acts he became its historian. He was particularly interested in the spiritual dynamic underlying the growth of the church. Thus in his writing he majored on the twin roles of prayer and the power of the Holy Spirit at work in the church. He has a great deal to say of importance, therefore, about the "power of the Spirit".

In the first chapter of Acts he makes clear that Jesus had warned his disciples to *"wait for the gift promised by the Father* (the Holy Spirit)" before starting on their work of witness in Jerusalem. Jesus said to them that they would receive *"power when the Holy Spirit comes upon you"*, indicating that the Spirit's power would be necessary for their witness. In the second chapter of Acts Luke gives

a full description of the nature of that "power" at work as the Spirit came upon disciples on the Day of Pentecost. First there were two "miraculous" signs. One was a violent wind, indicative of the sheer "power" of the Spirit, and the other was vision of a "ball" of tongues each of which was on fire and which separated so that one tongue came to rest on each of the disciples. These fiery tongues were indicative of speech that burned with great impact. Furthermore, the fiery tongues emerged from the apostles' mouths as languages foreign to the apostles but known to the many foreigners present in Jerusalem over Pentecost who were listening to them. The subject of those tongues was praise for "*the wonders of God*". There could scarcely be anything more appropriate as a visionary means of showing that the power of God would be manifest through the Spirit as Jesus' disciples testified "*with fire*" to Jesus, and that such testimony would be for all nations. "Tongues" as a phenomenon was a supreme prophetic statement that the gospel would be preached to the whole world and in all its languages.

There was much confusion and consternation at these happenings, and also mockery. So Peter, with the full backing of all the other disciples, stood up and in a loud voice addressed the crowd to deliver an explanation. He dismissed the mockery, and the proceeded to demonstrate in his preaching exactly what happens when a person becomes full of the "Holy Spirit". The first thing that stands out is the sheer boldness that enervated his words. Without the slightest hesitation and fearlessly he proclaimed Jesus; his death and resurrection, his glorification by God and the fact that what the people were witnessing was an outpouring of the Holy Spirit from the ascended Jesus. This was in the face of what could have been a large hostile crowd, and knowing full well that a very definite hostile ecclesiastical leadership would certainly get to hear of what he was saying. Not only did he proclaim Jesus, but he emphasised the fact that the Jewish leadership was responsible for the crucifixion of the Messiah.

The second thing that stands out in this Spirit-filled preaching of Peter was its impact on those who were listening. It is epitomised in the expression, "*They were cut to the heart*". Here was the Holy Spirit bringing, as Jesus had forewarned, conviction of "*sin, righteousness and judgement*". They were convicted of the fact that Jesus was the Messiah and was the "righteous one", they were convicted of their sin against him, and they were convicted of being

under the judgement of God for it. They demanded to know what they had to do to be saved. Whatever the impact of the earlier miracles might have been on the crowd it was the conviction brought about by the message of Peter that achieved God's purpose – three thousand were converted. It was not the consequence of oratory or clever speaking, but of the power of the Spirit.

The third feature of Peter's preaching was the extraordinary fluency and directness with which it flowed. This should not be overlooked. This was no prepared "sermon". This was the Holy Spirit giving words and shaping the direction and application of trenchant thoughts with incredible facility. It was an example of "preaching" in the power (enabling) of the Holy Spirit that many Spirit-filled preachers were to experience in the centuries which followed – and became commonly known as *"speaking with liberty"*. Peter had no script but what he did have was a store of teaching that he had acquired from Jesus himself (especially after the resurrection) and a wealth of experience of being with Jesus. This was spontaneous speaking not from an empty mind, but from a well-stocked mind and heart. Important for a Jewish audience, it was laced with appropriate Scripture, (Joel on the coming of the Spirit and The Psalms on the resurrection of Jesus).

6.   KEEPING IN STEP WITH THE SPIRIT

"Do not grieve the Holy Spirit of God, with whom you were sealed for the day of redemption."
Eph 4: 30ff NIV

It needs to be said, however, that even when we have received the Spirit there always remains the fact that we have to let Him have full sway and with his help crucify the flesh that still embodies us and seeks to influence us away from his working. We need also to be in personal fellowship with the Spirit so that He may give us an increasing fullness of his presence.

0800
6122302

13